The
QUICK RECIPE
COOKBOOK

The QUICK RECIPE COOKBOOK

WHITECAP
BOOKS

contents

special features

key for symbols

Although all the recipes in this collection have a quick preparation time, our 'super quick' symbol means the combined preparation and cooking time is no more than 25 minutes. 'Low-fat' recipes have a fat content of 10 g or less, and 'vegetarian' recipes are meat-free, but may contain dairy products.

 super quick   *low-fat*    *vegetarian*

the organized pantry

Organization is the key to successful 'quick' cooking. Before you begin, read through the recipe thoroughly, check your pantry and take note of the equipment you will need. As this book will show, it *is* possible to have a recipe that has a short list of ingredients and a relatively short preparation time, yet not be short on flavor.

pantry staples

A well-stocked pantry means fewer hurdles when answering the 'What's for dinner?' question, giving you the wherewithal to rustle up a wide range of creative and tasty possibilities. Gone are the days of frustration and disappointment, when, after finally deciding what to prepare, you discover you are missing the vital ingredient.

'Pantry staples' are non-perishable products common to many recipes such as flour, canned tomatoes and dried herbs, and those that make versatile accompaniments (rice, pasta and couscous).

purchase & storage tips

• Store dry ingredients, such as flour, sugar and nuts, in airtight containers as weevils can be a problem in open packages.
• Unopened canned products will last for months provided they are not rusty or damaged.
• Bottles and jars should be stored in the refrigerator once they have been opened.
• Pastes, such as tomato and curry, can be frozen in ice-cube trays. This allows you to keep it for much longer and in convenient small portions for easy use.
• Always check the sell-by or expiration date of products. Try to have a regular clean-out so you know which basics need restocking.

pantry staples

beans, canned
bread crumbs, dry
coconut cream/milk
couscous
curry paste
dried fruits
dried herbs and spices
flour (all-purpose, self-rising)
noodles
nuts (almonds, hazelnuts)
oil (olive, peanut)
rice (arborio, long-grain)
stock (cubes, tetra packs)
pasta
pasta sauce, tomato
sugar (brown, superfine)
tomato paste
tomatoes, canned

fresh produce

'Fresh produce' refers to fruit and vegetables, seafood, meat, chicken and dairy products. They should be stored in the refrigerator or freezer with the exception of potatoes, tomatoes and garlic. Fresh produce have a comparatively short shelf life and need to be restocked more frequently than pantry staples.

purchase & storage tips

• Buy fresh fruit and vegetables every few days to gain the best possible texture and flavor. Vegetables keep best in the crisper section of the refrigerator.
• Potatoes and onions are best stored in a cool, dark, dry place. Avoid storing them together as the potatoes will tend to rot. Onions can be kept in the refrigerator—this may also prevent teary eyes.
• Wrap fresh herbs in a clean, damp dish towel or in plastic bags and store in an airtight container. Fresh herbs, when chopped, can also be kept in sealable bags and stored in the freezer.
• Meat and chicken will keep for 2–3 days in the refrigerator. Always put the meat on a plate or tray, cover with plastic wrap or foil, and place on the bottom shelf in the refrigerator to prevent any juice dripping onto other foods.
• When freezing meat or chicken, wrap tightly in foil or plastic wrap and expel any excess air. Label and date the outside.
• Defrost meat or chicken overnight in the refrigerator to keep the meat at a temperature which limits bacterial growth. Never re-freeze meat unless it has been cooked first.
• When selecting meats that are quick to cook, look for boneless cuts. Most butchers can provide a wide range of meats that are pre-trimmed, pre-cut or cubed.
• Leftover bread can be made into bread crumbs and frozen in plastic bags ready for use.
• Products such as margarine, butter, milk, cheese and eggs should be stored in the refrigerator. Wrap block cheese in foil or kitchen paper—avoid using plastic wrap.

With the correct equipment, chopping and cooking can be a breeze. Carefully selected utensils and gadgets, pots and pans, glass and ceramic dishes and electrical appliances can help no end with the preparation of food and, in some cases, take over the job!

types & uses

• Utensils such as pancake turners, spatulas, tongs, whisks, ladles, and wooden and metal spoons are part of the most essential and versatile pieces of equipment in the kitchen. They are ideal for mixing cakes, stirring and serving soups, beating egg whites and flipping omelettes.

• Garlic presses, kitchen scissors, graters, zesters, potato mashers and good workable peelers are worth their weight in gold when trying to prepare a meal quickly.

• Measuring cups (liquid and dry) and measuring spoons are vital to accurately measure ingredients such as flour and milk, particularly for cakes and desserts. Electronic or manual scales may also be useful for other types of ingredients such as meat and vegetables.

• Good-quality knives made from stainless steel or carbon make slicing and dicing effortless. The most frequently used knives in the kitchen would be the chef's knife and a good paring knife.

• A set of good-quality saucepans can assist with quicker cooking by providing good even heat conduction. This allows fewer opportunities for food to scorch on the bottom of the pan.

• Large, non-stick skillets allow for quick evaporation. This is handy when reducing sauces or liquids.

• Many glass, enamel or ceramic dishes are heatproof, ovenproof and microwave safe. In many cases they are attractive enough to serve in. These dishes come in a range of sizes.

equipment

baking pan
pancake turner
food processor
skillet
garlic press
kitchen scissors
knives
ladle
measuring cups and spoons
metal and wooden spoons
pastry brush
potato masher
saucepans
scales
slotted spoon
spatula
tongs
vegetable peeler
whisk
wok

maintenance

• Wooden utensils such as spoons and pastry brushes are best washed well in hot soapy water. It is important that they are stored dry to help stop bacteria or mold forming when not in use.

• Non-stick skillets and pans may be easily scratched if you use metal utensils—use wooden or plastic.

• Line non-stick baking sheets with parchment paper to prevent baked-on stains accumulating on the sheet, and make washing up easy.

• Sharpen stainless steel or carbon knives with a steel when not in use. Store knives in a knife block to keep the edges sharp.

electrical

• Electrical appliances such as rice cookers can take over the cooking for you—there's no need to keep a watchful eye on the boiling pot.

• Electric woks are very convenient, but make sure you buy one with the highest wattage possible, otherwise it may not retain the heat throughout cooking. Woks are designed to cook food very quickly at a high temperature and can put a meal on the table in minutes.

• Electric mixers (portable and stand models) are great for preparing smooth batters and cake mixtures, taking the muscle out of beating by hand.

• Food processors and blenders should have a good motor, a strong blade and a bowl large enough to cope with different capacities. They are great for making purées, pesto, mayonnaise and sauces. Small food processors or spice grinders can also grind nuts and spices and make fresh bread crumbs.

• A handheld blender is useful for blending soups, sauces and drinks. The advantages of this blender are its compact size and its ability to process in any container (glass jug or saucepan), which means less washing up—always a bonus!

• Microwave ovens are commonly used for reheating and defrosting. They also allow you to make great meals in less time, leaving more flavor and nutrients in the food.

• Microwaves are handy for melting chocolate, toasting nuts and drying fresh bread crumbs in less time than the conventional methods.

You've got the right ingredients and time-saving equipment, but you've only got an hour to whip up a sumptuous meal. With these quick cooking techniques, you'll have that meal on the table with time to spare!

baking

- Preheating your oven is very important when baking, because the oven must reach the required temperature before you are ready to bake.
- When making cakes, always grease and flour or line the pan with parchment paper to prevent the mixture from sticking to the pan.

deep-frying

- Make sure that the saucepan you are using is secure on the stove top, and never leave the hot oil unattended—oil can ignite easily if it is overheated.
- Fill the saucepan one-third full of oil to reduce the possibilities of boiling over. A low to medium heat is sufficient to heat the oil to its required deep-frying temperature.
- Always test the oil before you deep-fry by dropping in a cube of bread. The bread should take 10–35 seconds to brown depending on the temperature required. For example, if the oil is heated to 350°F, the cube of bread will brown in 15 seconds. The hotter the oil, the less time the bread will take to brown.
- Cook the food in batches to prevent the food sticking together and to provide even cooking. Keep the cooked batch warm in an oven at 350°F.
- Be careful when lifting the food in and out of the hot oil with tongs or a metal slotted spoon—hot oil will burn you! Drain on several layers of crumpled paper towel.

techniques

> baking
> deep-frying
> grilling/broiling
> microwave cooking
> steaming
> stir-frying

grilling & broiling

- Grilling or broiling is a fast, healthy way to cook. Preheat the grill or broiler to hot before adding meats, seafood or vegetables.

microwave cooking

- Cooking in the microwave is quick and fuss-free—cooking times are reduced and you'll often be able to prepare, mix, cook and serve from the same dish.
- All ovenproof glass containers are suitable to use in the microwave, so too are paper or plastic plates. However, metal dishes or dishes with a metal trim are a big no-no as they will damage the microwave.
- When arranging food in a dish always remember that the food on the outer edges of the dish will cook the quickest—place the thickest part of the food at the edge.
- Vegetables should only take a few minutes to cook in the microwave. Keep in mind, microwaves vary in wattage, so cooking times will differ from brand to brand.
- The microwave is a great device for thawing soups and stews or reheating leftovers.

steaming

- Fish and vegetables are great served steamed and take very little time. Fish can be steamed in a covered bamboo steamer over a wok of boiling water or wrapped in foil and cooked in the oven. Steam vegetables in a metal steamer over a saucepan of boiling water. Make sure the bottom of either type of steamer doesn't touch the water.

stir-frying

- Prepare all your ingredients before you heat the wok. Bite-size pieces of meat and vegetables take very little time to cook over high heat and require constant stirring to avoid overcooking or burning. Organize your ingredients in the order that they will be added to speed up the process. Cut the meat across the grain to make it tender.
- Heat the wok before adding the oil. Add the oil and swirl it around to coat. If the oil sizzles when the first ingredient is added, it is ready.
- If there is a large quantity of an ingredient to be added to the wok at one time, such as meat, cook it in batches. This makes sure that the meat is cooked quickly, stays tender and doesn't stew.
- Be careful when adding wet ingredients such as washed vegetables and marinated foods to a hot wok; the oil will spit when the water hits the surface.
- Don't cover a wok during cooking because the food will steam.
- Stir-fries should be served as soon as they have been cooked.

chicken

ingredients

11 oz marinated artichokes in oil

4 oz button mushrooms, sliced

2/3 cup semi-dried tomatoes

1 red onion, cut into rings

1/4 cup slivered fresh basil

1 barbecued chicken

5 oz arugula leaves, trimmed

6 oz feta, cubed

preparation: 10 minutes
cooking: none
serves: 4–6

1 Place the artichokes and the oil marinade in a large bowl and add the mushrooms, tomatoes, onion and basil.

2 Remove the skin and bones from the chicken and cut the flesh into bite-size pieces. Add to the salad and toss well. Season to taste.

3 Arrange the arugula leaves on a serving plate and top with the salad. Scatter the feta over the top and serve with crusty bread.

nutrition per serve (6)
Protein 30 g; Fat 12 g; Carbohydrate 2.5 g; Dietary Fiber 3 g; Cholesterol 87 mg; 230 calories

handy tip...

Buy semi-dried tomatoes at good supermarkets and delicatessens. If not available, use sun-dried tomatoes.
Feta is a salty cheese made from sheep's milk. If the flavor is too strong, use chopped bocconcini.
This salad can also be made using 3 thinly sliced smoked chicken breasts.

ingredients

3 lb chicken drumsticks
3/4 cup buttermilk
2 tablespoons olive oil
1 cup polenta (cornmeal)
1 cup dry bread crumbs
1/2 teaspoon chili powder
   (optional)
2 eggs
2 tablespoons unsalted
   butter, melted

preparation: 15 minutes
cooking: 50 minutes
serves: 4–6

1 Preheat the oven to 350°F. Grease a foil-lined baking sheet. Cut two deep incisions into the thickest part of each of the drumsticks (this provides for even cooking). Place the drumsticks in a bowl, add the buttermilk and the oil, and turn to coat.

2 Place the polenta, bread crumbs and chili powder in another bowl. Season to taste, then mix together. Put the eggs in a small bowl and whisk with 1 tablespoon water.

3 Dip the chicken in the egg mixture, then coat with the polenta mixture, pressing with your fingers to make the crumbs stick. Arrange on the prepared sheet and drizzle with melted butter. Bake for 45–50 minutes, or until the chicken is crisp and golden. Serve with sweet potato mash and a green salad, if desired.

nutrition per serve (6)
Protein 56 g; Fat 27 g; Carbohydrate 30 g; Dietary Fiber 1.5 g; Cholesterol 287 mg; 592 calories

hint

Oven-frying delivers a crisp, crunchy crust with a lot less fat than traditional deep-frying. For an even leaner version, remove the skin from the chicken before coating.
To make the 'fried' chicken really moist, marinate the drumsticks in the buttermilk and oil for up to 8 hours.

ingredients

1 lb boneless chicken breast halves, with skin

2 tablespoons peanut or vegetable oil

2 green onions, diced

2 small hot red chiles, finely chopped

2 tablespoons soy sauce

2 tablespoons fish sauce

2 tablespoons grated palm sugar

1 cup loosely packed fresh basil

preparation: 10 minutes
cooking: 12 minutes
serves: 4

1 Cut the chicken breasts into small cubes. Heat the oil in the wok and swirl to coat. Add the chicken in batches and stir-fry over high heat for 5 minutes each batch, or until the chicken is tender.

2 Add the green onions and chiles and stir-fry for 1 minute. Add the soy sauce, fish sauce and sugar and toss briefly. Stir in the basil and serve with jasmine rice.

nutrition per serve
Protein 30 g; Fat 12 g; Carbohydrate 2.5 g; Dietary Fiber 0.5 g; Cholesterol 62 mg; 240 calories

handy tip...

Fish sauce is also known as Thai fish sauce or nam pla. Palm sugar is made from the sap of the coconut palm. It is sold in Asian supermarkets. If palm sugar is unavailable, use brown sugar.
The chicken may be substituted with fish or tofu.

2 in piece fresh galangal
2 cups unsweetened
   coconut milk
1 cup chicken stock
3 boneless, skinned
   chicken breast halves,
   cut into thin strips
1–2 teaspoons finely
   chopped fresh red chiles
2 tablespoons Thai fish
   sauce (nam pla)
1 teaspoon soft brown
   sugar
¼ cup fresh cilantro leaves

preparation: 15 minutes
cooking: 20 minutes
serves: 4

1 Peel the galangal and cut it into thin slices. Place the galangal, coconut milk and stock in a saucepan. Bring to a boil, then reduce the heat to low and simmer for 10 minutes, stirring occasionally.

2 Add the chicken and chiles to the pan and simmer for another 8 minutes. Stir in the fish sauce and brown sugar.

3 Add the cilantro leaves and serve immediately, garnished with extra sprigs of cilantro, if desired.

nutrition per serve
Protein 37 g; Fat 30 g; Carbohydrate 6.5 g; Dietary Fiber 2.5 g; Cholesterol 75 mg; 430 calories

hint

If fresh galangal is not available, you can use 5 large slices of dried galangal instead. Prepare it by soaking the slices in ½–1 cup boiling water for 10 minutes before slicing it into small shreds. Add the liquid to the chicken stock to make up 1 cup and use as above.

ingredients

1 lb 10 oz boneless, skinned chicken breast halves, cut into bite-size cubes
1/2 cup barbecue marinade
1 loaf thick flat bread or focaccia, halved horizontally
lettuce leaves, to serve

Salsa
2 large tomatoes, finely chopped
1 short, thin cucumber, finely chopped
1 peach or nectarine, finely chopped
1/2 cup chopped fresh cilantro leaves

preparation: 15 minutes
cooking: 10 minutes
serves: 4

1 Soak 8 skewers in a bowl of cold water to prevent them from burning while the kebabs are cooking. Preheat a broiler or barbecue grill.

2 Thread the chicken cubes onto the skewers and place in a shallow dish. Coat with the barbecue marinade, cover and refrigerate until ready to use.

3 To make the salsa, place the tomatoes, cucumber, peach or nectarine, and cilantro in a bowl and mix together well.

4 Remove the kebabs from the marinade (reserving the marinade) and place in a single layer under the hot broiler or on the barbecue. Cook for 3 minutes, then turn and cook for another 3 minutes, or until the chicken is cooked through. Baste with the reserved marinade during cooking.

5 Cut the bread into 8 slices, then broil or toast until golden.

6 Arrange the lettuce leaves on the bread. Remove the chicken cubes from the skewers and place on top of the lettuce. Serve with the fruity salsa.

nutrition per serve
Protein 54 g; Fat 8 g; Carbohydrate 60 g; Dietary Fiber 4 g; Cholesterol 100 mg; 516 calories

handy tip...

You could use mango or papaya instead of the peach. Sprinkle the salsa with balsamic vinegar or lemon juice for a more tangy taste.

ingredients

⅓ cup barbecue sauce
1 tablespoon honey
¼ cup mayonnaise
2 cloves garlic, crushed
2 teaspoons grated fresh ginger
4 boneless, skinned chicken breast halves (about 7 oz each)

preparation: 10 minutes + overnight marinating
cooking: 16 minutes
serves: 4

1 Place the barbecue sauce, honey, mayonnaise, garlic and ginger in a bowl and mix together well. Add the chicken and toss until well coated. Cover and refrigerate for at least 2 hours or preferably overnight.

2 Place the chicken breasts on a cold, lightly oiled broiler rack. Cook under a hot broiler, brushing occasionally with the remaining marinade, for 5–8 minutes. Turn and cook the other side for 5–8 minutes, or until the chicken is tender and cooked through. Slice the chicken and serve with a crisp mixed green salad, if desired.

nutrition per serve
Protein 46 g; Fat 9.5 g; Carbohydrate 17 g; Dietary Fiber 0.5 g; Cholesterol 105 mg; 335 calories

hint

This glaze is suitable for other cuts of chicken such as boneless thighs or wings and drumsticks. Try cooking the chicken on the barbecue instead of broiling.

ingredients

1 tablespoon oil
2 cloves garlic, crushed
4 green onions, sliced
1 quart chicken stock
1 lb broccoli florets
12 oz boneless, skinned
    chicken breast halves,
    cut into thin strips
½ cup sour cream

preparation: 15 minutes
cooking: 12 minutes
serves: 4

1 Heat the oil in a saucepan. Add the garlic and green onions and cook over medium heat for 1–2 minutes, or until softened.

2 Add the stock, bring to a boil, then reduce the heat and simmer. Add the broccoli to the stock and cook, covered, over low heat, for 3–5 minutes, or until the broccoli is tender but still green.

3 Transfer the soup to a blender or food processor and blend in batches until completely smooth.

4 Return to the pan and bring to a boil. Add the chicken strips, reduce the heat and simmer for 3–5 minutes, or until the chicken is cooked. Add the sour cream and season with salt and pepper. Reheat gently just before serving.

nutrition per serve
Protein 30 g; Fat 20 g; Carbohydrate 2.5 g; Dietary Fiber 5.5 g; Cholesterol 90 mg; 310 calories

handy tip...

If you are not planning to eat this soup right away, do not add the sour cream until just before serving. Reheating and boiling will separate the sour cream and give the soup a curdled appearance.

ingredients

12 oz farfalle pasta

3 chorizo sausages

1 lb 8 oz boneless, skinned
  chicken breast halves

2 small fresh red chiles,
  seeded and chopped

6 green onions, sliced

2/3 cup sun-dried
  tomato pesto

1 1/4 cups whipping cream

1/4 cup grated Parmesan

preparation: 15 minutes
cooking: 20 minutes
serves: 4–6

1 Cook the pasta in a large saucepan of boiling water according to the package instructions. Drain.

2 Meanwhile, cut the chorizo into 3/4 in slices and cut the chicken breasts into strips.

3 Heat a large skillet. Add the chorizo and cook, stirring, over high heat for 2 minutes. Add the chicken strips, chiles and green onions and cook, stirring, for 5 minutes, or until the chicken is lightly browned.

4 Stir in the pesto and cream and simmer for 5 minutes, or until the

chicken is tender. Remove from the heat and stir in the Parmesan. Toss with the pasta and serve at once.

nutrition per serve (6)
Protein 40 g; Fat 35 g; Carbohydrate 45 g; Dietary Fiber 4.5 g; Cholesterol 155 mg; 685 calories

hint

Chorizo is a spicy pork sausage widely used in Spanish and Mexican cuisine. It is available from good delicatessens. If unavailable, use a spicy salami instead.

1 lb 8 oz boneless, skinned
  chicken thighs

Satay sauce
1 tablespoon oil
1 onion, chopped
½ cup chunky peanut butter
1 tablespoon soy sauce
½ cup unsweetened
  coconut cream
2 tablespoons sweet chili
  sauce

preparation: 15 minutes
cooking: 15 minutes
serves: 4

1 Trim the chicken of excess fat and sinew, then cut into 1 in cubes. Soak 8 wooden skewers in water to prevent them from burning under the broiler.

2 To make the satay sauce, heat the oil in a small saucepan. Add the onion and cook over medium heat for 2–3 minutes, or until soft. Add the peanut butter, soy sauce, coconut cream and sweet chili sauce and cook gently, stirring, until heated through.

3 Thread the chicken cubes onto the skewers, then place on a cold, lightly oiled broiler rack. Cook under a hot broiler for 5 minutes, turn over and cook for another 5 minutes, or until tender. Brush with a little sauce during cooking, if desired. Serve with satay sauce and garnish with fresh cilantro.

nutrition per serve
Protein 52 g; Fat 30 g; Carbohydrate 7.5 g; Dietary Fiber 5 g; Cholesterol 95 mg; 520 calories

handy tip...

For extra flavor, the cubed chicken can be marinated in the satay sauce overnight, covered, in the refrigerator.

ingredients

1 lb 4 oz boneless, skinned chicken thighs
2 tablespoons olive oil
2 tablespoons brandy
½ cup chicken stock
10 oz button mushrooms, trimmed and thickly sliced (see hint)
2 teaspoons fresh thyme
¼ cup whipping cream

preparation: 15 minutes
cooking: 15 minutes
serves: 4

1 Cut the chicken into bite-size pieces. Heat the oil in a skillet until hot. Add the chicken in batches and cook over high heat for 4 minutes, or until browned. Reheat the pan between batches. Remove the chicken and drain the oil from the pan.

2 Heat the pan until slightly smoking, then pour in the brandy and allow it to bubble until nearly evaporated. Pour in the chicken stock and bring to a boil. Add the mushrooms and thyme. Return the chicken to the pan with any juices and cook for another 3 minutes, or until the mushrooms are soft. Stir in the cream and season well with salt and freshly ground black pepper. Serve over fettuccine or rice.

nutrition per serve
Protein 35 g; Fat 20 g; Carbohydrate 2 g; Dietary Fiber 2 g; Cholesterol 95 mg; 335 calories

hint

Do not wash mushrooms because they absorb water and will become mushy. Wipe them clean with a damp paper towel.

ingredients

1 lb boneless, skinned chicken breast halves

1²/₃ cup unsweetened coconut cream

1–2 tablespoons green curry paste

1²/₃ cup unsweetened coconut milk

5 oz green beans, cut into short lengths

4 kaffir lime leaves

1 tablespoon fish sauce

1 tablespoon brown sugar

preparation: 15 minutes
cooking: 20 minutes
serves: 4

1 Cut the chicken breasts into bite-size pieces.

2 Place coconut cream in a wok and stir in the curry paste. Bring to a boil, reduce the heat and simmer for 10 minutes, or until the oil separates from the coconut cream.

3 Add coconut milk, chicken, green beans and lime leaves. Bring back to a boil, then reduce the heat and simmer for 10 minutes, or until the chicken is cooked through.

4 Add fish sauce and brown sugar, stirring until combined. Serve immediately with steamed jasmine rice and garnish with chopped fresh cilantro leaves, if desired.

nutrition per serve
Protein 33 g; Fat 45 g; Carbohydrate 14 g; Dietary Fiber 4.5 g; Cholesterol 65 mg; 585 calories

handy tip...

Both unsweetened coconut milk and cream are available, canned, from Asian markets and some supermarkets. The cream is richer and thicker. If kaffir lime leaves are unavailable, you can use a small amount of fresh lemon or lime juice instead. Use good-quality Asian green curry paste.

ingredients

4 small boneless, skinned chicken breast halves
2 tablespoons honey
2 tablespoons Dijon mustard
1 cup pecans
2 tablespoons dry bread crumbs
2 tablespoons flour
2 tablespoons softened butter
¼ cup chopped chives

preparation: 15 minutes
cooking: 20 minutes
serves: 4

1 Preheat the oven to 425°F. Trim any excess fat from the chicken. Place the chicken in a 13 x 9 in shallow roasting pan and add 2 tablespoons water to the pan.

2 Place the honey and mustard in a bowl and mix together well.

3 Place the pecans, bread crumbs, flour, butter and chives in a food processor. Season with salt and freshly ground black pepper and process very quickly until the mixture is coarsely chopped and comes together.

4 Spread the honey mustard mixture over the chicken breasts, then firmly press on the pecan crumbs with your fingers. Bake for 15 minutes, or until the chicken is cooked and the crumbs are golden brown. Serve with a green salad, if desired.

nutrition per serve
Protein 33 g; Fat 30 g; Carbohydrate 20 g; Dietary Fiber 3 g; Cholesterol 88 mg; 470 calories

hint

Any nuts can be used in this recipe—walnuts, macadamias, cashews, or a combination. Store nuts in an airtight container in the freezer to stop them from going rancid.

ingredients

1 lb linguine
3 smoked chicken
  breast halves
  (about 7 oz each)
1¼ cups sour cream
1 tablespoon coarse grain
  mustard
1 tablespoon chopped,
  fresh flat-leaf parsley

preparation: 10 minutes
cooking: 15 minutes
serves: 6

1 Cook the linguine in a large saucepan of boiling water according to the package instructions. Drain the pasta, reserving ½ cup water in case you need to thin the sauce.

2 Meanwhile, cut the smoked chicken breasts into thin slices.

3 Place the sour cream in a skillet and warm it over low heat until it thins. Do not boil or the sour cream will curdle. Stir in the mustard and chicken and season with salt and freshly ground black pepper.

4 Toss the linguine into the sauce and mix well. Sprinkle with the parsley and serve immediately.

nutrition per serve
Protein 33 g; Fat 23 g; Carbohydrate 60 g; Dietary Fiber 4.5 g; Cholesterol 116 mg; 586 calories

handy tip...

Smoked chicken is usually sold in the deli section at the supermarket. If smoked chicken is not available, use 3 boneless, skinned chicken breast halves, lightly fried in a little olive oil. Allow to cool slightly before slicing.

ingredients

1 tablespoon oil
1 lb 10 oz boneless, skinned
    chicken breast halves
2 quarts chicken stock
3 green onions, sliced
3 oz dried thin egg
    noodles, broken
¾ cup chopped fresh
    parsley

preparation: 10 minutes
cooking: 25 minutes
serves: 4

1 Heat the oil in a large skillet. Add the chicken breasts and cook over medium heat for 15 minutes, or until golden, turning once. Remove from the pan and allow to cool. Shred finely.

2 Place the chicken stock in a large saucepan, bring to a boil, then reduce the heat. Add the chicken, green onions and noodles and simmer for 5–10 minutes, or until the noodles are just tender. Season to taste with salt and black pepper and stir in the parsley. Divide among four warm bowls and serve immediately.

nutrition per serve
Protein 30 g; Fat 8 g; Carbohydrate 20 g; Dietary Fiber 1 g; Cholesterol 60 mg; 275 calories

hint

Any noodles can be used in this recipe. Try replacing the dried egg noodles with fresh Hokkien, Udon or egg noodles. They will only need 5 minutes cooking. Separate them before adding to the saucepan.
This recipe is also delicious with barbecued pork.

ingredients

6 chicken thighs (about 7 oz each), skin removed

1³/₄ cups apricot nectar

1½ oz sachet French onion soup mix

15 oz can apricot halves, unsweetened, drained

¼ cup sour cream

preparation: 10 minutes
cooking: 1 hour
serves: 4–6

1 Preheat the oven to 350°F. Place the chicken thighs into an ovenproof dish.

2 Place the apricot nectar and soup mix in a bowl and mix together until well combined. Pour the mixture over the chicken.

3 Bake, covered, for 50 minutes, then add the apricot halves and bake, uncovered, for another 5 minutes. Stir in the sour cream just before serving. Serve with creamy mashed potatoes or rice to soak up the juices.

nutrition per serve (6)
Protein 23 g; Fat 6 g; Carbohydrate 10 g; Dietary Fiber 0 g; Cholesterol 63 mg; 187 calories

handy tip...

Any cut of chicken is suitable for this recipe.
Do not allow the sauce to boil after adding the sour cream or it will separate and give the dish a curdled appearance.

ingredients

12 chicken drumsticks
2 tablespoons soy sauce
2 tablespoons hoisin
   sauce
¼ cup ketchup
¼ cup honey
1 tablespoon lemon juice
2 tablespoons sesame
   seeds
½ teaspoon five-spice
   powder

preparation: 15 minutes +
   2 hours refrigeration
cooking: 50 minutes
serves: 4–6

1 Pat the chicken drumsticks dry with paper towels.

2 Place the soy sauce, hoisin sauce, ketchup, honey, lemon juice, sesame seeds and the five-spice powder in a large bowl and mix together.

3 Add the chicken and mix well to coat. Refrigerate, covered, for at least 2 hours, turning occasionally. Preheat the oven to 350°F.

4 Drain the chicken and discard the marinade. Place the legs on a rack in a roasting pan and bake for 40–50 minutes. Serve warm with rice and with steamed or stir-fried vegetables.

nutrition per serve (6)
Protein 40 g; Fat 7 g; Carbohydrate 6 g; Dietary Fiber 1.5 g; Cholesterol 83 mg; 246 calories

hint

This recipe is suitable for any cut of chicken.
The longer the chicken is left in the marinade the more developed the flavor will be.
These drumsticks can also be broiled or barbecued.

3 lb whole chicken
2 lemons, chopped
4 green onions, finely
    chopped
2 tablespoons chopped
    fresh lemon thyme
2 cloves garlic, crushed
1 tablespoon olive oil
6 sprigs fresh lemon
    thyme
4 thin slices prosciutto

preparation: 15 minutes
cooking: 1 hour 30 minutes
serves: 4

1 Preheat the oven to 350°F. Trim the chicken of any excess fat and sinew. Then rinse out the cavity and pat the chicken dry with paper towels.

2 Place the lemons, green onions, lemon thyme, crushed garlic and freshly ground black pepper in a bowl and mix together well. Spoon the lemon mixture into the cavity of the chicken.

3 Bend the chicken wings back and tuck them behind the body. Tie the drumsticks together with string. Place on a wire rack in a roasting pan, brush with the oil and top with the sprigs of lemon thyme. Cover the breast with overlapping slices of prosciutto.

4 Cover the chicken with foil and roast for 1 hour 15 minutes, or until cooked through. Remove the foil and cook for another 15 minutes, or until the chicken is tender and the skin is crispy. Allow the chicken to rest in a warm place for 15 minutes before carving. Discard the stuffing. Serve with roast vegetables, if desired.

nutrition per serve
Protein 65 g; Fat 45 g; Carbohydrate 4.5 g; Dietary Fiber 2 g; Cholesterol 215 mg; 675 calories

handy tip...

Prosciutto is the Italian word for ham or salt-cured pork that has been air-dried. If not available, use bacon with excess fat trimmed off.

ingredients

1/3 cup chopped fresh
flat-leaf parsley
2 cloves garlic, finely
chopped
1 tablespoon finely grated
lemon rind
4 chicken leg and thigh
quarters
olive oil, for brushing

preparation: 15 minutes
cooking: 45 minutes
serves: 4

1 Preheat the oven to 400°F.

2 Place the parsley, garlic and rind in a bowl and mix well. Season. Using your fingers, carefully loosen the skin from the chicken and fill with the parsley mixture. Pat the skin back to its original shape.

3 Put the chicken in a roasting pan, brush lightly with the olive oil and roast for 45 minutes, or until the chicken juices run clear when it is pierced with a skewer. Serve immediately, garnished with lemon wedges.

nutrition per serve
Protein 30 g; Fat 25 g; Carbohydrate 1 g; Dietary Fiber 0 g; Cholesterol 140 mg; 345 calories

hint

The gremolata is perfect for whole roast chicken. Simply lift the skin, press the mixture onto the chicken breast, brush with oil and roast until tender.

ingredients

2 sheets frozen ready-rolled butter puff pastry, thawed
2 tablespoons butter
1 lb 8 oz boneless, skinned chicken breast halves, finely sliced
2 large leeks, finely chopped
4 slices bacon, finely chopped
5 oz button mushrooms, sliced
⅓ cup chicken stock
¾ cup sour cream

preparation: 20 minutes
cooking: 30 minutes
serves: 4

1 Preheat the oven to 425°F. Lightly grease four 2-cup capacity ovenproof casseroles. Cut the thawed puff pastry into four rounds large enough to cover the tops of the casseroles.

2 Heat half the butter in a large, deep skillet and cook the chicken in batches for 3 minutes, or until lightly browned. Remove the chicken from the pan.

3 Heat the remaining butter in the same pan over high heat. Cook the leeks for 2 minutes, or until soft. Add the bacon and mushrooms and cook for 2 minutes. Return the chicken and any juices to the pan and stir. Add the stock and boil for 2 minutes, or until slightly thickened. Reduce the heat, then stir in the sour cream. Season.

4 Spoon the chicken mixture into the casseroles and top each with a pastry round. Pierce the pastry with a fork. Bake for 15 minutes, or until the pastry is puffed and golden. Serve immediately with salad or steamed vegetables.

nutrition per serve
Protein 56 g; Fat 37 g; Carbohydrate 40 g; Dietary Fiber 5 g; Cholesterol 235 mg; 712 calories

handy tip...

This recipe can be made into one large pie. Use a deep, 9 or 10 in pie plate or quiche dish and roll the sheets of pastry together before placing on top. Pierce a couple of holes in the top of the pastry.

ingredients

2 lb 4 oz boneless
chicken thighs
2 tablespoons lime juice
½ cup sweet chili sauce
¼ cup kecap manis
(see hint)

preparation: 15 minutes +
2 hours refrigeration
cooking: 20 minutes
serves: 6

1 Trim any excess fat and sinew from the chicken thighs and cut them in half. Transfer to a shallow glass or ceramic dish.

2 Place the lime juice, sweet chili sauce and kecap manis in a bowl and whisk to combine. Pour the marinade over the chicken, cover and refrigerate for 2 hours.

3 Barbecue or bake in a preheated 400°F oven for 20 minutes, or until the chicken is tender and cooked through and the marinade has caramelized. Serve with salad greens and garnish with lime wedges.

nutrition per serve
Protein 35 g; Fat 4.5 g; Carbohydrate 4 g; Dietary Fiber 1 g; Cholesterol 85 mg; 210 calories

hint

Kecap manis (ketjap manis) is a thick Indonesian sauce, similar to—but sweeter than—soy sauce, and is generally flavored with garlic and star anise. Store in a cool, dry place and refrigerate after opening. If not available, use soy sauce sweetened with a little soft brown sugar.

ingredients

2 boneless, skinned
  chicken breast halves
  (about 7 oz each)
2 ripe tomatoes, each cut
  into 4 slices
2 slices Swiss cheese
2 tablespoons tomato relish
²/₃ cup whole-egg
  mayonnaise
4 poppy-seed bagels,
  halved
3 oz baby spinach leaves
½ cup semi-dried
  tomatoes

preparation: 15 minutes
cooking: 15 minutes
serves: 4

1 Lightly spray a non-stick skillet with oil and heat over medium heat. Cook the chicken for 5–7 minutes on each side, or until cooked through. Remove from the skillet and keep warm.

2 In the same skillet, seal the tomato slices on each side.

3 While still hot, cut each chicken breast in half horizontally, through the center. Place a slice of cheese on two halves, then put the other half of chicken on top to melt the cheese slightly. Cut the chicken breasts crosswise in half to give four cheese-filled pieces.

4 Combine the tomato relish and the mayonnaise in a small bowl.

5 To assemble the burgers, spread both halves of each bagel with the tomato relish mayonnaise. Place the baby spinach leaves on the bottom half of the bagel, followed by the chicken breast, tomato slices and semi-dried tomatoes. Put the bagel lid on top and serve immediately.

nutrition per serve
Protein 38 g; Fat 27 g; Carbohydrate 44 g; Dietary Fiber 5 g; Cholesterol 82 mg; 572 calories

handy tip...

The tomato relish mayonnaise can be made in advance—a whole batch can be made up and kept in the refrigerator in an airtight container for up to 1 week.

ingredients

1 tablespoon oil
1 carrot, sliced
1 leek, chopped
1 lb 10 oz boneless,
    skinned chicken thighs,
    cut in bite-size pieces
¼ cup ditalini pasta
1 quart vegetable stock
2 ripe tomatoes, diced

preparation: 15 minutes
cooking: 15 minutes
serves: 4

1 Heat the oil in a saucepan. Add the carrot and leek and cook over medium heat for 4 minutes, or until softened. Add the chicken and cook for another 2 minutes, or until the chicken is browned.

3 Add the pasta and the vegetable stock, cover and bring to a boil. Reduce the heat and simmer for 10 minutes, or until the pasta is cooked. Add the tomatoes halfway through the cooking. Season with salt and freshly ground black pepper. Serve with fresh crusty bread, if desired.

nutrition per serve
Protein 48 g; Fat 10 g; Carbohydrate 9.5 g; Dietary Fiber 2.5 g; Cholesterol 100 mg; 317 calories

hint

Ditalini pasta can be replaced with any small soup pasta. Any vegetables can be added to this soup—try mixed frozen vegetables.

sweet potato and spinach chicken salad

Heat 2 tablespoons olive oil in a large skillet. Cook 1 lb thickly sliced (about ½ in) sweet potatoes in batches for 10 minutes, or until just tender. Set aside. Add 2 leeks cut into thin strips and cook until softened. Add 2 teaspoons brown sugar and cook over low heat for another 10 minutes, or until caramelized. Remove from the heat. In a small bowl, whisk together 2 tablespoons olive oil and 2 tablespoons balsamic vinegar. Remove the skin and bones from a barbecued chicken and chop the flesh into bite-size pieces. In a bowl, add 3 cups baby spinach leaves, ⅔ cup semi-dried tomatoes, the roasted sweet potatoes and chicken, then toss gently to combine. Pile the leeks on top of the salad, pour the dressing over the top and serve.

serves 4–6

lemon chicken and pancetta pasta

Remove the skin and bones from a barbecued chicken and shred the flesh. Bring a large saucepan of water to a boil. Add 1 lb fresh fettuccine to the water and cook until al dente. Drain and keep warm. Heat a large skillet, add 2 cups chopped pancetta and cook for 10 minutes, or until crisp. Add the chicken, 1¼ cups whipping cream, ½ cup lemon juice and 5 or 6 asparagus spears, cut into 2 in pieces. Simmer for 5 minutes, or until the sauce thickens slightly. Add the pasta and toss together with ⅓ cup grated Parmesan and ¼ cup shredded fresh basil.

serves 4

chicken wrap

Remove the skin and bones from half a barbecued chicken and shred the flesh. Combine ½ cup whole-egg mayonnaise with 1 tablespoon lime juice and 1 crushed clove garlic in a small bowl. Spread over 4 rounds of Lebanese bread. Top with some shredded chicken, about 1 cup thinly sliced broiled sweet peppers and ½ diced red onion. Roll up and serve either sliced or wrapped in waxed or silicone paper.

serves 4

From left to right: Sweet potato and spinach chicken salad; Lemon chicken and pancetta pasta; Chicken wrap; Chicken tacos; Cream of chicken and corn soup; Gourmet chicken pizza.

chicken tacos

Preheat the oven to 350°F. Remove the skin and bones from a barbecued chicken and shred the flesh. Heat a large skillet, then add a 7 oz can mexe beans, including ½ cup of the liquid, and a 7 oz jar taco sauce. Simmer for 2 minutes, add the shredded chicken and heat through. Combine ⅔ cup shredded Cheddar or jack cheese and 2 tablespoons chopped fresh cilantro in a bowl. Place 8 taco shells in the oven and bake for 5 minutes, or until heated through and crisp. Spoon some chicken mixture into each taco and top with the shredded cheese mixture and 1 tablespoon sour cream. Serve immediately.

serves 4

cream of chicken and corn soup

Remove the skin and bones from half a barbecued chicken and shred the flesh. Heat 2 tablespoons butter in a large saucepan and add 6 chopped green onions. Cook over medium heat, for 2 minutes. Add a 14 oz can creamed corn and stir to combine. Gradually stir in 1 quart chicken stock and ½ cup sour cream. Cook gently until the soup thickens, being careful not to boil. Add the chicken and cook until heated through. Stir in ¼ cup chopped fresh cilantro leaves and season to taste with salt and pepper. Garnish with some finely chopped green onions and serve with crusty bread.

serves 4

gourmet chicken pizza

Preheat the oven to 400°F. Cut 8 oz butternut squash into ¾ in cubes. Heat 1 tablespoon oil in a skillet, add the squash and cook for 10 minutes, or until tender and golden. Remove the skin and bones from half a barbecued chicken and chop the flesh into bite-size pieces. Spread a 12 in pizza base with ¼ cup mango chutney. Top with 1 cup shredded mozzarella cheese, 1 red onion cut into wedges, and the cubed chicken and squash. Bake for 20 minutes, or until the crust is golden and crisp. Serve with a dollop of thick yogurt and garnish with fresh cilantro leaves.

serves 4

ingredients

2 tablespoons olive oil
1 red onion, cut into thin
   wedges
1½ tablespoons butter
1 lb 10 oz boneless, skinned
   chicken breast halves,
   cut into bite-size pieces
2 teaspoons lemon rind,
   cut into thin strips
2 tablespoons salted
   baby capers, rinsed well
   and drained
⅓ cup lemon juice
¼ cup slivered fresh basil

preparation: 15 minutes
cooking: 15 minutes
serves: 4

1 Heat a wok until very hot, add 2 teaspoons of the oil and swirl it around to coat the side. Add the onion and stir-fry for 2–3 minutes, or until softened and golden. Remove from the wok and set aside.

2 Reheat the wok, add another 2 teaspoons oil and half the butter, and stir-fry the chicken in two batches for 3–5 minutes each batch, or until browned, adding the remaining oil and butter between batches. Return all the chicken to the wok with the onion.

3 Stir in the lemon rind, capers and lemon juice. Toss well and cook until warmed through. Add the slivered basil; season with salt and freshly ground black pepper. Serve with mashed potatoes.

nutrition per serve
Protein 45 g; Fat 20 g; Carbohydrate 2.5 g; Dietary Fiber 1 g; Cholesterol 115 mg; 370 calories

handy tip...

Capers are the flower bud of a shrub native to the Mediterranean region. They are sold in jars in a vinegar brine or sold packed in salt. Salted capers need to be rinsed before adding them to dishes.

ingredients

4 boneless, skinned
  chicken breast halves
  (about 4 oz each)
2 tablespoons oil
4 small zucchini, sliced
2 leeks, thinly sliced
2 small fresh red chiles,
  finely chopped
5 oz oyster mushrooms
1 tablespoon lime juice
¼ cup whipping cream

preparation: 15 minutes
cooking: 20 minutes
serves: 4

1 Trim the chicken of any excess fat and sinew. Heat the oil in a skillet. Add the chicken and cook over medium heat for 5–7 minutes on each side, or until tender. Remove, drain on paper towels and keep warm.

2 Add the zucchini, leeks and chiles to the pan and cook over high heat for 2 minutes. Add the mushrooms and cook for another 3 minutes, or until tender.

3 Stir in the lime juice and cream and cook for 2 minutes, or until heated through. Season to taste with salt and pepper. Serve with roasted red sweet bell peppers and warm crusty bread rolls, if desired.

nutrition per serve
Protein 12 g; Fat 17 g; Carbohydrate 3.5 g; Dietary Fiber 3 g; Cholesterol 40 mg; 217 calories

hint

This dish should be served immediately after cooking. If oyster mushrooms are not available, use button mushrooms, sliced.
To protect your hands, wear rubber gloves when chopping hot chiles and rinse them afterwards. Avoid touching your face, as the chile juice can burn your eyes.

ingredients

1 lb boneless, skinned chicken breast halves

5 oz snow peas

1 tablespoon sesame oil

⅓ cup roasted unsalted cashews

1 tablespoon honey

2 tablespoons kecap manis (*see hint page 33*)

1–2 tablespoons chopped fresh cilantro leaves

preparation: 10 minutes
cooking: 15 minutes
serves: 4

1 Cut the chicken breast halves into bite-size pieces. Slice the snow peas on the diagonal.

2 Heat a wok until very hot, add sesame oil and swirl it to coat the side. Add the chicken and stir-fry in three batches, tossing, for 1–2 minutes, or until golden brown.

3 Return all the chicken to the wok and add the snow peas. Cook, tossing, for 3 minutes. Add the cashews, honey and kecap manis and cook for 1–2 minutes, or until the chicken is cooked. Scatter with the cilantro leaves and serve with rice or noodles, if desired.

nutrition per serve
Protein 33 g; Fat 15 g; Carbohydrate 13 g; Dietary Fiber 3 g; Cholesterol 60 mg; 307 calories

handy tip...

To roast the cashews, preheat the oven to 350°F. Place the cashews on a baking sheet and roast for 5–8 minutes. Keep a close eye on them as they will burn easily.

ingredients

4 boneless, skinned
chicken breast halves
(about 7 oz each)
1/4 cup all-purpose flour
2 tablespoons olive oil
1 tablespoon chopped
fresh lemon thyme
2 teaspoons dry sherry
1/2 cup whipping cream

preparation: 10 minutes
cooking: 15 minutes
serves: 4

1 Trim the chicken of any excess fat and sinew, then toss the breasts in the flour, shaking off any excess.

2 Heat the oil in a large non-stick skillet. Cook the chicken breasts for 5 minutes on each side, or until golden brown.

3 Sprinkle with lemon thyme, then turn the chicken over. Add sherry, pour in half the cream and boil for 2–3 minutes. Turn the breasts over again and drizzle with the remaining cream. Season to taste. Serve with a salad or vegetables.

nutrition per serve
Protein 45 g; Fat 20 g; Carbohydrate 5 g; Dietary Fiber 0 g; Cholesterol 125 mg; 395 calories

hint

Any herb could be used in the sauce instead of the lemon thyme. Try tarragon, chervil or basil for a deliciously different flavour.

ingredients

3 lb chicken pieces
2 tablespoons oil
3 lb potatoes, thickly
    sliced
3 large onions, thinly
    sliced
3 cups rich chicken stock
¼ cup butter, melted

preparation: 15 minutes
cooking: 1 hour 50 minutes
serves: 6

1 Trim the chicken pieces of any excess fat. Pat dry with paper towels, then rub with salt and freshly ground black pepper.

2 Heat the oil in a large Dutch oven. Cook the chicken in batches over medium heat until well browned. Remove from the pot.

3 Arrange one quarter of the potatoes over the base of the pot. Top with one quarter of the onions and four pieces of chicken. Repeat the layering process, ending with the onions.

4 Pour the chicken stock and butter over the top and cover with a sheet of greased parchment paper and the lid. Bring to a boil, then reduce the heat and simmer, covered, for 1 hour 30 minutes, or until the chicken is tender. Garnish with chopped fresh herbs.

nutrition per serve
Protein 45 g; Fat 19 g; Carbohydrate 37 g; Dietary Fiber 5 g; Cholesterol 109 mg; 499 calories

handy tip...

This Scottish dish is sometimes called 'stovies'. It is derived from the French *étouffer*, to cook in a closed pot, and dates back to the strong link between the Scottish and the French in the 17th century.

ingredients

4 boneless, skinned chicken breast halves (about 7 oz each)

flour, for dusting

2 tablespoons olive oil

4 oz button mushrooms, sliced

3 green onions, sliced

½ cup whipping cream

1 tablespoon brandy

¾ cup shredded Gruyère or Swiss cheese

preparation: 10 minutes
cooking: 15 minutes
serves: 4

1 Flatten the chicken breasts with the palm of your hand until they are ½ in thick. Dust the breasts with the flour, shaking off any excess. Heat the oil in a skillet, add the chicken and cook for 4–5 minutes on each side, or until golden brown. Transfer to a baking sheet lined with parchment paper or foil and then cover with foil.

2 Add the mushrooms and green onions to the skillet and cook for 2 minutes, or until onions are soft. Add cream and brandy and bring to a boil. Reduce the heat and simmer for 1 minute, or until the sauce reduces slightly. Season with salt and freshly ground black pepper.

3 Spoon the sauce over the chicken and top with the cheese. Place under a hot broiler until the cheese melts and begins to brown. Serve with roasted vegetables.

nutrition per serve
Protein 60 g; Fat 35 g; Carbohydrate 6 g; Dietary Fiber 1.5 g; Cholesterol 166 mg; 568 calories

hint

Gruyère has a strong distinctive flavor. If you would prefer something a little milder, use Cheddar.

beef & veal

ingredients

4 rib eye or New York
strip steaks (about
7 oz each)

1/4 cup soy sauce

1/2 cup teriyaki sauce

2 tablespoons mirin or
sweet sherry

2 tablespoons honey

2 cloves garlic, crushed

2 teaspoons grated fresh
ginger

green onions, finely
chopped, to garnish

preparation: 15 minutes +
overnight refrigeration
cooking: 20 minutes
serves: 4

1 Trim the meat of any excess fat and sinew. Place the soy sauce, teriyaki sauce, mirin, honey, garlic and ginger in a glass or ceramic dish and mix together. Add the steaks and turn well to coat. Cover and refrigerate for at least 2 hours or preferably overnight. Drain the meat and reserve the marinade.

2 Place the steaks in a non-stick skillet and cook over high heat for 2 minutes on each side to seal. For rare steaks, cook for another 1 minute on each side. For medium steaks, reduce the heat and cook another 2–3 minutes on each side. For well-done steaks, cook another 4–6 minutes on each side.

3 Bring the reserved marinade to a boil in a saucepan. Pour over the steaks during the last few minutes of cooking.

4 Serve the steaks with the marinade drizzled over the top. Garnish with the green onions.

nutrition per serve
Protein 44 g; Fat 12 g; Carbohydrate 18 g; Dietary Fiber 0.5 g; Cholesterol 100 mg; 365 calories

handy tip...

For a different flavor, try a red wine sauce: substitute the soy sauce with balsamic vinegar, the teriyaki sauce with red wine, and the ginger with extra garlic and follow the instructions as directed.

ingredients

1 lb boneless sirloin steak
1 short, thin cucumber,
 cut into cubes
4 green onions, chopped
10–12 cherry tomatoes,
 halved

Dressing
2 tablespoons fish sauce
2 tablespoons lime juice
2 tablespoons sweet chili
 sauce
1 tablespoon chopped
 fresh cilantro leaves

preparation: 15 minutes
cooking: 10 minutes
serves: 4

1 Heat a non-stick skillet. Add the steak and cook over high heat for 4 minutes on each side. Remove from the pan and allow to cool for 5 minutes.

2 To make the dressing, place the fish sauce, lime juice, sweet chili sauce and chopped cilantro leaves in a bowl and mix together.

3 Cut the cooled steak into thin strips and place in a bowl with the cucumber, green onions and tomatoes. Toss until well mixed and transfer to a serving dish—line the dish with a few lettuce leaves, if desired. Drizzle with the dressing and serve immediately, garnished with cilantro leaves.

nutrition per serve
Protein 30 g; Fat 4 g; Carbohydrate 5 g; Dietary Fiber 2 g; Cholesterol 85 mg; 178 calories

hint

Steak, lamb or chicken can be used in this recipe. The meat can be cooked on the barbecue.
Try mint or basil in place of the cilantro for a different flavor.

ingredients

2 tablespoons oil
1 lb top round steak,
   cut into thin strips
1 onion, sliced
10 oz sugar snap peas
2 tablespoons honey
2 tablespoons soy sauce
2 tablespoons oyster sauce
1 tablespoon finely
   cracked black pepper

preparation: 15 minutes
cooking: 15 minutes
serves: 4

1 Heat a wok until very hot, then add 1 tablespoon oil and swirl to coat. Stir-fry the beef in batches over high heat for 3–4 minutes each batch, or until browned, then remove and drain on paper towels.

2 Reheat the wok, add the remaining oil and stir-fry the onion and sugar snap peas until softened. Remove from the wok.

3 Add the honey, soy sauce, oyster sauce and pepper to the wok. Bring to a boil, then reduce the heat and simmer for 3–4 minutes, or until the sauce thickens slightly.

4 Increase the heat, return meat and vegetables to the wok, and toss for 2–3 minutes, or until well combined and heated through. Serve with steamed rice or noodles.

nutrition per serve
Protein 30 g; Fat 15 g; Carbohydrate 20 g; Dietary Fiber 4.5 g; Cholesterol 70 mg; 335 calories

handy tip...

If sugar snap peas are not available, use snow peas, broccoli or asparagus.
To crush the pepper, place into a pepper or spice grinder, food processor or mortar and pestle, and process until you reach the desired consistency.

ingredients

1 lb boneless sirloin steak, cut into thin strips

3 stems lemon grass, white part only, finely chopped

1 onion, finely chopped

3 cloves garlic, finely chopped

2 tablespoons fish sauce

2 teaspoons sugar

1 tablespoon oil

¼ cup chopped roasted peanuts

preparation: 15 minutes + 3–4 hours marinating
cooking: 15 minutes
serves: 4

1 Place the beef strips in a large glass or ceramic bowl. Put the lemon grass, onion, garlic, fish sauce and sugar in a separate bowl and mix together well. Pour the marinade over the meat and toss to coat. Cover and refrigerate for 3–4 hours.

2 Heat the oil in a wok until very hot and stir-fry the beef in batches over high heat for 3 minutes, or until just browned. Toss constantly to make sure the small pieces of onion and lemon grass don't scorch on the surface of the wok and burn.

3 Return all the meat to the wok. Add the peanuts and toss quickly until combined. Serve immediately with noodles or rice.

nutrition per serve
Protein 35 g; Fat 8.5 g; Carbohydrate 6 g; Dietary Fiber 2 g; Cholesterol 85 mg; 235 calories

hint

Lemon grass can be purchased fresh or dried from Asian markets. Remove the coarse outer layer and use only the white part of the fresh plant. Soak dried lemon grass in hot water before chopping.

nutrition per serve
Protein 27 g; Fat 28 g; Carbohydrate
2 g; Dietary Fiber 1.5 g; Cholesterol
117 mg; 372 calories

ingredients

2 tablespoons olive oil

2 oz sliced prosciutto,
  cut into wide strips

7 oz button mushrooms,
  stalks trimmed

4 rib eye or New York
  strip steaks (about
  7 oz each)

2 cloves garlic, crushed

2 tablespoons chopped,
  fresh flat-leaf parsley

¼ cup dry white wine

½ cup whipping cream

preparation: 15 minutes
cooking: 25 minutes
serves: 4

1 Preheat the oven to 400°F. Heat the oil in a deep ovenproof skillet (large enough to hold the steaks in one layer without overlapping). Add the prosciutto and mushrooms and toss until the mushrooms start to brown.

2 Arrange the steaks on top of the mushroom mixture, sprinkle with the garlic and parsley, then pour in the white wine. Bring to a boil, then remove the skillet from the heat. Bake, covered tightly (with a lid or with foil), for 10–15 minutes, or until the steaks are cooked to taste. Remove only the steaks from the skillet.

3 Return the skillet to the stove top over medium heat. Add the cream and simmer for 3–5 minutes, or until the sauce thickens slightly. Pour the sauce over the steaks and serve immediately with roasted potatoes or steamed vegetables.

handy tip...

Flat-leaf parsley is also known as Italian or continental parsley. It has a stronger, more dominant flavor than curly leaf parsley. It is important to bring the wine to a boil to evaporate the alcohol.

ingredients

1 lb boneless rib or rib
    eye (Delmonico) roast
¼ cup sesame oil
¼ cup soy sauce
2 cloves garlic, crushed
2 tablespoons grated
    fresh ginger
1 tablespoon lemon juice
2 tablespoons chopped
    green onions
¼ cup firmly packed soft
    brown sugar

preparation: 15 minutes +
    overnight marinating
cooking: 25 minutes
serves: 4

1 Trim the beef of any excess fat or sinew.

2 Combine the sesame oil, soy sauce, garlic, ginger, lemon juice, green onions and brown sugar in a glass or ceramic dish. Add the beef and coat well with the marinade. Cover and refrigerate for at least 2 hours, or preferably overnight. Drain and reserve the marinade.

3 Preheat a lightly oiled barbecue. When it is very hot, add the beef and brown on all sides to seal the meat. Remove the roast, wrap it in foil and cook on the barbecue, turning occasionally, for another 15–20 minutes, depending on how rare or well done you like your beef. Rest the beef for 10 minutes before slicing.

4 Meanwhile, place the reserved marinade in a small saucepan and boil for 5 minutes. Drizzle over the beef just before serving. Serve with a fresh mixed salad, if desired.

nutrition per serve
Protein 28 g; Fat 20 g; Carbohydrate 15 g; **Dietary Fiber** 0.5 g; Cholesterol 84 mg; 345 calories

hint

If you prefer, individual steaks can be used instead and cooked on the barbecue. However, there is no need to wrap them in foil.

ingredients

1 tablespoon oil

1 lb 4 oz top round steak, cut into cubes

2 onions, chopped

1 tablespoon madras curry paste

2 cups beef stock or water

2 tablespoons chopped fresh cilantro leaves

2 tablespoons chopped fresh mint

1/3 cup plain yogurt

preparation: 10 minutes
cooking: 1 hour 45 minutes
serves: 4

1 Heat the oil in a saucepan. Cook the beef over medium heat, in batches, until browned all over. Return all the meat to the pan.

2 Add the onions and stir for 3 minutes, or until golden. Add the curry paste and cook for 1 minute. Pour in the beef stock and bring to a boil. Reduce the heat and simmer, covered, for 1 hour. Check, then cook for up to 30 minutes more (if necessary), or until the meat is tender and the liquid has reduced and thickened slightly. Stir occasionally during cooking.

3 Add the chopped cilantro, mint and yogurt and stir until well combined. Garnish with a sprig of cilantro and serve with steamed basmati rice and some curried vegetables, if desired.

nutrition per serve
Protein 33 g; Fat 12 g; Carbohydrate 4 g; Dietary Fiber 1 g; Cholesterol 90 mg; 255 calories

handy tip...

This curry can be cooked up to 3 days ahead and stored, covered, in the refrigerator. If you choose to do this, do not add the yogurt until you reheat the curry, or it will separate. Any curry paste may be used in this recipe. For a richer curry, add 1 3/4 cups canned chopped tomatoes.

ingredients

2 lb 4 oz top round steak
3 slices bacon
12 small boiling onions
1 cup red wine
2 cups beef stock
1 teaspoon dried thyme
7 oz button mushrooms
2 bay leaves

preparation: 10 minutes
cooking: 1 hour 45 minutes
serves: 4–6

1 Trim the top round steak of any fat and sinew and then cut into ¾ in cubes. Cut the bacon slices into ¾ in squares.

2 Heat a large saucepan. Add the bacon and quickly cook over medium heat for 3 minutes, or until browned. Remove from the pan. Add the steak, in batches, and cook for 3 minutes each batch, or until browned. Remove from the pan. Add the onions to the pan and cook for 3 minutes, or until golden.

3 Return the bacon and meat to the saucepan with the red wine, stock, thyme, mushrooms and bay leaves. Bring to a boil, then reduce the heat and simmer, covered, for 1 hour 30 minutes, or until the meat is very tender, stirring occasionally. Remove the bay leaves before serving. Serve with mashed potatoes and steamed green beans, if desired.

nutrition per serve (6)
Protein 40 g; Fat 7 g; Carbohydrate 5 g; Dietary Fiber 1 g; Cholesterol 90 mg; 275 calories

hint

This dish can be stored in an airtight container in the refrigerator for up to 3 days. For a richer, slightly sweeter flavor, substitute the red wine with port.
This dish can also be cooked in the oven in a covered baking dish. If the sauce is too thin after cooking, remove the lid and boil until reduced slightly.

ingredients

5 lb 8 oz beef rib roast
2 cloves garlic, crushed
1 tablespoon flour
2 tablespoons red wine
1¼ cups beef stock

Yorkshire puddings
¾ cup all-purpose flour
½ cup milk
2 eggs

preparation: 15 minutes
cooking: 1 hour 45 minutes
serves: 6

1 Preheat the oven to 475°F. Rub the beef with the garlic and some pepper. Place the beef on a rack in a roasting pan, and roast for 15 minutes.

2 Meanwhile, to make the Yorkshire puddings, sift the all-purpose flour and ½ teaspoon salt into a large bowl, make a well in the center and whisk in the milk. In a separate bowl, whisk the eggs until fluffy, then add them to the batter and mix well. Add ½ cup water and whisk until large bubbles form on the surface. Cover with plastic wrap and refrigerate for 1 hour.

3 Reduce the oven temperature to 350°F, and then roast the meat for another 50–60 minutes for a rare result, or a little longer for well done. Cover the meat loosely with foil and rest in a warm place for 10–15 minutes. Increase the oven temperature to 425°F.

4 Pour off all the meat juices into a bowl and reserve for making gravy later. Put ½ teaspoon of the juices

into each of twelve ⅓-cup capacity muffin cups. Whisk the batter again until bubbles form on the surface. Pour the batter into each muffin cup to three-quarters full. Bake for 10 minutes, then reduce the oven to 350°F and cook for another 10 minutes, or until puffed and light golden.

5 Put the roasting pan on the stove, add the reserved meat juices and cook over low heat. Add the flour and stir, scraping the bottom of the pan to release any sediment. Cook over medium heat, stirring constantly, until the flour is browned. Combine the wine and stock, and then gradually stir it into the flour mixture. Cook, stirring constantly, until the gravy boils and thickens. Then simmer the gravy for 3 minutes.

6 Serve the roast beef with the gravy, Yorkshire puddings, Brussels sprouts and roasted potatoes.

nutrition per serve
Protein 100 g; Fat 16 g; Carbohydrate 14 g; Dietary Fiber 1 g; Cholesterol 267 mg; 585 calories

handy tip...

It is important to let the roast stand for up to 15 minutes before slicing. This allows the meat to relax and prevents the juices from spilling out onto the chopping board.

ingredients

1 lb lean ground beef
1 small onion, grated
1 tablespoon light olive oil
4 lettuce leaves
4 buttered hamburger buns
4 slices cheese
1 tomato, sliced
1 small red onion,
    finely sliced

preparation: 10 minutes
cooking: 10 minutes
serves: 4

1 Place the ground beef in a large mixing bowl with the grated onion, then season with salt and freshly ground black pepper. With clean hands, gently mix to just combine (too much handling will cause the meat juices to run out and escape during cooking). Shape the beef mixture into four patties, handling the meat quickly and lightly.

2 Heat the olive oil in a wide skillet and cook the patties over medium heat for 5 minutes on each side, or until cooked through. Drain well on paper towels.

3 Place a lettuce leaf on the bottom half of each bun. Top with a beef patty, slice of cheese, tomato and red onion slices. Season to taste with salt and freshly ground black pepper and top with the other half of the bun. Serve immediately with ketchup or barbecue sauce.

nutrition per serve
Protein 35 g; Fat 18 g; Carbohydrate 47 g; Dietary Fiber 5 g; Cholesterol 80 mg; 495 calories

hint

Add some chopped fresh herbs such as parsley or rosemary to the beef mixture. Use a combination of pork and beef for extra flavor.

ingredients

12 oz boneless sirloin or
 top round steak
12 long sprigs rosemary
12 button mushrooms,
 halved
1 tablespoon oil
1 tablespoon honey
1 tablespoon soy sauce

preparation: 15 minutes
cooking: 10 minutes
serves: 4

1 Trim the meat of any excess fat and sinew and cut into 1 in cubes. Trim the leaves from the stems of the rosemary sprigs, leaving 2 in at one end. Thread the meat alternately with the mushrooms onto the rosemary skewers. Place the oil, honey and soy sauce in a small bowl and mix together well.

2 Place the skewers on a lightly oiled broiler rack and brush the meat with the oil and honey mixture. Cook the skewers under a hot broiler for 10 minutes, or until tender, turning occasionally and brushing with the oil and honey mixture. Serve immediately with a green salad.

nutrition per serve
Protein 20 g; Fat 2.5 g; Carbohydrate 6 g; Dietary Fiber 0.5 g; Cholesterol 60 mg; 130 calories

handy tip...

Rosemary sprigs make great alternative skewers to wooden or metal skewers. In addition to holding the meat and vegetables, the rosemary aroma permeates throughout the meat and vegetables while cooking.

ingredients

1 tablespoon olive oil
1 onion, chopped
1 lb lean ground beef
15 oz can crushed
    tomatoes
1¼ oz sachet chili
    seasoning mix
½ teaspoon dried oregano
2 tablespoons tomato paste
15 oz can red kidney
    beans, rinsed and
    drained

preparation: 10 minutes
cooking: 30 minutes
serves: 4

1 Heat the oil in a large saucepan. Add the onion and cook, stirring occasionally, over medium heat for 5 minutes, or until the onion is soft and golden. Add the beef and cook over high heat for 5 minutes, or until the meat is brown, breaking up any lumps with the back of a wooden spoon. Drain off any excess liquid.

2 Add the tomatoes, seasoning mix, oregano, tomato paste and ½ cup water, and bring to a boil. Reduce the heat, cover and then simmer for 15 minutes, stirring occasionally.

3 Add the red kidney beans and simmer for 3–4 minutes, or until heated through. Season with salt and freshly ground black pepper. Serve hot with corn chips and a dollop of sour cream, or with rice.

nutrition per serve
Protein 28 g; Fat 16 g; Carbohydrate 20 g; Dietary Fiber 9 g; Cholesterol 65 mg; 340 calories

hint

The ground beef can be substituted with ground fresh chicken.
If chili seasoning mix is not available, use ½ teaspoon chili powder or 2 finely chopped fresh red chiles.

ingredients

13 oz can unsweetened
coconut cream
1–2 tablespoons Thai red
curry paste
13 oz can unsweetened
coconut milk
1 lb 8 oz beef sirloin strips
6 green onions
7 oz green beans
1 tablespoon grated palm
sugar
2 tablespoons fish sauce

preparation: 15 minutes
cooking: 25 minutes
serves: 4–6

1 Heat a wok and add the coconut cream. Bring to a boil, reduce the heat slightly and simmer rapidly for 10 minutes, or until the oil separates from the coconut cream.

2 Stir in the curry paste, add the coconut milk and beef strips and cook for 5 minutes. Cut the green onions into pieces and the beans into 1¼ in lengths. Stir in the green onions, beans, palm sugar and fish sauce and cook for 10 minutes, or until meat is tender. Serve with jasmine rice and garnish with shredded lime leaves, if desired.

nutrition per serve (6)
Protein 32 g; Fat 40 g; Carbohydrate 14 g; Dietary Fiber 4.5 g; Cholesterol 81 mg; 540 calories

handy tip...

If palm sugar is unavailable, use soft brown sugar. Any vegetables can be added to this dish, including bamboo shoots, baby corn and baby eggplant.
To make a simple mussaman curry, omit the beans, add 2 tablespoons chunky peanut butter, 8 baby potatoes and 8 baby onions. Serve sprinkled with chopped nuts.

ingredients

1 lb 10 oz lean ground
   beef
1 onion, grated
2 cloves garlic, crushed
¼ cup fruit chutney
2 teaspoons chopped
   fresh oregano
1 egg, lightly beaten
1½ cups fresh, soft
   bread crumbs
8 slices bacon

preparation: 15 minutes
cooking: 20 minutes
serves: 4

1 Place the beef, onion, garlic, fruit chutney, oregano, egg and bread crumbs in a large bowl and mix together well (you will find it easier to use your hands for this). Season to taste with salt and freshly ground black pepper. Divide the mixture into eight even portions, shaping each into a 3½ in patty.

2 Cut each slice of bacon in half lengthwise. Wrap one length of bacon around the patty and then wrap another length around in the other direction, forming a cross. Secure with a cocktail pick.

3 Heat a lightly greased skillet over medium heat and then add the beef patties in batches. Cook for 5 minutes on each side, or until the patties are well browned and cooked through. Drain well on paper towels and remove the cocktail picks before serving.

nutrition per serve
Protein 80 g; Fat 28 g; Carbohydrate 18 g; Dietary Fiber 1.5 g; Cholesterol 215 mg; 560 calories

hint

This mixture can also be made into meatballs or a meat loaf. Finely chop the bacon and fold it into the beef mixture.

ingredients

3 lb beef short ribs
½ cup apricot nectar
1 tablespoon soy sauce
1 tablespoon sweet chili
  sauce
2 cloves garlic, crushed
2 teaspoons grated fresh
  ginger

preparation: 5 minutes
cooking: 30 minutes
serves: 4

1 Preheat the oven to 425°F. Arrange the ribs in a single layer in a roasting pan.

2 Place the apricot nectar, soy sauce, sweet chili sauce, the garlic and ginger in a bowl and mix together. Pour the glaze mixture over the ribs.

3 Bake for 30 minutes, or until the ribs are tender and well browned. Brush the ribs occasionally with the glaze, turning a couple of times during cooking. Serve immediately with a green salad, if desired.

nutrition per serve
Protein 80 g; Fat 15 g; Carbohydrate 5.5 g; Dietary Fiber 0.5 g; Cholesterol 205 mg; 466 calories

handy tip...

This dish can also be cooked under the broiler or on the barbecue.
The apricot nectar can be replaced with orange juice.

ingredients

1 lb boneless sirloin or top
    round steak
1 teaspoon olive oil
1 onion, finely diced
1 cinnamon stick
4 cloves
1 bay leaf
2 cups beef stock
8 x 8 in tortillas

preparation: 15 minutes
cooking: 1 hour 35 minutes
serves: 4

1 Trim the steak of any excess fat and sinew and cut the flesh into ¾ in cubes.

2 Heat the oil in a skillet. Add the onion and cook over medium heat for 2–3 minutes, or until golden brown.

3 Add the meat, cinnamon stick, cloves, bay leaf and beef stock. Bring to a boil, then reduce the heat and simmer, covered, for 1 hour 30 minutes, or until the meat is soft and the liquid is almost absorbed. Remove the cinnamon stick, cloves and bay leaf.

4 Shred the meat with two forks. Place the meat evenly down the center of each tortilla. Roll up the burrito. Serve with bottled salsa and red onion, or with green vegetables or a salad, if desired.

nutrition per serve
Protein 40 g; Fat 7 g; Carbohydrate 60 g; Dietary Fiber 3.5 g; Cholesterol 84 mg; 462 calories

hint

The burritos can be cooked in the oven to become enchilladas. Place them in an ovenproof dish, pour on a jar of tomato salsa and sprinkle with shredded jack cheese. Bake in a 400°F oven for 20 minutes, or until the cheese is golden.

ingredients

Lemon mustard butter
½ cup butter
1 tablespoon French
   mustard
2 teaspoons finely grated
   lemon rind
1 tablespoon finely
   chopped fresh chives

4 filet mignon steaks
   (about 5 oz each)
1 tablespoon olive oil
2 cloves garlic, crushed
1 teaspoon ground
   rosemary

preparation: 10 minutes
cooking: 12 minutes
serves: 4

1 To make the lemon mustard butter, cream the butter with the mustard and rind. Stir in the chives. Shape into a log, wrap in plastic wrap and freeze until required.

2 Trim the meat of any excess fat and sinew.

3 Flatten the steaks to an even thickness and nick the edges to prevent curling. Combine the oil, garlic and rosemary and brush evenly over each steak.

4 Place the meat on a lightly oiled hot barbecue. Cook over high heat for 2 minutes on each side, turning once. For a rare result, cook for another minute on each side. For medium and well done results, move the meat to a cooler part of the barbecue, cook for another 2–3 minutes on each side for medium and 4–6 on each side for well done.

5 Serve the steaks with a slice of lemon mustard butter and a wedge of lemon.

nutrition per serve
Protein 33 g; Fat 27 g; Carbohydrate 0.5 g; Dietary Fiber 0.5 g; Cholesterol 154 mg; 370 calories

handy tip...

The lemon mustard butter can be prepared a day ahead and refrigerated.
A little sesame or walnut oil added to the mixture rubbed on the steaks will give them a pleasant, slightly nutty taste.

ingredients

1 lb 8 oz lean ground beef

²/₃ cup sour cream

1³/₄ sachet tomato
   soup mix

1 onion, finely chopped

2 cloves garlic, crushed

1 tablespoon ground
   paprika

1 teaspoon chopped fresh
   red chile

preparation: 10 minutes
cooking: 1 hour
serves: 6

1 Preheat the oven to 350°F. Grease an 8½ x 4½ x 2½ in loaf pan and line the base and sides with parchment paper.

2 Place the beef in a large bowl with the sour cream, soup mix, onion, garlic, paprika and chile and mix together well.

3 Press the mixture firmly into the prepared pan. Bake for 1 hour, or until well browned and firm—insert a skewer in the center to check for firmness. Turn out of the pan and serve sliced. Serve with salad, if desired.

nutrition per serve
Protein 26 g; Fat 24 g; Carbohydrate 2 g; Dietary Fiber 0.5 g; Cholesterol 114 mg; 327 calories

hint

Meat loaf can be served hot or cold. If serving hot, cook just before serving. If serving cold, meat loaf can be cooked up to 2 days before required. Store, covered, in the refrigerator.

simple steak sauces

creamy mustard sauce

Remove the steaks from the skillet and drain off any excess oil. Add ¼ cup white wine and cook, stirring, to remove any pan juices from the bottom of the skillet. Boil until the wine has nearly evaporated. Reduce the heat to low and stir in 1 teaspoon honey, 2 tablespoons coarse grain mustard and 1¼ cups sour cream for 5 minutes, or until heated through.

From left to right: Creamy mustard sauce; Chunky tomato sauce; Quick herb butter; Rich red wine sauce; Creamy mushroom sauce; Green peppercorn sauce.

serves 4

chunky tomato sauce

Remove the steaks from the skillet and drain off any excess oil. Stir in 2 tablespoons tomato chutney, 1 tablespoon balsamic vinegar and 1¾ cups bottled tomato pasta sauce. Bring to a boil and cook until it is thick and pulpy. Sprinkle 1 tablespoon chopped fresh parsley over the sauce when served.

serves 4

quick herb butter

Remove the steaks from the skillet and drain off any excess oil. Add ⅓ cup butter, 2 crushed cloves garlic, 1 tablespoon lemon juice and ¼ cup chopped fresh mixed herbs (eg. chives, parsley). Stir until the butter melts and turns a nutty brown color.

serves 4

rich red wine sauce

Remove the steaks from the skillet and drain off any excess oil. Add 1 cup red wine to the pan and bring to the boil, stirring to release any pan juices that may be stuck to the bottom of the skillet. Stir in ½ cup beef stock and 2 tablespoons redcurrant jelly. Then simmer the sauce for 5 minutes, or until the sauce is reduced by half and becomes syrupy.

serves 4

creamy mushroom sauce

Remove the steaks from the skillet and drain off any excess oil. Melt 3 tablespoons butter and then add 2 crushed cloves garlic, 3 sliced green onions and 1 cup thinly sliced button mushrooms. Cook over medium heat until the mushrooms are golden brown. Add 1 tablespoon brandy and 1 cup whipping cream. Bring to a boil, then simmer for 5 minutes, or until the sauce has thickened slightly.

serves 4

green peppercorn sauce

Remove the steaks from the skillet and drain off any excess oil. Add 1 tablespoon chicken stock, ½ teaspoon Worcestershire sauce, 1¼ cups whipping cream, 2 tablespoons brandy and 2 tablespoons canned green peppercorns, coarsely chopped. Bring to a boil, stirring to release any pan juices that may be stuck to the bottom of the skillet. Simmer for 5 minutes, or until the sauce has thickened slightly.

serves 4

ingredients

¼ cup olive oil
¼ cup butter
1 lb veal leg round steak,
    ¼ in thick
flour, for coating
2 tablespoons lemon juice
2 tablespoons finely
    chopped fresh parsley
lemon slices, to garnish

preparation: 15 minutes
cooking: 15 minutes
serves: 4

1 Heat the oil and half the butter in a large skillet over medium heat. Cut the veal into 8 pieces, coat in the flour, shake off any excess and add to the pan, cooking in batches if necessary. Cook for 1 minute, or until lightly browned on one side. Turn over and cook for another minute, or until brown. (Thin veal steaks should only take 1 minute to brown on each side—any longer and it will toughen the meat.) Transfer to a warm plate and season with salt and pepper.

2 To make the lemon sauce, reduce the heat to low and add the lemon juice, parsley and remaining butter to the skillet. Stir to combine, then add the veal and turn in the sauce for 1 minute, or until heated through.

3 Serve the veal with the lemon sauce and garnish with lemon slices. Serve with a green salad or vegetables, if desired.

nutrition per serve
Protein 40 g; Fat 30 g; Carbohydrate 4 g; Dietary Fiber 0.5 g; Cholesterol 178 mg; 443 calories

handy tip...

For thin veal steaks, cover them with plastic wrap and pound with a rolling pin or meat mallet to ⅛ in thickness. This sauce is delicious with the addition of white wine. Add ½ cup white wine, bring to a boil, then add the lemon juice and remaining ingredients.

ingredients

4 veal loin chops
flour, for dusting
2 tablespoons milk
1 egg, beaten
¾ cup dry bread crumbs
1 tablespoon finely
   chopped fresh sage,
   or 2 teaspoons dried
   sage
2 tablespoons butter
1 tablespoon olive oil

preparation: 10 minutes
cooking: 10 minutes
serves: 4

1 Trim any excess fat from the veal chops.

2 Dust the chops with the flour. Add the milk to the beaten egg. Combine the bread crumbs and sage. Brush the chops with the combined egg and milk mixture, then coat in the bread crumbs.

3 Heat the butter and oil in a large skillet. Add the chops in a single layer and cook over medium heat for 5 minutes on each side, or until cooked through. Serve with a green salad and garnish with lemon wedges, if desired.

nutrition per serve
Protein 19 g; Fat 13 g; Carbohydrate 15 g; Dietary Fiber 1 g; Cholesterol 80 mg; 254 calories

hint

To make your own dry bread crumbs, place slices of stale bread and crusts on a baking sheet. Bake in a 300°F oven until golden brown, dry and crisp. Process to crumbs in a food processor or blender.

ingredients

1 lb veal leg round steak,
    ¼ in thick, cut into
    serving pieces
2 tablespoons flour
⅓ cup butter
⅓ cup Marsala
½ cup chicken stock

preparation: 10 minutes
cooking: 20 minutes
serves: 4

1 Trim the steaks of any excess fat and pat dry with paper towels.

2 Season the flour with salt and freshly ground black pepper. Then toss the veal lightly in the seasoned flour and shake off any excess from the veal.

3 Heat ¼ cup of the butter in a skillet. Cook the veal over medium heat for 1 minute on each side, turning once. Remove from the pan and keep warm.

4 Add the Marsala and stock to the skillet and bring to a boil. Boil for 2 minutes, stirring constantly. Return the veal to the pan, reduce the heat and simmer, covered, for 10 minutes, basting the veal occasionally. Transfer the veal to a serving dish.

5 Boil the Marsala sauce rapidly for 2–3 minutes, or until syrupy. Stir in the remaining butter and spoon the sauce over the veal. Serve with pasta and a green salad, if desired.

nutrition per serve
Protein 21 g; Fat 20 g; Carbohydrate 5 g; Dietary Fiber 0 g; Cholesterol 127 mg; 293 calories

handy tip...

Marsala is a sweet fortified wine.
To make the sauce richer, add ½ cup whipping cream with the Marsala. Bring to a boil, then simmer until the sauce coats the back of a spoon.

ingredients

8 veal loin chops
1/3 cup olive oil
1 large leek, sliced
3 cloves garlic, crushed
6 fresh sage leaves
2 x 13 oz cans cannellini
   beans, rinsed and
   drained
1/2 cup chicken stock

preparation: 10 minutes
cooking: 25 minutes
serves: 4–6

1 Trim the chops of any excess fat and sinew.

2 Heat 2 tablespoons of the oil in a large saucepan. Add the leek and cook for 3 minutes, or until softened. Stir in the garlic and sage and add the beans. Pour in the stock and season with salt. Cook, covered, over medium heat for 10 minutes, stirring occasionally, and adding extra stock or water if necessary. Mash a few beans into the liquid to make a thick sauce. Keep warm until ready to serve.

3 Heat the remaining oil in a large non-stick skillet. Add the chops and cook over medium heat for 4 minutes each side.

4 Just before serving, season the beans with plenty of salt and freshly ground black pepper. Serve the chops with the beans and a green salad, if desired.

nutrition per serve (6)
Protein 30 g; Fat 15 g; Carbohydrate 15 g; Dietary Fiber 9 g; Cholesterol 78 mg; 316 calories

hint

Dried white beans can be used instead of canned, but they will need extra liquid and a much longer cooking time. Chickpeas are a good substitute for the beans.

ingredients

2 tablespoons oil
3 tablespoons butter
2 onions, thinly sliced
2 tablespoons flour
1 lb 4 oz calves' liver, thinly sliced (ask your butcher to do this)
½ cup good-quality Riesling
1 cup finely chopped fresh parsley

preparation: 15 minutes
cooking: 20 minutes
serves: 4

1 Heat a wok or skillet until very hot. Add one tablespoon of the oil with 2 teaspoons of the butter and swirl it around to coat the side. Stir-fry the onions over medium-high heat for 3–4 minutes, or until soft. Remove from the wok.

2 Season the flour with salt and freshly ground black pepper. Toss the liver in the seasoned flour.

3 Reheat the wok. Add the remaining oil and the remaining butter, and stir-fry the floured liver in four batches for 3 minutes, or until browned. Remove from the wok and keep warm.

4 Reheat the wok, then add the wine and boil until it has reduced by two-thirds. Return the onions and the liver to the wok, add the parsley and toss well to combine. Season with salt and freshly ground black pepper. This is delicious served with creamy polenta or mashed potatoes.

nutrition per serve
Protein 30 g; Fat 35 g; Carbohydrate 10 g; Dietary Fiber 1.5 g; Cholesterol 440 mg; 485 calories

handy tip...

It is very important not to overcook the liver or it will be tough and dry.
If you would like this recipe to have a gravy, add 1 cup water or beef stock with the wine and bring to a boil.
Stir until thickened.

ingredients

1 lb veal leg round steak,
    ¼ in thick
flour, for coating
1 egg, lightly beaten
dry bread crumbs,
    for coating
2 tablespoons butter
¼ cup oil
⅔ cup bottled chunky
    tomato pasta sauce
1 cup shredded mozzarella

preparation: 15 minutes +
    1 hour refrigeration
cooking: 30 minutes
serves: 4

1 Cut the veal into serving-size pieces and pat dry with paper towels. Coat the veal in the flour and shake off any excess. Dip in the egg and coat with bread crumbs. Refrigerate for 1 hour.

2 Preheat the oven to 350°F. Grease a baking dish large enough to lay the veal slices in a single layer.

3 Heat the butter and oil in a large skillet. Add the crumbed veal to the skillet and cook for 2–3 minutes on each side, or until golden. Drain on paper towels.

4 Place in a single layer in the prepared dish. Spoon the tomato sauce onto each piece of veal, then sprinkle with the mozzarella. Bake for 20–25 minutes, or until the mozzarella is golden and melted. Serve with a green salad.

nutrition per serve
Protein 32 g; Fat 32 g; Carbohydrate 4 g; Dietary Fiber 0.5 g; Cholesterol 158 mg; 425 calories

hint

This recipe can be made up to baking stage several hours ahead and stored, covered, in the refrigerator. Cook just before serving. It can also be frozen, without cheese, for up to 1 month. Allow to defrost completely in the refrigerator, and sprinkle the mozzarella on top just before cooking. Wonderful for unexpected dinner guests!

ingredients

12 thin veal scallops
  (escalopes)
12 fresh sage leaves
12 slices cooked leg ham
12 slices mozzarella
flour, for coating
⅓ cup butter
1 cup white wine

preparation: 10 minutes
cooking: 30 minutes
serves: 6

1 Flatten the veal scallops with a meat mallet to make them as thin as possible.

2 On each scallop, place a sage leaf, a slice of ham and a slice of cheese. Fold the scallops in half and secure each with a cocktail pick. Lightly coat in flour.

3 Heat the butter in a skillet. When foaming, add the scallops in two batches and cook over medium-high heat for 5–6 minutes on each side, or until light golden. Remove the veal and keep warm.

4 Add the wine to the skillet and stir over high heat until reduced by half to make a sauce. Season with salt and freshly ground black pepper. Remove the cocktail picks from the scallops, pour the sauce over the top and serve.

nutrition per serve
Protein 30 g; Fat 15 g; Carbohydrate 0 g; Dietary Fiber 0 g; Cholesterol 132 mg; 295 calories

handy tip...

One teaspoon of dried sage sprinkled over each scallop can be used in place of fresh.

ingredients

8 veal rib chops
1/2 cup chicken stock
1 lime, cut into wedges
8 oz button mushrooms,
    finely sliced
3/4 cup sour cream

preparation: 15 minutes
cooking: 1 hour 25 minutes
serves: 4

1 Preheat the oven to 300°F. Trim the veal of any excess fat and sinew.

2 Place the chops, chicken stock and lime wedges in a roasting pan. Cover and bake in the oven for 1 hour 15 minutes, or until tender.

3 Remove the lime and stir in the sliced mushrooms. Return to the oven and cook, uncovered, for 5 minutes, or until the mushrooms are wilted and heated through, taking care not to cook too long.

4 Transfer the mushrooms and the chops to a hot serving dish and keep warm.

5 Place the roasting pan with the pan juices over high heat and bring to a boil. Cook for 4–5 minutes, or until the liquid is reduced by half.

6 Whisk the sour cream into the sauce. Pour the sauce over the veal and mushrooms and serve immediately with pasta or rice.

nutrition per serve
Protein 33 g; Fat 22 g; Carbohydrate 2 g; Dietary Fiber 0 g; Cholesterol 180 mg; 340 calories

hint

For a thicker sauce, add up to twice the amount of sour cream.

lamb

ingredients

1 lb lamb's liver
1 tablespoon olive oil
1 large onion, sliced
4 oz bacon, cut into strips
2 tablespoons butter
1 tablespoon flour
1¼ cups beef stock
2 tablespoons chopped
fresh parsley

preparation: 10 minutes
cooking: 10 minutes
serves: 4

1 Remove the membrane and tubes from the liver and slice horizontally into ¼ in slices.

2 Heat the oil in a large skillet. Cook the onion and bacon until browned, then remove from the pan and keep warm.

3 Increase the heat and add the butter to the skillet until it sizzles. Quickly cook the liver, in batches, over high heat for 1 minute on each side—do not overcook or it will become tough.

4 Return all the liver to the pan with the bacon and onion. Sprinkle the flour over the top and toss to coat. Gradually add the stock and stir until the sauce boils and thickens. Season. Stir in the parsley and serve with fried tomato slices and mashed potatoes.

nutrition per serve
Protein 35 g; Fat 22 g; Carbohydrate 7 g; Dietary Fiber 0.5 g; Cholesterol 578 mg; 364 calories

handy tip...

Liver is an excellent source of Vitamin A, iron and protein.
This recipe can also be made with calves' liver, which is larger, darker and stronger in flavor.

ingredients

Mint sauce
⅓ cup sugar
2 tablespoons malt or
    cider vinegar
⅓ cup finely chopped
    fresh mint

8 Frenched lamb rib chops
1 tablespoon olive oil

preparation: 10 minutes
cooking: 10 minutes
serves: 4

1 To make the mint sauce, combine the sugar and ⅓ cup water in a saucepan. Stir over low heat, without boiling, until the sugar has dissolved. Bring to a boil, then reduce the heat and simmer for 3 minutes. Remove from the heat and pour into a bowl. Then add the vinegar and mint and mix together well.

2 Trim the excess fat and sinew from each chop with a small, sharp knife. Scrape all the sinew from the bone until it is clean.

3 Heat the oil in a skillet. Cook the chops (in batches if necessary) over high heat for 2 minutes on each side, to seal, then for another 1 minute on each side.

4 Serve the mint sauce at room temperature over the lamb chops. This dish is delicious served with boiled new potatoes, squash and zucchini.

nutrition per serve
Protein 15 g; Fat 9.5 g; Carbohydrate 22 g; Dietary Fiber 0 g; Cholesterol 48 mg; 232 calories

hint

To save you time, ask your butcher to 'French' (trim) the lamb chops for you.
This recipe can also be made using lamb loin chops.

ingredients

2 large tomatoes
1 tablespoon oil
1 onion, finely chopped
2 teaspoons soft brown
 sugar
1 tablespoon red wine
 vinegar
1 tablespoon finely
 chopped fresh mint
8 lamb loin chops
fresh mint sprigs, to
 garnish

preparation: 10 minutes
cooking: 25 minutes
serves: 4

1 To make the salsa, cut a small cross on the bottom of each tomato with a sharp knife. Plunge the tomatoes into boiling water for 30 seconds, then into chilled water for 1 minute. Peel the skin down from the cross, then finely chop the tomatoes.

2 Heat the oil in a small saucepan, then add the onion and cook over low heat for 5 minutes, or until softened. Add the tomatoes, sugar and vinegar and simmer for 5 minutes, stirring occasionally. Add the chopped mint and mix well.

3 Place the chops on a cold, lightly oiled broiler rack and cook under a hot broiler for 2 minutes on each side to seal. For a rare result, cook the chops for another 1 minute on each side. For a medium or well-done result, lower the broiler rack, or reduce the heat to medium, and cook for another 2–3 minutes on each side for medium and 4–6 minutes on each side for a well-done result.

4 Serve the chops immediately with the tomato and mint salsa (the salsa can be served either warm or cold). Garnish with a fresh sprig of mint.

nutrition per serve
Protein 24 g; Fat 9 g; Carbohydrate 4 g; Dietary Fiber 1.5 g; Cholesterol 65 mg; 192 calories

handy tip...

The salsa can be made up to 2 days before required. Add the mint just before serving. Store, covered, in the refrigerator and reheat just before serving.
This dish is great served with mashed potatoes and steamed peas or beans.
For a slight variation, use a different cut of lamb, such as leg chops or fillets.

ingredients

12 Frenched lamb
    rib chops
1/4 cup all-purpose flour
2 eggs, lightly beaten
1 1/2 cups dry bread
    crumbs
1/4 cup oil

preparation: 10 minutes +
    30 minutes refrigeration
cooking: 20 minutes
serves: 4

1 Trim the lamb chops of any excess fat and sinew.

2 Season the flour on a plate. Toss the chops lightly in the seasoned flour and shake off any excess.

3 Dip each flour-coated chop into the egg, then quickly coat with the bread crumbs. Using your fingers, press the bread crumbs firmly onto the chops, then shake off any excess.

4 Place the chops in a single layer on a baking sheet. Cover and refrigerate for 30 minutes.

5 Heat the oil in a large skillet (make sure the oil isn't too hot or the crumbs will burn before the meat is cooked through). Add the chops in three batches and cook over medium heat for 3 minutes on each side, or until golden and tender. Drain on paper towels.

nutrition per serve
Protein 32 g; Fat 25 g; Carbohydrate 30 g; Dietary Fiber 2 g; Cholesterol 160 mg; 475 calories

hint

For a variation, replace the dry bread crumbs with cornflake crumbs, or stir some chopped fresh mixed herbs and grated lemon rind into the bread crumbs.

ingredients

4 racks of lamb
    (4 rib chops each)
1 cup mint jelly
2 tablespoons white wine
¼ cup finely chopped
    fresh chives

preparation: 15 minutes
cooking: 45 minutes
serves: 4

1 Preheat the oven to 400°F. Trim any excess fat from the racks of lamb, leaving a thin layer of fat. Clean any meat or sinew from the bones. Cover the bones with foil and place them on a rack in a roasting pan.

2 Place the mint jelly and wine in a small saucepan. Cook, stirring, over high heat for 4 minutes, or until the mixture has reduced and thickened. Cool slightly, then add the chives.

3 Brush the racks of lamb with the glaze. Roast for 35 minutes for a rare result, or 40 minutes for medium-rare result, brushing with the glaze every 10 minutes. Remove the foil from the lamb and allow to rest for 5 minutes before serving. Serve with steamed or roasted vegetables.

nutrition per serve
Protein 30 g; Fat 9 g; Carbohydrate 0 g; Dietary Fiber 0 g; Cholesterol 95 mg; 215 calories

handy tip...

For a variation to the mint glaze, substitute the mint jelly with redcurrant jelly or cranberry jelly.

ingredients

1 tablespoon oil

1 lb 8 oz lean boneless lamb, cubed

2 cups beef or chicken stock

2 small onions, chopped

½ cup pitted prunes, halved

½ cup dried apricots, halved

1 teaspoon ground ginger

1 teaspoon ground cinnamon

preparation: 15 minutes
cooking: 1 hour 10 minutes
serves: 4

1 Heat the oil in a large saucepan. Add the meat in small batches, and cook over medium heat for 2 minutes, or until well browned. Return all the meat to the pan.

2 Add the stock, onions, prunes, apricots, ginger and cinnamon to the saucepan and season with pepper. Bring to a boil, then reduce the heat and simmer, covered, for 1 hour, or until the meat is tender. Garnish with toasted slivered almonds, if desired, and serve with rice or couscous (see hint).

nutrition per serve
Protein 44 g; Fat 12 g; Carbohydrate 26 g; Dietary Fiber 5 g; Cholesterol 125 mg; 386 calories

hint

This recipe is delicious served with spiced couscous. Place the couscous, a large piece of butter, 1 cinnamon stick and 1 strip of orange rind in a heatproof bowl and cover with boiling water. Allow to stand until the water has been absorbed.

ingredients

4 lb leg of lamb
2 cloves garlic, sliced
3 large strips lemon rind,
   cut into ½ in pieces
½ cup chopped fresh
   cilantro leaves
¼ cup chopped fresh
   parsley
2 tablespoons olive oil

preparation: 15 minutes
cooking: 1 hour 20 minutes
serves: 4–6

1 Preheat the oven to 350°F. Trim the lamb of any excess fat and sinew. Using a sharp knife, make deep cuts in the flesh and place a slice of garlic and a piece of lemon rind into each cut.

2 Place the cilantro, parsley, oil and 1 teaspoon freshly ground black pepper in a bowl and mix together well. Coat the lamb with the herb mixture and place on a rack in a roasting pan. Pour 1 cup water into the pan.

3 Roast for 1 hour 20 minutes, or until the lamb is cooked to your liking. Add extra water to the roasting pan during cooking if it starts to dry out. Allow the lamb to rest for 10 minutes before cutting into slices. Serve with a selection of vegetables, if desired. Drizzle with the pan juices for extra flavor.

nutrition per serve (6)
Protein 46 g; Fat 11 g; Carbohydrate 0 g; Dietary Fiber 0 g; Cholesterol 132 mg; 282 calories

handy tip...

Cilantro is a pungent, leafy green herb, readily available at most greengrocers.
Water is added to the roasting pan for several reasons. It keeps the meat moist, it prevents the juices from burning, and it provides a delicious liquid base for making gravy.

ingredients

4 large lamb leg sirloin chops (about 6 oz each)

2 tablespoons oil

16 oz can cream of mushroom soup

1 tablespoon Worcestershire sauce

¾ cup chicken stock

½ cup dry sherry

8 oz button mushrooms, sliced

2 large onions, sliced

preparation: 15 minutes
cooking: 2 hours 15 minutes
serves: 4

1 Preheat the oven to 350°F. Trim the chops of any excess fat and sinew. Heat 1 tablespoon oil in a skillet. Cook the chops for 1 minute on each side, or until well browned. Drain on paper towels.

2 Place the chops in a 2-quart capacity covered casserole. Then mix together the mushroom soup, Worcestershire sauce, chicken stock and sherry and pour over the chops. Cover and bake for 1 hour 30 minutes.

3 Heat the remaining oil in the skillet and cook the mushrooms for 3 minutes, or until lightly browned. Remove from the pan. Add the onions and cook for 5 minutes, or until soft and golden.

4 Stir the mushrooms into the casserole and top with the onion slices. Return to the oven and cook, uncovered, for 30 minutes, or until the onions are crisp and the lamb is tender. Serve with steamed fresh vegetables, if desired.

nutrition per serve
Protein 40 g; Fat 22 g; Carbohydrate 13 g; Dietary Fiber 4 g; Cholesterol 118 mg; 446 calories

hint

The sherry can be replaced with white wine. The lamb leg chops can be substituted with shoulder blade or arm chops.

ingredients

2 tomatoes
2 teaspoons oil
1 lb 4 oz boneless lamb leg
   center slice, thinly sliced
3 cloves garlic, chopped
1 teaspoon cumin seeds
2 teaspoons finely chopped
   fresh rosemary
2 tablespoons balsamic
   vinegar
10½ oz can cannellini
   beans, rinsed and drained

preparation: 15 minutes
cooking: 10 minutes
serves: 4

1 Score a cross in the base of each tomato. Cover with boiling water for 30 seconds, then transfer to iced water before peeling them and removing the stalks. Scoop out the seeds and finely chop the flesh into cubes.

2 Heat the wok until very hot, add the oil and swirl it around to coat the side. Stir-fry the lamb in two batches over very high heat for 2–3 minutes, or until browned.

3 Return all the lamb to the wok and add the garlic, cumin seeds and rosemary. Cook for 1 minute. Reduce the heat and add the vinegar. Stir well, scraping any sediment off the base of the wok.

4 Add the tomatoes and cannellini beans and stir-fry until warmed through. Season with salt and black pepper, then garnish with flat-leaf parsley leaves.

nutrition per serve
Protein 35 g; Fat 6 g; Carbohydrate 3 g; Dietary Fiber 3 g; Cholesterol 100 mg; 210 calories

handy tip...

This is a delightfully versatile recipe so feel free to experiment with different types of beans—try borlotti or lima beans.

ingredients

4 lb 8 oz leg of lamb
2 cloves garlic, cut into
    thin slivers
2 tablespoons fresh
    rosemary sprigs
2 teaspoons oil

preparation: 15 minutes
cooking: 1 hour 30 minutes
serves: 6

1 Preheat the oven to 350°F. Using a small sharp knife, cut small slits all over the lamb. Insert the slivers of garlic and sprigs of rosemary into the slits.

2 Brush the lamb with the oil and sprinkle with salt and freshly ground black pepper. Place on a wire rack in a roasting pan and pour in ½ cup water.

3 Roast the lamb in the oven for 1 hour 30 minutes for a medium result, or until cooked as desired, basting often with the pan juices. Keep warm and rest the lamb for 10–15 minutes before serving.

nutrition per serve
Protein 75 g; Fat 9 g; Carbohydrate 0 g; Dietary Fiber 0 g; Cholesterol 220 mg; 390 calories

hint

Always carve meat across the grain. To make sure the lamb cooks evenly, return to room temperature before roasting.

ingredients

½ cup olive oil

3 x 8 oz lamb tenderloins
(see handy tip)

½ small head red
cabbage, shredded

1 tablespoon caraway
seeds

1 tablespoon chopped
fresh rosemary

2 tablespoons pine nuts,
lightly toasted

Vinaigrette
1 tablespoon Dijon
mustard
1 tablespoon white wine
vinegar

preparation: 10 minutes
cooking: 20 minutes
serves: 6

1 Preheat the oven to 350°F. Heat 2 tablespoons of the oil in a skillet. Add the lamb and cook over high heat for 2 minutes on each side. Place the lamb on a wire rack in a roasting pan and bake for 5–7 minutes. Remove from the oven and rest for 10 minutes.

2 To make the vinaigrette, whisk together the mustard and vinegar in a bowl. Season with salt and freshly ground black pepper. Gradually whisk in the remaining olive oil until the mixture thickens, then adjust the seasoning to taste.

3 Place the shredded cabbage in a salad bowl, pour on the vinaigrette and mix together well. Add the caraway seeds and rosemary and toss. To serve, place the cabbage on a serving platter. Cut the lamb into ½ in slices and arrange over the cabbage. Sprinkle with the pine nuts and serve immediately.

nutrition per serve
Protein 29 g; Fat 29 g; Carbohydrate 1 g; Dietary Fiber 1.5 g; Cholesterol 82 mg; 380 calories

handy tip...

Lamb tenderloins are cut from the rib roast. For best results, turn the meat over halfway during baking for more even heat distribution. When the meat is cooked, remove from the oven and wrap completely in foil. Rest for 10 minutes before carving or slicing.

ingredients

1/3 cup ghee or butter
1 lb lamb tenderloins
    or leg center slice,
    cubed
1 onion, sliced
1 carrot, cut into strips
2 cups long-grain rice
3 1/2 cups boiling chicken
    stock
1/2 cup golden raisins
fresh parsley, chopped

preparation: 15 minutes
cooking: 30 minutes
serves: 4

1 Melt the ghee in a large skillet. Add the lamb in batches and cook until lightly browned. Add the onion and carrot and cook for 2 minutes. Season. Stir in the rice until coated.

2 Pour in the boiling stock, then reduce the heat and cook, covered, for 20 minutes, or until the rice is tender and all the liquid has been absorbed. Add the raisins, cover, and let stand until plumped. Garnish with the chopped parsley.

nutrition per serve
Protein 35 g; Fat 28 g; Carbohydrate 92 g; Dietary Fiber 4 g; Cholesterol 148 mg; 760 calories

hint

Pilaf originated in the Near East and is traditionally cooked, covered, in the oven, but can also be made on the stove. Pilaf is always made with medium- or long-grain rice.

ingredients

2 lb 4 oz boneless lamb leg
3 leeks, cut into ¼ in slices
3 carrots, thickly sliced
2 onions, cut into small
  cubes
1 cup medium pearl
  barley, well rinsed
2 cloves garlic, crushed
¼ cup chopped fresh
  parsley
parsley sprigs, to garnish

preparation: 15 minutes
cooking: 2 hours
serves: 6–8

1 Cut the lamb into cubes and place in a Dutch oven. Add the leeks, carrots, onions, barley and 10 cups water. Bring to a boil, then reduce the heat and simmer, covered, for 1 hour. Remove any scum as it rises to the surface.

2 Add the garlic and parsley, season with freshly ground pepper and simmer gently, uncovered, for another hour.

3 Season to taste with salt and freshly ground black pepper. Spoon into warm soup bowls and garnish with sprigs of parsley.

nutrition per serve (8)
Protein 30 g; Fat 5.5 g; Carbohydrate 20 g; Dietary Fiber 5 g; Cholesterol 82 mg; 258 calories

handy tip...

This recipe is best
prepared a day ahead.
Refrigerate and remove any
fat from the top of the broth.
The flavor of the soup will
develop and improve
on standing.
Diced lamb from the leg
is best suited to this recipe.

ingredients

2 lb 4 oz boneless lean
  lamb leg
1 green sweet bell pepper
1 red sweet bell pepper
2/3 cup olive oil
1/3 cup lemon juice
2 cloves garlic, crushed
1 tablespoon dried
  oregano
2 bay leaves, crumbled

preparation: 15 minutes +
  overnight refrigeration
cooking: 10 minutes
serves: 4

1 Trim the lamb of any excess fat and sinew. Cut the lamb into 1¼ in cubes. Cut the red and green sweet bell peppers into ¾ in squares.

2 Soak the wooden skewers in a bowl of cold water to prevent them from burning during cooking. Thread the meat and pepper pieces alternately onto the skewers, then place in a glass or ceramic dish.

3 Place the oil, lemon juice, garlic, oregano and bay leaves in a bowl. Season with salt and freshly ground black pepper and mix together. Pour the marinade over the skewers. Cover with plastic wrap and refrigerate overnight,
turning occasionally. Drain and reserve the marinade.

4 Place the skewers on a lightly greased barbecue grill or under a hot broiler. Cook over medium heat for 10 minutes, or until tender, brushing with the reserved marinade several times during cooking. This is delicious served with warm pita bread, Greek salad and Tzatziki (cucumber yogurt dip).

nutrition per serve
Protein 56 g; Fat 47 g; Carbohydrate 2.5 g; Dietary Fiber 1 g; Cholesterol 165 mg; 658 calories

hint

Uncooked kebabs can be frozen in marinade in an airtight container for up to a month. Thaw the kebabs in the container, then cook as directed.

ingredients

6–8 lamb shoulder arm
    chops
1 lemon
1 teaspoon oil
1 large onion, finely
    chopped
⅓ cup redcurrant jelly
1 tablespoon barbecue
    sauce
1 tablespoon ketchup
2 cups chicken stock

preparation: 15 minutes
cooking: 1 hour 15 minutes
serves: 4

1 Preheat the oven to 325°F. Trim the lamb of any excess fat and sinew. Grate 1 teaspoon of rind from the lemon and squeeze 1 tablespoon juice.

2 Heat the oil in a large skillet. Then add the chops and cook over medium heat, turning once, for 2–3 minutes, or until well browned. Remove from the pan and place in a baking dish.

3 Add the onion to the skillet and cook over medium heat, stirring frequently, for 5 minutes, or until the onion has softened. Add the redcurrant jelly, lemon rind and juice, barbecue sauce, ketchup and the stock. Stir for 2–3 minutes, or until heated through. Pour the sauce over the chops and stir to coat.

4 Bake, covered, for 1 hour, or until the meat is tender, turning 2–3 times during cooking. Lift the chops out onto a side plate and keep warm.

5 Pour the sauce into a skillet and boil rapidly for 5 minutes, or until the sauce has thickened and reduced. Return the chops to the sauce before serving.

nutrition per serve
Protein 31 g; Fat 11 g; Carbohydrate 6 g; Dietary Fiber 1.5 g; Cholesterol 96 mg; 250 calories

handy tip...

This casserole will keep, covered and refrigerated, for up to 2 days, and is suitable to freeze for up to 1 month.
Other lamb chop cuts can be used instead of shoulder arm, if preferred.

ingredients

2 tablespoons oil
1 lb lamb leg center slice,
  cut into thin strips
2 cloves garlic, crushed
4 green onions,
  thickly sliced
2 tablespoons soy sauce
1/3 cup dry sherry
2 tablespoons sweet chili
  sauce
2 teaspoons sesame
  seeds, toasted (see hint)

preparation: 15 minutes
cooking: 12 minutes
serves: 4

1 Heat a wok until very hot. Add 1 tablespoon oil and swirl it around to coat the side. Add the lamb strips in two batches and stir-fry over high heat for 3 minutes each batch, or until browned. Remove all the lamb from the wok.

2 Reheat the wok and add the remaining oil. Add the garlic and green onions and stir-fry for 2 minutes, then remove from the wok. Add the soy sauce, sherry and sweet chili sauce to the wok. Bring to a boil, then reduce the heat and simmer for 3–4 minutes, or until the sauce thickens slightly.

3 Return the meat, with any juices, and the green onions to the wok, and toss to coat with the sauce. Serve sprinkled with the toasted sesame seeds.

nutrition per serve
Protein 30 g; Fat 15 g; Carbohydrate 3 g; Dietary Fiber 1 g; Cholesterol 82 mg; 285 calories

hint

It is well worth toasting the sesame seeds as it really brings out the flavor. Simply place them in a non-stick skillet and cook over medium heat until golden, shaking the pan frequently.

pork

ingredients

4 pork loin butterfly chops
1 tablespoon oil
1 teaspoon grated
fresh ginger
1 cup apple cider
1 teaspoon cornstarch
1 tablespoon chopped
fresh chives

preparation: 10 minutes
cooking: 10 minutes
serves: 4

1 Trim the butterfly chops of any excess fat and sinew.

2 Heat the oil in a skillet and add the pork. Cook over medium heat for 2–3 minutes on each side, or until tender, turning once during cooking. Remove and keep warm.

3 Add the ginger to the pan, stirring and scraping with a wooden spoon. Place 1 tablespoon cider in a small bowl, add the cornstarch and stir until smooth. Add the remaining cider, mix well, and add to the pan. Bring to a boil, then reduce the heat and simmer, stirring, for 2 minutes, or until the sauce has thickened and reduced. Stir in the chives. Pour the sauce over the chops and serve with steamed vegetables.

nutrition per serve
Protein 28 g; Fat 6 g; Carbohydrate 7 g; Dietary Fiber 0 g; Cholesterol 62 mg; 194 calories

handy tip...

Either sweet or hard cider is suitable for this recipe. If you use hard cider, add it to the skillet before thickening and boil rapidly to evaporate the alcohol. Mix the cornstarch with 1 tablespoon water and stir into the cider.

ingredients

14 oz sweet potato,
  coarsely shredded
2 large potatoes,
  coarsely shredded
2 eggs, lightly beaten
1 tablespoon flour
2 tablespoons oil
8 slices bacon
8 thick pork sausages
⅓ cup fruit chutney, to serve

preparation: 15 minutes
cooking: 30 minutes
serves: 4

1 Place sweet potato, potatoes, eggs and flour in a bowl and mix together well. Season to taste with salt and freshly ground black pepper. Divide into eight portions and, using your hands, shape each portion into a 4 in flat patty.

2 Heat the oil in a non-stick skillet and cook the rosti in batches for 3–4 minutes on each side, or until golden brown and cooked through. Set aside and keep warm.

3 Wrap a piece of bacon around each sausage and secure with a cocktail pick.

4 Cook the sausages under a hot broiler for 10–15 minutes, or until cooked through, turning often. Remove the cocktail pick. Divide among the serving plates and top with a dollop of chutney. Serve with the potato rosti and a mixed green salad, if desired.

nutrition per serve
Protein 35 g; Fat 38 g; Carbohydrate 40 g; Dietary Fiber 5 g; Cholesterol 200 mg; 640 calories

hint

The sweet potato can be replaced with white potato (use a floury potato such as Russet, Idaho or Spunta). Make sure you squeeze the shredded potato to remove any excess moisture.

nutrition per serve
Protein 27 g; Fat 30 g; Carbohydrate
60 g; Dietary Fiber 4 g; Cholesterol
225 mg; 637 calories

ingredients

1 lb spaghetti
8 slices bacon, cut into
    thin strips
4 eggs
½ cup freshly grated
    Parmesan
1¼ cups whipping cream

preparation: 10 minutes
cooking: 20 minutes
serves: 6

1 Cook the spaghetti in a large saucepan of boiling water according to the package instructions. Drain well and return the spaghetti to the saucepan.

2 Meanwhile, heat a skillet. Add the bacon and cook over medium heat until crisp. Remove and drain on paper towels.

3 Place the eggs, Parmesan and cream in a bowl and beat together well. Add the bacon and the sauce to the warm pasta. Toss gently until the pasta is well coated.

4 Return the pan to the heat and cook over very low heat for 30–60 seconds, or until slightly thickened. Season with freshly ground black pepper and serve. Garnish with herb sprigs, if desired.

handy tip...

There are two thoughts as to the origin of this dish. Some say it appeared in Rome during the Second World War, when the GIs combined their rations of bacon and eggs with the local spaghetti. The other possibility suggests it was a quick and easy meal developed by the coal vendors, or *carbonari*.

ingredients

2 tablespoons olive oil
12 oz small mushrooms, quartered
4 slices bacon, chopped
6 eggs
1/3 cup heavy whipping cream
1 tablespoon tomato paste
2 teaspoons chopped fresh basil
1/2 cup shredded Cheddar

preparation: 10 minutes
cooking: 15 minutes
serves: 4–6

1 Heat the oil in a large skillet. Add the mushrooms and bacon and stir over medium heat for 5 minutes, or until golden and almost all the liquid is absorbed. Remove the pan from the heat.

2 Place the eggs, cream, tomato paste, basil and Cheddar in a bowl and season to taste. Beat with a whisk until mixed together.

3 Return the skillet to the heat. Pour the egg mixture over the mushrooms and bacon and stir. Shake the pan to spread the mixture evenly over the base. Cook over medium heat for 5 minutes, or until the omelette has almost set.

Place the pan under a hot broiler; cook for 2–3 minutes, or until the top is set. Cut into wedges and serve.

nutrition per serve (6)
Protein 16 g; Fat 22 g; Carbohydrate 2 g; Dietary Fiber 1.5 g; Cholesterol 220 mg; 265 calories

hint

Omelettes are great for a late breakfast or light lunch. They may be prepared with either savory (cheese, asparagus, shrimp) or sweet (macerated fruit) fillings.

pork rib chops with fried pear

ingredients

4 pork rib chops,
  well trimmed
1 tablespoon olive oil
1 tablespoon butter
1 ripe pear, peeled, cored,
  sliced into thin wedges
2 green onions, sliced
1 tablespoon flour
1 cup chicken stock
¼ cup apple juice or cider

preparation: 10 minutes
cooking: 20 minutes
serves: 4

1 Trim the chops of any fat. Heat the oil and butter in a skillet. Add the pear and cook over medium heat until lightly browned, turning occasionally. Remove.

2 Season the pork with salt and pepper. Add to the skillet and cook over medium heat for 4–5 minutes on each side, or until the pork is cooked through. Remove from the pan and keep warm.

3 Add the green onions to the skillet and cook until just soft. Stir in the flour and cook for 2 minutes. Remove from the heat and stir in the combined stock and apple juice. Return the pan to the heat and cook, stirring, until the sauce boils and thickens. Reduce the heat and simmer for 2 minutes. Add any pork juices to the pan.

4 Serve the pork topped with the pear slices and drizzled with the sauce. Serve with baby potatoes and beans. Sprinkle with chopped sage leaves, if desired.

nutrition per serve
Protein 25 g; Fat 10 g; Carbohydrate 9 g; Dietary Fiber 1 g; Cholesterol 58 mg; 225 calories

handy tip...

If pork rib chops are not available, use pork loin chops. Apple may be used instead of pear—Golden Delicious or Granny Smith are best for cooking.

ingredients

1 tablespoon oil
1 onion, coarsely
    chopped
4 slices prosciutto,
    coarsely chopped
5 small potatoes, cut into
    ½ in cubes
1½ cups chicken stock
2 cups frozen peas
1 tablespoon shredded
    fresh sage leaves

preparation: 10 minutes
cooking: 25 minutes
serves: 4

1 Heat the oil in a saucepan and add the onion and prosciutto. Cook, stirring constantly, over high heat for 2–3 minutes, or until the onion is golden. Add the potatoes and cook for another minute.

2 Pour in the stock and 2½ cups water. Cook over medium heat for 15 minutes. Add the peas and cook for another 5 minutes. Stir in the sage and season to taste with salt and freshly ground black pepper.

3 Divide the soup among four warm serving bowls. Serve with crusty bread and butter.

nutrition per serve
Protein 7 g; Fat 5.5 g; Carbohydrate 15 g; Dietary Fiber 6 g; Cholesterol 1.5 mg; 130 calories

hint

Trimmed slices of bacon can be used instead of prosciutto, and minted or fresh peas are a nice alternative to frozen peas. For a richer soup, replace the water with more stock, but don't be tempted to use bouillon granules—the soup will be too salty.

ingredients

1 tablespoon oil
4 pork loin chops
1 cup white wine
⅓ cup redcurrant jelly

preparation: 5 minutes
cooking: 25 minutes
serves: 4

1 Heat the oil in a skillet. Add the chops and cook over medium heat for 8 minutes on each side, or until they are tender and browned. Remove from the pan and keep the chops warm.

2 Add the wine and jelly to the pan and stir until blended with the pan juices. Bring the sauce to a boil, then reduce the heat and simmer for 10 minutes, or until reduced by half. Divide the chops among the serving plates and pour the sauce over the chops. Serve with a green salad, if desired.

nutrition per serve
Protein 23 g; Fat 6.5 g; Carbohydrate 0 g; Dietary Fiber 0 g; Cholesterol 45 mg; 195 calories

handy tip...

Orange or lime-and-ginger marmalade can be used instead of the redcurrant jelly. The sauce will thicken as it boils and reduces.
Pork rib or butterfly chops can be used instead of loin chops.

nutrition per serve
Protein 25 g; Fat 23 g; Carbohydrate
36 g; Dietary Fiber 2.5 g; Cholesterol
70 mg; 465 calories

ingredients

12 in purchased pizza
base

½ cup purchased pizza
sauce

1 cup shredded
mozzarella or Cheddar

⅓ cup thinly sliced
pepperoni

¼ cup thinly sliced salami

¼ cup mortadella slices,
cut into quarters

preparation: 15 minutes
cooking: 20 minutes
serves: 4

1 Preheat the oven to 425°F. Place the pizza base on a lightly oiled pizza pan.

2 Spread the sauce evenly over the pizza base. Sprinkle ¾ cup of the mozzarella over the sauce, then arrange the pepperoni, salami and mortadella on top. Sprinkle with the remaining mozzarella.

3 Bake for 20 minutes, or until the cheese has melted and the crust is crunchy and golden. Cut into wedges and serve with a green salad and garlic bread, if desired.

hint

Other meats, such as pancetta, prosciutto or any hot or spicy salami can also be used.
If you prefer a really spicy pizza, use a pinch of chili powder in the pizza sauce.

pork with mustard and cream sauce

ingredients

1 lb pork tenderloin
2 tablespoons olive oil
1 onion, sliced into rings
2 cloves garlic, crushed
½ cup white wine
1 cup whipping cream
2 tablespoons coarse
    grain mustard
2 tablespoons chopped
    fresh parsley

preparation: 10 minutes
cooking: 25 minutes
serves: 4

1 Cut the pork into 6–8 pieces and pound pieces thinly. Heat the oil in a large skillet. Add pork and cook for 3–4 minutes on each side, or until golden. Remove from the pan.

2 Reduce the heat and add the onion. Cook for 3 minutes, or until golden. Add the garlic and cook for 1 minute more. Add the wine, bring to a boil and cook until the liquid is reduced by half.

3 Stir in the cream and mustard and simmer gently for 5 minutes. Add the pork and simmer for another 5 minutes. Stir in the parsley and season. Divide the pork among the serving plates. Spoon the sauce over the pork and serve immediately.

nutrition per serve
Protein 30 g; Fat 38 g; Carbohydrate 4 g; Dietary Fiber 1 g; Cholesterol 150 mg; 490 calories

handy tip...

To make a quick mustard sauce, omit the wine and cream and stir in 1½ cups sour cream. Gently heat, but do not boil.

ingredients

⅓ cup honey

⅓ cup plum sauce

⅓ cup cold, strong tea

2 tablespoons soy sauce

1 tablespoon grated fresh ginger

2 cloves garlic, crushed

½ teaspoon Chinese five-spice powder

3 lb pork spare ribs

preparation: 10 minutes + overnight marinating
cooking: 45 minutes
serves: 4

1 Place the honey, plum sauce, tea, soy sauce, ginger, garlic and five-spice powder in a bowl and mix together well.

2 Place the pork ribs in a shallow glass or ceramic dish. Pour on the marinade and brush over the ribs to coat thoroughly. Cover and refrigerate for 2 hours or preferably overnight.

3 Preheat the oven to 350°F. Drain the ribs and reserve the marinade. Place the spare ribs on a rack in a large roasting pan and bake for 45 minutes, or until tender and golden. Turn the pork occasionally and brush with the reserved marinade during cooking. Garnish with strips of green onions, if desired, and serve immediately.

nutrition per serve
Protein 60 g; Fat 7.5 g; Carbohydrate 25 g; Dietary Fiber 0.5 g; Cholesterol 130 mg; 405 calories

hint

This marinade is also delicious used on chicken wings or drumsticks, as well as beef short ribs. Simmer beef ribs for 20 minutes and drain before adding to marinade.

ingredients

8 lb 8 oz leg of pork with
 rind attached
oil, to rub on pork
salt, to rub on pork

Gravy
1 tablespoon brandy or
 Calvados
2 tablespoons flour
1½ cups chicken stock
½ cup unsweetened apple
 cider

preparation: 15 minutes
cooking: 3 hours 15 minutes
serves: 6–8

1 Preheat the oven to 500°F. Score the rind of the pork with a sharp knife at ¾ in intervals. Rub in some oil and salt to provide a crisp crackling.

2 Place the pork, rind-side up, on a rack in a large roasting pan, then add a little water to the pan. Roast for 30 minutes, or until the rind begins to crackle and bubble. Reduce the oven heat to 325°F, then roast for 2 hours 40 minutes (20 minutes per pound). The pork is cooked if the juices run clear when the flesh is pierced with a fork and a meat thermometer placed in the thickest portion of the muscle registers 170°F. Rest in a warm place for 10 minutes.

3 To make the gravy, drain off all except 2 tablespoons of the pan juices from the roasting pan. Place on top of the stove over medium heat, add the brandy and stir quickly to lift the sediment from the bottom of the pan. Cook for 1 minute. Remove from the heat, stir in the flour and mix well. Return the pan to the heat and cook for 2 minutes, stirring constantly. Gradually add the stock and apple cider, and cook, stirring constantly, until the gravy boils and thickens. Season to taste with salt and freshly ground black pepper. Slice the pork and serve with the crackling and gravy. May also be served with apple sauce and baked apple wedges, if desired.

nutrition per serve (8)
Protein 120 g; Fat 4 g; Carbohydrate 0 g; Dietary Fiber 0 g; Cholesterol 230 mg; 515 calories

handy tip...

To produce delicious crisp crackling, it is essential to score the pork skin and rub it with a generous amount of oil and salt. For 8–9 lb, you will need approximately ¼ cup oil and ¼ cup salt. Do not cover or turn the pork over during roasting or the crackling will go soft.

ingredients

2 sheets frozen short or
   puff pastry, thawed
4 teaspoons butter
1 onion, chopped
4 slices bacon, cut into
   thin strips
2 tablespoons chopped
   chives
2 eggs
1 cup whipping cream
3 oz Swiss cheese,
   shredded

preparation: 15 minutes +
   20 minutes refrigeration
cooking: 1 hour 5 minutes
serves: 4–6

1 Line a shallow, loose-based, round, 10 in fluted tart pan with two sheets of pastry, pressing the pastry well into the pan base and sides. Trim off any excess pastry by using a sharp knife or by rolling a rolling pin across the top of the pan. Place the pan in the refrigerator for 20 minutes. Preheat the oven to 375°F.

2 Cover the pastry shell with parchment paper and then fill evenly with pie weights or rice. Bake for 15 minutes. Remove the paper and weights, and bake the pastry for another 10 minutes, or until it is golden. Remove from the oven, then reduce the temperature to 350°F.

3 To make the filling, heat the butter in a skillet. Add the onion and bacon and cook, stirring frequently for 10 minutes, or until the onion is soft and the bacon is cooked. Stir in the chives, then allow to cool.

4 Place the eggs and cream in a bowl and whisk until well combined. Season with pepper.

5 Spread the onion and bacon mixture evenly over the base of the pastry shell. Pour the egg mixture over the top, then sprinkle with the cheese. Bake for 30 minutes, or until the filling has set and the top is golden.

nutrition per serve (6)
Protein 16 g; Fat 44 g; Carbohydrate 27 g; Dietary Fiber 1.5 g; Cholesterol 170 mg; 560 calories

hint

If the flavor of Swiss cheese is too strong, use Cheddar. If bacon is not available, try ham.
The quiche originated in Lorraine, on the French-German border and was originally made with bread dough—Quiche Lorraine, with its filling of egg and bacon or ham, is a specialty of the region.

quick snacks with ham

crispy bacon, egg, bocconcini and tomato salad

Broil 4 bacon slices until crisp, allow to cool, then break into large pieces. Hard-cook 4 eggs, peel and cut in half. Arrange 3–4 cups baby spinach leaves in a large flat salad bowl. Top with the eggs, 5 oz sliced baby bocconcini and 12–16 halved mixed cherry and yellow pear tomatoes. Make a simple dressing by combining ⅓ cup plain yogurt with 2 tablespoons orange juice and 2 teaspoons coarse grain mustard. Drizzle over the salad and serve immediately.

serves 4

blt

Broil 8 slices bacon until crisp. Cut 4 pieces of flat bread, focaccia or whole wheat breadrolls in half and spread both sides with whole-egg mayonnaise. Top one half with a few lettuce leaves, slices of tomato and 2 slices of crispy bacon. Drizzle with a little tomato sauce and top with the remaining half of bread.

serves 4

fried ham, cheese and mustard sandwiches

Divide 8 oz sliced cooked leg ham among 4 thick slices white bread and top each piece of bread with a slice of Swiss cheese. Spread another 4 slices of bread with Dijon mustard, and place them mustard-side down on the cheese. Butter the outside of the bread. Heat a skillet and cook the sandwiches, in batches, over medium heat until the outside is crisp and golden brown and the cheese has melted.

serves 4

chicken skewers wrapped in ham

Cut 4 boneless, skinned chicken breast halves into 1¼ in cubes and place in a bowl with ½ cup classic French dressing. Cover and refrigerate for 20 minutes. Wrap each cube in a piece of sliced cooked leg ham—you will need 6–8 slices in total. Thread the chicken pieces onto bamboo skewers, which have been soaked in water, alternating with cherry tomatoes and bay leaves. Cook under a hot broiler, brushing lightly with the reserved dressing and turning frequently, for 5 minutes, or until cooked through.

serves 4–6

From left to right: Crispy bacon, egg, bocconcini and tomato salad; BLT; Fried ham, cheese and mustard sandwiches; Chicken skewers wrapped in ham; Eggs on toast with bacon and cheese; Chicken cordon bleu.

eggs on toast with bacon and cheese

Place 1 cup shredded Cheddar, 2 tablespoons butter, ½ teaspoon mustard powder and a pinch of paprika in a small saucepan and cook over low heat for 2 minutes, or until the cheese has melted. Remove from the heat. Poach 4 eggs until cooked to your liking and broil 8 slices bacon until crisp. Toast 4 thickly cut slices of whole wheat bread. Place the bacon onto the toast, top with the egg, pour the sauce over the egg and broil until bubbling. Serve immediately.

serves 4

chicken cordon bleu

Cut a pocket into the side of 4 boneless chicken breast halves and fill each pocket with 1 slice of Swiss cheese and 1 slice of smoked leg ham, then skewer with a cocktail pick. Heat 1 tablespoon oil in a large skillet and cook the chicken in batches until golden brown on both sides. Transfer to a baking sheet and bake in a 350°F oven for 15 minutes, or until cooked through.

serves 4

ingredients

2 tablespoons oil
2 cloves garlic, chopped
1 onion, cut into wedges
1 lb pork tenderloin,
   cut into thin slices
2 tablespoons cornstarch
¼ cup plum sauce
1 tablespoon soy sauce
2 teaspoons hoisin sauce

preparation: 15 minutes
cooking: 15 minutes
serves: 4

1 Heat half the oil in a wok and swirl around to coat the side. Add the garlic and onion and stir-fry over medium heat for 2 minutes, or until softened. Remove.

2 Coat the pork lightly in the cornstarch and season well with salt and pepper. Add the remaining oil to the wok and when it is extremely hot, stir-fry the pork in two batches for 5–6 minutes, or until dark golden brown. Set aside with the garlic and onion.

3 Add the plum, soy and hoisin sauces to the wok. Return the garlic, onion and pork to the wok. Toss well to coat the meat and serve immediately with rice.

nutrition per serve
Protein 30 g; Fat 15 g; Carbohydrate 20 g; Dietary Fiber 1 g; Cholesterol 60 mg; 345 calories

handy tip...

The cornstarch is added to thicken the sauce. For a thinner sauce, simply omit the cornstarch.

ingredients

2 tablespoons oil
2 tablespoons butter
5 oz fennel bulb, thinly
    sliced
1 lb 4 oz pork tenderloin,
    cut into thin strips
1 tablespoon lemon juice
¼ cup chicken or
    vegetable stock
2 tablespoons baby capers,
    drained and rinsed

preparation: 15 minutes
cooking: 15 minutes
serves: 4

1 Heat the wok until very hot, add half the oil and half the butter, and swirl it around to coat the side. When the butter begins to sizzle, add the fennel and stir-fry for 3–5 minutes, or until golden and tender. Remove and keep warm.

2 Reheat the wok and add the remaining oil and remaining butter. Stir-fry the pork in two batches until browned.

3 Return the pork and fennel to the wok. Add the lemon juice, stock and capers and stir, scraping any sediment from the wok. Season with salt and freshly ground pepper. For a slight Italian twist to this recipe, garnish with shaved Parmesan.

nutrition per serve
Protein 40 g; Fat 20 g; Carbohydrate 2 g; Dietary Fiber 1 g; Cholesterol 105 mg; 365 calories

hint

Be sure to trim the tough base and outer leaves from the fennel.
Fennel has a mild aniseed flavor. If it is not available, use 1 leek instead.

ingredients

14 lb whole leg of ham
cloves, to garnish

Glaze
2/3 cup soft brown sugar
1/4 cup honey
1 tablespoon hot English
   mustard

preparation: 20 minutes
cooking: 65 minutes
serves: 20

1 Preheat the oven to 350°F. Using a sharp knife, cut through the ham rind about 2½ in from the shank end. To remove the rind from the ham, run your thumb around the edge, under the rind, and carefully pull the rind back. Using a sharp knife, remove and discard the excess fat from the ham.

2 With the sharp knife, score the fat with cuts crosswise and then diagonally to make a diamond pattern. Do not cut all the way through to the ham or the fat will fall off during cooking. Press a clove into the center of each diamond.

3 To make the glaze, place the sugar, honey and mustard in a bowl and mix together. Spread carefully over the ham with a flexible metal spatula.

4 Place the ham on a rack in a deep roasting pan. Add 2 cups water to the pan. Cover the ham and pan securely with foil, and cook for 45 minutes. Increase the oven temperature to 425°F and bake for 20 minutes, or until the surface is slightly caramelized. Rest for 15 minutes before carving.

nutrition per serve
Protein 53 g; Fat 10 g; Carbohydrate 10 g; Dietary Fiber 0 g; Cholesterol 144 mg; 345 calories

handy tip...

It may not be that often that you get to cater for 20 people, however do not let that deter you from trying this recipe. Leftovers are great for quick soups, pies, quiches, toasted sandwiches and salads. Leftover ham can be stored in the refrigerator, wrapped in a clean, damp dish towel, for up to 10 days.

ingredients

2 bunches Chinese
   broccoli
1 tablespoon peanut oil
3/4 in piece fresh ginger,
   julienned
2 cloves garlic, crushed
1 lb Chinese barbecued
   pork, thinly sliced
1/4 cup chicken or
   vegetable stock
1/4 cup oyster sauce
1 tablespoon kecap manis
   (see hint page 33)

preparation: 10 minutes
cooking: 10 minutes
serves: 4

1 Trim the broccoli and cut it into 2 in lengths. Place the broccoli in a steamer over a saucepan of simmering water and cook for 5 minutes, or until just tender but still crisp. Set aside.

2 Heat a wok until very hot, add the oil and swirl around to coat the side. Add the ginger and garlic and stir-fry for 30 seconds, or until fragrant. Add the broccoli and barbecued pork and toss together.

3 Place the stock, oyster sauce and kecap manis in a small bowl and mix together well. Add to the wok and stir-fry until heated through. Serve with steamed rice or noodles.

nutrition per serve
Protein 50 g; Fat 10 g; Carbohydrate 5 g; Dietary Fiber 5.5 g; Cholesterol 116 mg; 312 calories

hint

If Chinese broccoli is not available, try choy sum or bok choy. Some Asian vegetables are available at supermarkets. If not, try an Asian market.

seafood

ingredients

12 taco shells

2 x 6½ oz cans tuna in brine, drained

½ cup sour cream

½ small red onion, finely chopped

10½ oz can cannellini or butter beans, rinsed and drained

2 cups shredded lettuce

3 tomatoes, thinly sliced

preparation: 15 minutes
cooking: 10 minutes
serves: 6

1 Preheat the oven to 350ºF. Warm the taco shells for 5–10 minutes while preparing the filling.

2 Place the tuna in a large bowl and flake with a fork. Add the sour cream, red onion and beans and mix together well. Season with salt and freshly ground black pepper.

3 Place some of the lettuce and a couple of slices of tomato in each taco, then fill with the tuna and bean mixture. Serve immediately.

nutrition per serve
Protein 20 g; Fat 15 g; Carbohydrate 8 g; Dietary Fiber 4.5 g; Cholesterol 60 mg; 297 calories

handy tip...

The filling for the tacos also makes a good lunch box salad. Put it in an airtight container and serve the tacos or corn chips on the side. Salmon can be used instead of the tuna.

ingredients

4 boneless white fish fillets
(about 6 oz each)
1/4 cup plain yogurt
1 1/2 teaspoons garam
masala
1 clove garlic, crushed
1/2 teaspoon chili flakes

preparation: 10 minutes +
20 minutes marinating
cooking: 6 minutes
serves: 4

1 Arrange the fish fillets in a large glass or ceramic dish.

2 Place the yogurt, garam masala, garlic and chili flakes in a small bowl, season to taste with salt and mix together well. Spread the marinade evenly over the fillets, cover, and then refrigerate for 20 minutes.

3 Drain the fish fillets and place on a lightly oiled broiler pan. Cook under a hot broiler for 2–3 minutes on each side, or until the flesh can be flaked easily with the point of a knife. Serve immediately with steamed white rice.

nutrition per serve
Protein 38 g; Fat 5.5 g; Carbohydrate
1 g; Dietary Fiber 0 g; Cholesterol
130 mg; 210 calories

hint

To make tandoori fish fillets, simply add 2 tablespoons of bottled tandoori paste to the yogurt.

ingredients

1 lb squid (calamari) tubes
1 tablespoon finely
    chopped fresh ginger
2–3 teaspoons finely
    chopped fresh red chile
3 cloves garlic, chopped
1/4 cup oil
2 onions, thinly sliced
1 lb baby bok choy,
    coarsely chopped

preparation: 10 minutes +
    2–3 hours marinating
cooking: 15 minutes
serves: 4

1 Wash the squid well and dry with paper towels. Cut into 1/2 in rings and place in a shallow glass or ceramic bowl.

2 Place the ginger, chile, garlic and oil in a bowl and mix together. Pour the mixture over the squid and toss well. Cover and refrigerate for 2–3 hours.

3 Heat the wok until very hot. Stir-fry the squid over high heat in three batches for 1–2 minutes each batch, reserving the marinade. Remove from the wok as soon as the squid turns white. Do not overcook or the squid will be rubbery. Remove all the squid from the wok.

4 Pour the reserved marinade into the wok and bring to a boil. Add the onions and cook over medium heat for 3–4 minutes, or until slightly softened. Add the bok choy and steam, covered, for 2 minutes, or until it has wilted slightly.

5 Return the squid to the wok and toss until well combined. Season with salt and freshly ground black pepper. Remove from the wok and serve immediately. Serve with rice or noodles, if desired.

nutrition per serve
Protein 25 g; Fat 15 g; Carbohydrate 7 g; Dietary Fiber 2 g; Cholesterol 250 mg; 265 calories

handy tip...

Reheat the wok in between the batches of squid—if it is not hot enough, the squid will become tough.

ingredients

ingredients

4 thick salmon fillet portions
(about 5 oz each)
3 tablespoons butter

Leek and caper sauce
3 tablespoons butter
1 leek, chopped
1 cup white wine (Riesling
or chardonnay)
2 tablespoons capers,
drained
1 tablespoon chopped,
fresh flat-leaf parsley

preparation: 10 minutes
cooking: 20 minutes
serves: 4

1 Lightly grease a shallow baking pan and arrange the salmon fillets in a single layer. Melt the butter and brush each fillet with it. Cook under a medium broiler, without turning, for 10 minutes, or until the fillets are just cooked. Remove and cover loosely with foil to keep the fillets warm while making the sauce.

2 To make the leek and caper sauce, melt the butter in a saucepan. Add the leek and cook gently for 5 minutes, or until soft, but not brown. Add the wine and boil for 3–4 minutes. Add the capers and parsley and season to taste with salt and freshly ground black pepper. Remove the pan from the heat.

3 Spoon the hot sauce over the salmon and serve immediately with steamed potatoes.

nutrition per serve
Protein 70 g; Fat 29 g; Carbohydrate 1 g; Dietary Fiber 0.7 g; Cholesterol 182 mg; 463 calories

hint

The salmon can be pan-fried, baked or barbecued instead of broiled.
Use only the white part of the leek and cut it in half and rinse well to remove any dirt before chopping.

ingredients

18 baby octopus
2 teaspoons finely grated
    lemon rind
1/4 cup lemon juice
1/4 cup olive oil
2 cloves garlic, crushed
1/4 cup chopped fresh
    parsley
1 tablespoon ground
    sweet paprika

preparation: 15 minutes +
    3 hours marinating
cooking: 6 minutes
serves: 4–6

1 To clean the octopus, use a small sharp knife and remove the gut by either cutting off the head entirely or by slitting open the head and removing the gut.

2 Pick up the body and use your index finger to push the beak up. Remove, then clean the octopus thoroughly. Remove the eyes and cut the sac into two or three pieces.

3 Place the lemon rind and juice, olive oil, garlic, parsley and paprika in a large bowl and mix together well. Add the prepared octopus, cover with plastic wrap and marinate for 2–3 hours.

4 Lightly oil a broiler pan. Arrange the octopus evenly over the surface. Cook under a hot broiler for 3 minutes on each side, or until tender, basting with the marinade during cooking. Serve immediately with a green salad, if desired.

nutrition per serve (6)
Protein 28 g; Fat 12 g; Carbohydrate 0.5 g; Dietary Fiber 0 g; Cholesterol 332 mg; 220 calories

handy tip...

Look for small octopus with curly tentacles. This means they have been tenderized at the markets and your octopus is less likely to be chewy.
This recipe is also suitable for barbecuing.

ingredients

4 salmon steaks or fillet portions (about 7 oz each) (*see hint*)
½ cup unsalted butter
2 green onions, finely chopped
1 cup whipping cream
1 tablespoon lemon juice
8 fresh sorrel leaves

preparation: 10 minutes
cooking: 20 minutes
serves: 4

1 Season the salmon portions with freshly ground black pepper. Heat half the butter in a skillet, and quickly cook the salmon in batches for 3–4 minutes on each side, or until golden. This will vary depending on the thickness of the fish. Test by gently prising the flesh apart—if it pulls away easily, the fish is cooked. Be careful not to overcook.

2 To prepare the sauce, melt the remaining butter in a saucepan and cook the green onions over low heat for 1 minute, or until softened. Add the cream and lemon juice. Bring to a boil, then reduce the heat and simmer gently for 1 minute. Remove the stems from the sorrel and slice the leaves into strips. Add to the pan and cook for 2 minutes. Season to taste.

3 Place the salmon on a serving dish. Spoon on the warm sauce and serve immediately with a green salad, if desired.

nutrition per serve
Protein 37.5 g; Fat 60 g; Carbohydrate 2.5 g; Dietary Fiber 0 g; Cholesterol 160 mg; 833 calories

hint

If salmon steaks are not readily available, use fresh trout fillets. As an alternative to frying, steam the salmon on a bed of sorrel leaves over simmering water.

ingredients

2 cups all-purpose flour
2 teaspoons baking powder
3/4 cup beer
light olive oil,
   for deep-frying
1 lb 8 oz potatoes, cut into
   thick finger shapes
4 white fish fillets
   (about 6 oz each),
   skinned and boned

preparation: 15 minutes +
  20 minutes standing
cooking: 25 minutes
serves: 4

1 Sift the flour, baking powder and 1/2 teaspoon salt into a large bowl. Make a well in the center and gradually add the beer and 3/4 cup cold water, whisking to form a smooth batter. Cover and allow to stand for 20 minutes.

2 Fill a deep heavy-based saucepan one-third full of oil. Heat the oil to 325°F, or until a bread cube dropped into the oil browns in 30–35 seconds. Add potatoes, in two or more batches if necessary, and deep-fry until tender, but pale in color. Drain on paper towels.

3 Heat the same oil to 350°F, or until a bread cube browns in 15 seconds. Cut each fillet in half diagonally and pat dry with paper towels. Dip the fish in the batter, gently shaking off the excess. Deep-fry for 3–4 minutes, depending on the thickness, or until crisp, golden and cooked through. Drain on paper towels.

4 Reheat the oil to 350°F and gently return the potatoes to the pan. Cook for 1–2 minutes, or until crisp and golden. Drain on paper towels and serve with the fish.

nutrition per serve
Protein 26 g; Fat 13 g; Carbohydrate 25 g; Dietary Fiber 3 g; Cholesterol 72 mg; 334 calories

handy tip...

For best results, the fish fillets should have moist, resilient flesh with no discoloration or dryness and should not be waterlogged.

ingredients

1 lb 8 oz raw shrimp
1 cup white wine
14 oz scallops
8 green onions, chopped
2 cloves garlic, crushed
2 tablespoons chopped
    fresh dill
½ cup chilled butter,
    chopped
⅓ cup heavy whipping
    cream

preparation: 15 minutes
cooking: 8 minutes
serves: 4

1 Shell the shrimp, leaving the tails intact. Gently pull out the vein from the tail, starting at the head.

2 Place the wine in a saucepan and bring to a boil. Add the shrimp and the scallops and simmer for 1 minute, or until the shrimp and the scallops are just cooked through. Remove the seafood with a slotted spoon.

3 Add the green onions, garlic and dill to the wine and bring to a boil. Cook for 5 minutes, or until the sauce has reduced by half.

4 Reduce the heat to low. Add the butter gradually, whisking after each addition until it has melted. Add the cream and seafood and stir until heated through. Season to taste with salt and freshly ground black pepper. Garnish with a sprig of fresh dill and serve with rice or steamed vegetables, if desired.

nutrition per serve
Protein 50 g; Fat 36 g; Carbohydrate 3 g; Dietary Fiber 1 g; Cholesterol 420 mg; 578 calories

hint

Remove the black muscle from the outside of the scallop before cooking.
This recipe can also be made using a good marinara mix from your local fish retailer. It is delicious served with boiled rice or pasta.

ingredients

1 lb 8 oz fresh tuna,
    finely chopped
3 green onions,
    finely chopped
1 tablespoon mirin
1 teaspoon soy sauce
1 tablespoon lime juice

preparation: 15 minutes +
    2 hours refrigeration
cooking: 10 minutes
serves: 4

1 Place the tuna, green onions, mirin, soy sauce and lime juice in a bowl and mix together. Divide into four portions and shape into patties. Cover and refrigerate for 2 hours.

2 Cook the patties on a preheated barbecue grill or in a hot skillet for 4–5 minutes on each side, or until cooked through. Serve hot or cold with lime wedges, your favorite relish and salad leaves.

nutrition per serve
Protein 35 g; Fat 5.5 g; Carbohydrate 0 g; Dietary Fiber 0 g; Cholesterol 67.5 mg; 205 calories

handy tip...

To make tuna meatballs, shape heaped tablespoons of the chopped mixture into balls and refrigerate for 2 hours. Preheat the oven to 350°F. Add a little oil to a skillet and cook in batches for 3 minutes, or until just brown. Place the meatballs on a baking sheet and bake for 5 minutes.

nutrition per serve
Protein 32 g; Fat 16 g; Carbohydrate 27 g; Dietary Fiber 2 g; Cholesterol 90 mg; 382 calories

ingredients

1 cup chopped mixed fresh herbs *(see hint)*

8 slices day-old bread, crusts removed

1 egg

2 tablespoons milk

4 tuna steaks

2 tablespoons olive oil

preparation: 15 minutes + 15 minutes refrigeration
cooking: 6 minutes
serves: 4

1 Place the mixed herbs and bread in a food processor and process for 30 seconds, or until the bread forms very fine crumbs.

2 Place the egg and milk together in a small bowl and whisk together well. Dip each tuna steak in the egg mixture, then coat evenly with the herbed bread crumbs, pressing firmly with your fingers. Refrigerate for 15 minutes.

3 Heat the oil in a skillet, add the tuna and cook over medium heat for 2–3 minutes on each side, or until tender. Serve immediately with a green salad, if desired.

hint

Try to avoid using strong-flavored herbs such as rosemary, tarragon and oregano because they will overpower the fish. Try parsley, basil and thyme.

This recipe is suitable for any thick fish steaks or fillets. Try salmon, swordfish or marlin.

ingredients

2 tablespoons butter
1 tablespoon flour
2/3 cup milk
1/3 cup finely shredded
    Cheddar
24 fresh oysters in half
    shells
2 tablespoons grated
    fresh Parmesan

preparation: 10 minutes
cooking: 7 minutes
serves: 4

1 Heat the butter in a small saucepan and stir in the flour. Cook over medium heat for 1 minute, or until golden. Take the pan off the heat and add the milk. Stir until smooth then return to the heat. Stir constantly until the sauce boils and thickens. Simmer for 1 minute, then add the Cheddar. Stir until the cheese melts.

2 Place the oysters on a broiler rack. Spoon a level tablespoon of the sauce onto each oyster and sprinkle with the Parmesan. Broil under a hot broiler for 2–3 minutes, or until the sauce is hot and the cheese is light golden brown. Serve immediately.

nutrition per serve
Protein 10 g; Fat 14 g; Carbohydrate 4.5 g; Dietary Fiber 0 g; Cholesterol 63 mg; 177 calories

handy tip...

Oysters vary in flavor depending on their size and where they are grown. As a general rule, smaller oysters tend to be milder than larger ones.
Oysters Kilpatrick is another popular way to serve oysters. Melt 2 tablespoons butter in a small saucepan. Add 2 tablespoons Worcestershire sauce and 1 tablespoon ketchup, season with pepper and cook for 1 minute. Place 24 fresh oysters in half shells on a broiler rack. Sprinkle 3 slices finely chopped bacon over the oysters, then spoon on the butter mixture. Broil for 2–3 minutes, or until the bacon is cooked. Garnish with freshly chopped parsley and serve immediately.

ingredients

4 skinless and boneless
    white fish fillets
    (about 7 oz each)
²/₃ cup butter, melted
3 cloves garlic, crushed
2 cups fresh white bread
    crumbs (made from
    Italian bread)
1 tablespoon finely
    chopped fresh parsley
lemon wedges, to serve

preparation: 15 minutes
cooking: 15 minutes
serves: 4

1 Preheat the oven to 400°F. Grease a baking dish with a little oil or melted butter and arrange the fish fillets in a single layer.

2 Mix together the melted butter and garlic in a bowl and set aside. Place the bread crumbs and parsley in a bowl and mix well. Scatter the bread crumb mixture in a thick layer over the fillets, then drizzle with the garlic butter.

3 Bake for 10–15 minutes, or until fish is white and flakes easily, and bread crumbs are golden brown. If the bread crumbs are not golden but the fish is cooked, flash under a hot broiler for a couple of minutes, or until golden—don't take your eyes off it because it can burn very quickly. Garnish with lemon wedges and, if desired, serve with steamed vegetables or a salad.

nutrition per serve
Protein 16 g; Fat 18 g; Carbohydrate 27 g; Dietary Fiber 2 g; Cholesterol 83 mg; 335 calories

hint

Fresh bread crumbs are very simple to make. Remove the crusts from slightly stale (at least one-day old) slices of bread. Put the bread in a food processor and mix until crumbs form. Use ordinary bread or, as in this recipe, Italian bread.

ingredients

1 cup vegetable oil

¼ cup butter, chopped

8 cloves garlic, finely chopped

2 small fresh red chiles, seeded and finely chopped

20 raw large shrimp, shelled and deveined, with tails intact

¼ cup finely chopped fresh parsley

preparation: 15 minutes
cooking: 5 minutes
serves: 4

1 Heat the oil and butter in a large, deep skillet. When very hot, but not smoking, carefully add the garlic, chiles and shrimp all at once. Cook, stirring, for 3 minutes, or until the shrimp turn pink. Take care not to overcook the shrimp.

2 Using a large spoon, quickly transfer the shrimp into four hot individual serving dishes and drizzle with some of the garlic butter. Sprinkle with the parsley and serve with crusty bread to soak up the juices.

nutrition per serve
Protein 20 g; Fat 43 g; Carbohydrate 1 g; Dietary Fiber 1.5 g; Cholesterol 180 mg; 463 calories

This recipe is traditionally cooked in small cast-iron pots (available from kitchenware shops). Preheat the oven to 500°F. Place the oil and butter in the pots and heat in the oven for 5–10 minutes, or until hot. Add the shrimp, return to the oven and bake for 5 minutes, or until cooked. Stir in the garlic and serve immediately.
Although there appears to be a high amount of fat used, not all is generally consumed. The nutritional analysis is based on half the oil being eaten.

nutrition per serve
Protein 37 g; Fat 15 g; Carbohydrate 11 g; Dietary Fiber 0.5 g; Cholesterol 125 mg; 322 calories

ingredients

White sauce
3 cups milk
1 onion, peeled and
    halved
1 clove
1 bay leaf
1/4 cup butter
1/3 cup all-purpose flour
1/3 cup chopped fresh
    chives or parsley

2 lb 4 oz smoked cod or
    haddock fillets

preparation: 15 minutes
cooking: 30 minutes
serves: 6

1 Preheat the oven to 350°F.

2 To make the white sauce, place the milk in a saucepan with the onion, clove and bay leaf, then heat slowly to a simmer. Remove the sauce from the heat. Allow to stand for 3 minutes, then strain into a bowl.

3 Melt the butter in a saucepan, then add the flour. Stir constantly over low heat for 2–3 minutes, or until light golden. Gradually add the strained milk to the pan, stirring until the mixture is smooth. Stir constantly over medium heat for 8–10 minutes, or until the sauce boils and thickens. Reduce the heat, and simmer for another minute. Remove from the heat. Season lightly with salt and pepper and stir in the chives or parsley.

4 Grease a baking dish. Cut the fillets into serving-sized pieces and then arrange in the prepared dish. Pour the white sauce over the fish and bake for 10–15 minutes, or until the fish is tender and the flesh flakes at the thickest part. Serve with the white sauce and garnish with snipped fresh chives, if desired.

hint

Smoked fish is often very salty. If you want to make it less salty, combine 1/2 cup milk and 1/2 cup water in a bowl. Add the fish and soak for several hours before cooking. Discard the soaking liquid. Instead of baking the fish, poach the fillets in 1/2 cup milk and 1/2 cup water, in a skillet, until tender and flaking at the thickest part. Transfer to heated plates and pour the white sauce over the fish.

ingredients

4 salmon steaks
   (about 5 oz each)
1 tablespoon finely
   shredded fresh ginger
2 green onions, finely
   sliced on the diagonal
1 tablespoon soy sauce
½ teaspoon sesame oil

preparation: 5 minutes
cooking: 15 minutes
serves: 4

1 Preheat the oven to 375°F. Cut out four 12 in squares from foil and also four from parchment paper. Place the parchment paper on top of the foil and then put one steak on each square. Scatter the shredded ginger and green onions over the steaks.

2 Place the soy sauce, sesame oil and 2 tablespoons water in a small bowl and mix together well. Spoon over the salmon and seal the foil to make parcels. Place the parcels in a shallow baking pan.

3 Bake for 15 minutes, or until the fish flakes easily. Open the parcels and serve the fish immediately with rice or noodles and steamed Asian greens.

nutrition per serve
Protein 27.5 g; Fat 18.5 g; Carbohydrate 0.5 g; Dietary Fiber 0 g; Cholesterol 105 mg; 270 calories

handy tip...

This recipe can also be cooked in a bamboo steamer over simmering water in a wok.
Any type of fish steak is suitable for this recipe—try tuna or snapper.

ingredients

Herbed butter
1/4 cup butter, softened
1 tablespoon lemon juice
2 tablespoons chopped
    fresh mixed herbs
    (parsley, chives and
    tarragon or dill)

4 firm white fish fillets
    (about 6 oz each)
1/2 cup dry white wine
2 slices lemon
lemon wedges, to
    garnish

preparation: 10 minutes +
    refrigeration
cooking: 10 minutes
serves: 4

1 To make the herbed butter, place the butter, lemon juice and mixed herbs in a small bowl and mix together well. Season to taste with salt and freshly ground black pepper. Shape the butter into a log, wrap in plastic wrap and freeze until firm.

2 Place the fish in a large shallow skillet. Add the wine, lemon slices and enough water to just cover the fish. Bring to a boil, then reduce the heat and simmer for 5 minutes, or until the fish is tender, and the thickest part of the fish flakes when tested with a fork. Drain the fish on paper towels.

3 Serve on warm plates, topped with slices of the herbed butter and garnished with lemon wedges.

nutrition per serve
Protein 8.5 g; Fat 13 g; Carbohydrate 0.5 g; Dietary Fiber 0 g; Cholesterol 66 mg; 176 calories

hint

This recipe also works well with caper and lime herb butter. Add 1 tablespoon chopped, drained capers and 1 teaspoon lime zest to the butter. Stir in 2 tablespoons chopped fresh parsley. Wrap and chill.

ingredients

1 lb raw shrimp

1 tablespoon oil

2–3 tablespoons laksa
paste

2 cups unsweetened
coconut milk

8 ready-made fried fish
balls, sliced

14 oz fresh rice spaghetti
(laksa noodles)

3 oz bean sprouts, trimmed

1/2 cup Vietnamese mint
leaves or cilantro

preparation: 15 minutes
cooking: 1 hour 15 minutes
serves: 4

1 Set aside four shrimp. Shell the rest, and place the heads, shells, tails and legs in a deep saucepan, without any oil. Cook over medium heat, shaking the pan occasionally, for about 10 minutes, or until the shells are aromatic and a bright, dark orange.

2 Stir in 1 cup water. When it has almost evaporated, stir in another cup of water and bring to a boil. Add 4 cups water. (Adding the water gradually will produce a rich, dark, flavorsome stock.)

3 Bring the stock to a boil, then reduce the heat and simmer gently for 30 minutes. Add the four reserved shrimp and cook until they turn pink. Remove from the pan. Strain the stock and discard the peelings. You should have between 2–3 cups stock.

4 Heat the oil in a wok, add the laksa paste and cook, stirring constantly, over low heat for 4 minutes, or until aromatic. Stir in the shrimp stock and coconut milk. Bring to a boil, then reduce the heat and simmer for 5 minutes. Add the shelled shrimp and fish ball slices and simmer until the shrimp turn pink.

5 Separate the noodles and cook in boiling water for 30 seconds (they will fall apart if overcooked). Drain well and divide among four deep soup bowls.

6 Ladle the soup over the noodles in the bowls. Garnish with bean sprouts, mint and a whole shrimp. Serve at once.

nutrition per serve
Protein 35 g; Fat 35 g; Carbohydrate 30 g; Dietary Fiber 4 g; Cholesterol 200 mg; 530 calories

handy tip...

Laksa paste is available at Asian supermarkets. If rice spaghetti is not available, use dried rice vermicelli and soak it in boiling water for 15 minutes, or until tender. Drain before using. If fried fish balls are not available, substitute with extra shrimp.

ingredients

1 lb 8 oz raw medium
   shrimp
1/3 cup sun-dried tomatoes
   in oil
4 green onions, finely
   chopped
1 cup chicken stock
1/2 cup dry white wine
1 cup heavy whipping
   cream
2 tablespoons finely
   chopped fresh basil

preparation: 15 minutes
cooking: 15 minutes
serves: 4

1 Shell the shrimp, leaving tails intact, and gently pull out the vein. Drain the oil from the sun-dried tomatoes and reserve 2 teaspoons. Cut the tomatoes into strips.

2 Heat the oil in a wok or skillet over high heat, and swirl it around to coat the side. Add the shrimp and green onions in batches and stir-fry for 5 minutes, or until the shrimp are pink and cooked. Remove from the wok.

3 Add the sun-dried tomatoes, stock, white wine and cream to the wok and bring to a boil. Reduce the heat and simmer for 7 minutes, or until the sauce has thickened and reduced.

4 Return the shrimp to the wok with the basil. Stir-fry over high heat for 1 minute, or until heated through. Serve with pasta.

nutrition per serve
Protein 40 g; Fat 28 g; Carbohydrate 3 g; Dietary Fiber 0.5 g; Cholesterol 364 mg; 443 calories

hint

This recipe is also delicious using scallops or a seafood marinara mix.

1 tablespoon vegetable oil

1 tablespoon Thai red curry paste

2 cups unsweetened coconut milk

2 tablespoons fish sauce

2 tablespoons soft brown sugar

3 fresh or dried kaffir lime leaves, finely shredded

1 lb 8 oz firm white fish fillets, cut into ³/₄ in pieces

¹/₃ cup fresh cilantro leaves

preparation: 10 minutes
cooking: 15 minutes
serves: 4

1 Heat the oil in a wok or skillet and swirl it around to coat the side. Add the red curry paste and cook over medium heat for 2 minutes, or until fragrant.

2 Stir in the coconut milk, fish sauce, sugar and lime leaves and bring to a boil. Reduce the heat and simmer for 5 minutes.

3 Add the fish and simmer, covered, for 5 minutes, or until the fish is cooked. Stir in the cilantro leaves and serve over steamed rice. Garnish with thinly sliced green onions and lime wedges, if desired.

nutrition per serve
Protein 42 g; Fat 36 g; Carbohydrate 15 g; Dietary Fiber 2.5 g; Cholesterol 132 mg; 547 calories

handy tip...

To make a green fish curry, substitute the red curry paste for green curry paste. For a milder flavor, use 1 tablespoon curry paste, and, increase it to 2–3 tablespoons, if you like your curries with a bit more heat.
Always use a good-quality Asian brand of paste, available from Asian markets.

ingredients

8 thin white fish fillets, boned and skinned
flour, to coat
1 egg, lightly beaten
dry bread crumbs, to coat
2 tablespoons oil
1/3 cup butter
grated rind and juice from 4 limes *(see hint)*
1/4 cup chopped fresh parsley

preparation: 15 minutes + 20 minutes refrigeration
cooking: 10 minutes
serves: 4

1 Pat the fillets dry with paper towels. Coat in the flour, shaking off any excess. Dip in the egg, then coat in the bread crumbs. Cover and refrigerate for 20 minutes.

2 Heat the oil in a skillet over medium heat. Add the fillets and cook for 3 minutes, then turn over and cook for another 2 minutes, or until cooked through. Drain on paper towels, then place on warm serving plates. Wipe out the skillet with paper towels to remove any burnt crumbs.

3 Add the butter, lime rind and juice to the clean skillet. Stir over low heat until the butter has melted. Stir in the parsley. Spoon the sauce over the fillets and serve immediately.

nutrition per serve
Protein 30 g; Fat 35 g; Carbohydrate 9 g; Dietary Fiber 0.5 g; Cholesterol 200 mg; 472 calories

hint

You should be able to get 1 tablespoon grated rind and 1/4 cup juice from 4 limes. Most skinless and boneless types of fish fillets are suited to this recipe—try John Dory, snapper, rainbow trout or bream (porgy).

smoked salmon bagel

Cut 4 bagels in half. Combine 4 oz (½ cup) spreadable cream cheese, 2 finely chopped gherkins and 1 tablespoon chopped fresh dill. Spread evenly over the base of each bagel. Divide 7 oz smoked salmon and 1 tablespoon baby capers among the bagel bases, and season with cracked black pepper. Cover each with the remaining bagel half and serve.

serves 4

From left to right: Smoked salmon bagel; Creamy salmon herb pasta; Avocado and salmon salad.

creamy salmon herb pasta

Cook 1 lb spaghetti in boiling water until *al dente*. Place 1¼ cups sour cream, 1 teaspoon lime rind, 1 tablespoon lime juice, ½ cup milk, 2 chopped green onions and 2 tablespoons snipped fresh chives in a large bowl and whisk together well. Season to taste with salt and pepper. Drain the pasta, then toss in 7 oz thinly sliced smoked salmon and the cream mixture.

serves 4

avocado and salmon salad

Place 5 oz (3–4 cups) baby spinach leaves, 1 avocado cut into large pieces, 3 oz sliced Camembert, 3 oz thinly sliced smoked salmon and 1⅔ cups fresh raspberries in a large salad bowl and toss together well. Place 1 tablespoon honey mustard, 1 tablespoon lemon juice and ⅓ cup olive oil in a small bowl and whisk together. Pour the dressing over the salad and serve.

serves 4

smoked salmon
puff pastry rounds

Preheat the oven to 400°F. Cut out 2 in rounds with a fluted cutter from 2 sheets thawed ready-rolled butter puff pastry. Place onto non-stick baking sheets, brush lightly with milk and bake for 10 minutes, or until crisp and golden. Allow to cool. Place 3 oz thick sour cream and 2 teaspoons chopped fresh dill in a small bowl and mix together well. Spoon 1 teaspoonful of the mixture onto each pastry round. Cut 3 oz smoked salmon into strips and place on top of the sour cream. Garnish with a sprig of dill.

makes 32

mini smoked
salmon frittatas

Preheat the oven to 350°F. Place 12 eggs, 1 cup whipping cream, ¼ cup chopped smoked salmon, 3 green onions, finely sliced, and 2 tablespoons finely chopped fresh parsley in a bowl and whisk together well. Divide the mixture between twelve ½-cup muffin cups and bake for 20 minutes, or until set.

makes 12

From left to right: Smoked salmon puff pastry rounds; Mini smoked salmon frittatas; Quick smoked salmon benedict.

quick smoked
salmon benedict

Melt ⅓ cup butter in a saucepan. Process 2 teaspoons tarragon vinegar and 2 egg yolks in a food processor until combined. With the motor running, gradually add the melted butter and process until the sauce is thick enough to coat the back of a spoon. Cut 4 English muffins in half and toast under a hot broiler until golden. Butter and keep warm. Poach 8 eggs, in batches, in warm water until cooked to your liking. Divide 3 oz smoked salmon among the English muffins and top with the poached eggs and sauce. Garnish with chopped fresh chives.

serves 4

creamy lemon shrimp sandwiches

Shell and devein 1 lb 4 oz cooked large shrimp, then coarsely chop. Place the shrimp, 3–4 tablespoons lemon juice, 2 tablespoons whole-egg mayonnaise, 2 tablespoons seafood cocktail sauce and 2 tablespoons chopped fresh cilantro leaves in a bowl and mix together well. Serve sandwiched between thick slices of buttered sourdough bread.

serves 6

shrimp cocktail

Cut 2 avocados in half and remove the stones. Shell and devein 10 oz cooked large shrimp and arrange the shrimp in the hole of each avocado. Place 2 teaspoons concentrated lime juice syrup, 2 tablespoons plain yogurt and 2 tablespoons whole-egg mayonnaise in a bowl and mix together well. Spoon the dressing over the shrimp, season with ground pepper and a squeeze of fresh lime juice.

serves 4

mediterranean shrimp salad

Shell and devein 10 oz cooked large shrimp. Place 1 chopped red sweet bell pepper, 1 sliced red onion, ½ cup marinated Kalamata olives, 7 oz feta broken into large pieces and 1 bunch arugula leaves in a salad bowl. Place 2 tablespoons extra virgin olive oil and 1 tablespoon balsamic vinegar in a small bowl and mix together well. Drizzle the dressing over the salad and toss the salad gently before serving.

serves 2–4

spicy shrimp pasta

Cook 1 lb pasta in a large saucepan of boiling water until *al dente*. Drain and keep warm. Shell and devein 1 lb cooked large shrimp. Heat 1 tablespoon oil in a skillet, add 1 thinly sliced onion and cook over medium heat for 3 minutes, or until golden. Add the shrimp, 1¼ cups bottled tomato salsa and 1¼ cups sour cream, then reduce the heat to low and stir until heated through. Stir in 2 tablespoons chopped fresh basil. Toss the sauce with the pasta and serve.

serves 4–6

From left to right: Creamy lemon shrimp sandwiches; Shrimp cocktail; Mediterranean shrimp salad; Spicy shrimp pasta; Cajun shrimp burritos; Pappadam shrimp cups with mango yogurt.

cajun shrimp burritos

Preheat the oven to 350°F. Place 4 flour tortillas on a baking sheet, cover with foil, and then bake for 10 minutes or until heated through. Shell and devein 1 lb cooked large shrimp, then halve lengthwise. Heat 1 tablespoon oil in a skillet. Add 3 thinly sliced green onions, 1 tablespoon cajun seasoning, 1 tablespoon lemon juice and the shrimp. Cook, stirring gently to coat the shrimp in the seasoning, for 3 minutes, or until heated through. Divide the shrimp among the tortillas. Serve with shredded lettuce, chopped tomatoes and shredded cheese. Dollop with sour cream and taco sauce, if desired.

serves 4

pappadam shrimp cups with mango yogurt

Cut 8 chili pappadams into quarters with a sharp knife or scissors. Cook, according to the package instructions. Place ⅓ cup plain yogurt, 1 tablespoon mango chutney and 2 teaspoons chopped fresh mint in a bowl and mix together well. Divide the yogurt mixture among the pappadams and top with 5 oz cooked shelled small shrimp. Garnish with a wedge of lime and a sprig of mint.

makes 32

creamy salmon pie

Preheat the oven to 425°F. Heat 1 tablespoon oil in a skillet, add 1 thinly sliced leek and cook over medium heat for 5 minutes, or until golden. Add 2 tablespoons flour and cook, stirring, for 1 minute. Gradually pour in 1½ cups milk and bring to a boil, stirring constantly, until the mixture boils and thickens. Then add 1 cup shredded Cheddar, 15 oz can pink salmon, drained and bones removed, 1 tablespoon lemon juice, 1 teaspoon lemon rind and 2 tablespoons chopped fresh dill. Season. Spoon the mixture into a 9 in pie dish and allow to cool slightly before covering with 1 sheet of thawed ready-rolled puff pastry. Brush lightly with milk and bake for 20 minutes, or until golden.

serves 6

simple low-fat niçoise

Place the torn leaves of 1 romaine lettuce, 8 oz halved cherry tomatoes, 1 cup Kalamata olives, 7 oz chopped low-fat feta, 7 oz blanched green beans, 4 peeled and quartered hard-cooked eggs and 15 oz can salmon in brine, drained and broken into bite-size chunks, in a serving bowl. Drizzle with your favorite oil-free dressing and toss.

serves 6

salmon salad on crispy french bread

Drain a 15 oz can pink salmon, then flake in a bowl. Add 3 chopped green onions, ¼ cup sour cream, ¼ cup thousand island dressing and 2 tablespoons chopped fresh chives. Season with freshly ground black pepper and mix together well. Serve on a baguette with arugula leaves.

serves 4

From left to right: Creamy salmon pie; Simple low-fat niçoise; Salmon salad on crispy French bread.

tuna pasta bake

Preheat the oven to 400°F. Boil 14 oz macaroni until *al dente*, then drain well. Combine 3 chopped green onions, 16 oz can tuna in brine, drained and flaked, 14 oz can drained asparagus pieces, 15 oz can creamy chicken soup, 1¼ cups sour cream, ¼ cup milk and 1 cup shredded Cheddar in a bowl, then stir in the macaroni. Spoon into four 2½-cup greased casseroles and sprinkle with an extra ½ cup shredded Cheddar. Bake for 20 minutes, or until crisp and golden.

serves 4

tuna patties

Place 1 lb 6 oz floury potatoes, cooked and mashed, 15 oz can drained tuna, 2 tablespoons sweet chili sauce, 1–2 tablespoons lemon juice, 1 lightly beaten egg, 2 finely chopped green onions and 2 tablespoons chopped fresh parsley in a large bowl and mix well. Shape into 8 patties and roll in 1–2 cups dry bread crumbs. Shallow-fry in batches in a large skillet for 3–5 minutes on each side, or until crisp and golden.

serves 4

salmon and brie turnovers

Preheat the oven to 425°F. Cut 2 sheets thawed ready-rolled puff pastry into four squares on each sheet. Divide 15 oz can drained pink salmon among the pastry squares—in a triangle shape, in the bottom corner—top with 3 oz thinly sliced Brie, 2 teaspoons grated lemon rind and a large sprig of dill. Fold into a triangle and press to seal the edges with the tip of a teaspoon. Place the triangles on a non-stick baking sheet and brush lightly with a beaten egg. Bake for 20 minutes, or until crisp and golden brown.

serves 4

From left to right: Tuna pasta bake; Tuna patties; Salmon and brie turnovers.

noodles, grains, pasta & rice

ingredients

1 cup orange juice
1½ cups vegetable stock
2¼ cups instant couscous
2 cloves garlic, crushed
¼ cup golden raisins
¼ cup butter
2 tablespoons grated orange rind

preparation: 10 minutes
cooking: 10 minutes
serves: 4

1 Place the orange juice in a saucepan with the stock and bring to a boil. Stir in the couscous, garlic and raisins. Reduce the heat to low, and simmer, covered, for 5 minutes, stirring occasionally.

2 Remove the pan from the heat and add the butter and orange rind. Mix together well, then cover and set aside for 5 minutes. Separate the grains with a fork before serving.

nutrition per serve
Protein 6 g; Fat 13 g; Carbohydrate 55 g; Dietary Fiber 3 g; Cholesterol 40 mg; 350 calories

handy tip...

Couscous is a cereal made from semolina and wheat flour pressed into tiny bead-like grains. It is traditionally served hot as an accompaniment to vegetable tagine.

ingredients

2 cloves garlic, crushed
1 cup instant polenta
½ cup whipping cream
2½ tablespoons butter,
 chopped
⅓ cup grated Parmesan
¼ teaspoon paprika, and
 extra to garnish
shaved Parmesan,
 to garnish

preparation: 10 minutes
cooking: 10 minutes
serves: 4

1 Place 3½ cups water in a large saucepan and bring to a boil. Add the garlic and 1 teaspoon salt. Stir in the polenta with a wooden spoon, breaking up any lumps. Cook, stirring frequently, over medium heat for 4–5 minutes, or until smooth.

2 Add half the cream and cook for 2–3 minutes, or until the polenta is thick and comes away from the pan. Stir in the butter. Remove from the heat and stir in the Parmesan, paprika and remaining cream. Transfer to a warm serving bowl and sprinkle with extra paprika. Garnish with the shaved Parmesan and serve at once. This dish is a delicious accompaniment to chili beans.

nutrition per serve
Protein 7 g; Fat 25 g; Carbohydrate 30 g; Dietary Fiber 1 g; Cholesterol 80 mg; 360 calories

hint

Instant polenta (cornmeal) cooks in half the time of regular polenta. If it is not available, your polenta will take about 20 minutes to cook. Polenta must be served hot to keep its creamy, light consistency. Use a vegetable peeler to peel cheese shavings from a block of Parmesan.

ingredients

¼ cup butter
3 onions, sliced
2 cloves garlic,
    crushed
2 cups basmati rice
5 cups vegetable stock
1½ cups shelled peas
    (1 lb 8 oz in pod)
½ cup grated Parmesan
½ cup chopped fresh
    parsley

preparation: 10 minutes
cooking: 20 minutes
serves: 6

1 Melt the butter in a large saucepan over low heat. Add the onions and garlic and stir for 5 minutes, or until soft and golden.

2 Add the rice and stock, then bring to a boil, stirring once. Reduce the heat and simmer for 5 minutes, or until almost all the liquid has been absorbed.

3 Stir in the peas and cook, covered, over very low heat for 10 minutes, or until the rice is tender. Stir in the Parmesan and parsley and serve immediately.

nutrition per serve
Protein 11 g; Fat 12 g; Carbohydrate 60 g; Dietary Fiber 5 g; Cholesterol 34 mg; 385 calories

handy tip...

Basmati, meaning 'fragrant', is a creamy long-grain rice and is grown in the foothills of the Himalayas. The grains separate when cooked and have a sweet, nutty, dusky flavor and aroma.

ingredients

1 cup basmati rice
1 cup red lentils
¼ cup ghee
2 onions, sliced
2 teaspoons garam
  masala

preparation: 10 minutes
cooking: 50 minutes
serves: 4–6

1 Wash the rice two or three times, and then drain. Wash the lentils and drain. Heat 2 tablespoons ghee in a large saucepan, add half the onions and cook, stirring frequently, over low heat for 10 minutes, or until golden.

2 Add the rice and lentils and stir over low heat for 2–3 minutes. Add the garam masala and 1 teaspoon salt and stir for 1 minute, then slowly add 3½ cups hot water. Bring to a boil, stirring, then reduce the heat to very low and cover with a tight-fitting lid. Cook for 20–25 minutes, checking after about 20 minutes.

3 Heat the remaining ghee in a small skillet. Add the remaining onions and cook over moderate heat for 15 minutes, or until golden and caramelized. Drain on paper towels. Serve the kitchri immediately, garnished with the caramelized onion.

nutrition per serve (6)
Protein 13 g; Fat 9.5 g; Carbohydrate 43 g; Dietary Fiber 7 g; Cholesterol 25 mg; 311 calories

hint

Also known as clarified butter, ghee is the result of removing the milk solids from unsalted butter. Once the milk solids have been removed, butter will keep longer without becoming rancid. It also has a high smoke point and can be heated to higher temperatures than ordinary butter without the risk of burning. This means it is ideal for sautéing and frying.

ingredients

Pesto
2 cups firmly packed
  fresh basil leaves
¼ cup pine nuts,
  lightly toasted
2 large cloves garlic,
  chopped
⅓ cup extra virgin
  olive oil
½ cup grated Parmesan

1 clove garlic, crushed
1¼ cups whipping
  cream
1 lb fresh potato gnocchi

preparation: 15 minutes
cooking: 10 minutes
serves: 4

1 To make the pesto, place the basil, pine nuts and garlic in a blender or food processor. Process until smooth. Reserve 2 teaspoons of the oil. With the motor running, slowly pour in the remaining oil. Add the Parmesan and process until smooth.

2 Heat the reserved oil in a small saucepan. Add the garlic and cook over medium heat for 1 minute. Add the cream and ¼ cup of the pesto and bring to the boil. Be careful because it will boil over easily. Reduce the heat to low and simmer for 3 minutes.

3 Meanwhile, cook the gnocchi in a large saucepan of boiling water according to the packet instructions. Drain and place the gnocchi in a large bowl. Pour on the sauce and toss thoroughly. Season. Transfer to a serving bowl. Garnish with basil and serve with lemon wedges.

nutrition per serve
Protein 4 g; Fat 22 g; Carbohydrate 8 g; Dietary Fiber 1 g; Cholesterol 42 mg; 230 calories

handy tip...

Store the remaining pesto in an airtight container and cover the surface with a thin layer of extra virgin olive oil. Seal and refrigerate for up to 7 days.
Fresh gnocchi is available from supermarkets and delicatessens.

ingredients

1 lb fresh potato gnocchi
2 tablespoons oil
1 leek, sliced
1 cup bottled tomato
   pasta sauce
2/3 cup vegetable stock
1/3 cup chopped black
   olives
6 canned anchovy fillets,
   chopped

preparation: 10 minutes
cooking: 10 minutes
serves: 4

1 Cook the gnocchi in a large saucepan of boiling water according to the packet instructions. Drain.

2 Meanwhile, heat the oil in a saucepan and add the leek. Cook over medium heat for 5 minutes, or until golden. Add the tomato sauce, stock, olives and anchovies. Stir the mixture for 5 minutes, or until heated through. Pour over the gnocchi and serve.

nutrition per serve
Protein 6 g; Fat 11 g; Carbohydrate 24 g; Dietary Fiber 4 g; Cholesterol 3.5 mg; 219 calories

hint

The sauce can be cooked a day ahead and stored, covered, in the refrigerator. Reheat just before serving.
Purchase good-quality fresh gnocchi or make your own. Use any other dried or fresh pasta, if preferred.

ingredients

1 lb fresh mixed tagliatelle
  (spinach and plain)
1 tablespoon olive oil
1 cup pine nuts
10 oz arugula leaves
2 cups fresh mint
1/2 cup olive oil

preparation: 10 minutes
cooking: 10 minutes
serves: 6

1 Preheat the oven to 350°F. Cook the tagliatelle in a large saucepan of boiling water according to the package instructions. Drain, toss with the tablespoon of oil and keep warm. Scatter the pine nuts on a baking sheet and bake for 5 minutes, or until golden.

2 Place the arugula and mint in a food processor or blender and process for 10 seconds. Add the pine nuts and oil and process another 20 seconds, or until the mixture is finely chopped and well combined. Season to taste.

3 Place the pasta on a serving platter and top with the pesto. Serve with shaved Parmesan, if desired.

nutrition per serve
Protein 13 g; Fat 40 g; Carbohydrate 60 g; Dietary Fiber 6 g; Cholesterol 0 mg; 665 calories

handy tip...

Arugula is a salad green with a peppery mustard flavor.

ingredients

10 oz pasta spirals
1 cup sun-dried tomatoes
    in olive oil, drained
½ cup fresh basil
⅓ cup pine nuts
½ cup finely grated
    Parmesan
⅓ cup oil

preparation: 15 minutes
cooking: 15 minutes
serves: 6

1 Cook the pasta spirals in a large saucepan of boiling water according to the package instructions.

2 Meanwhile, place the sun-dried tomatoes in a food processor with the basil, pine nuts and Parmesan. Using the pulse action, process for 1 minute, or until finely chopped. With the motor running, pour in the oil in a steady stream.

3 Drain the pasta well and place in a large serving bowl. Add the sun-dried tomato pesto and toss to combine well. Serve immediately.

nutrition per serve
Protein 10 g; Fat 22 g; Carbohydrate 36 g; Dietary Fiber 3 g; Cholesterol 8 mg; 380 calories

hint

This dish can be made 1 hour ahead and served at room temperature.
Sun-dried tomato pesto can be made up to one day in advance and stored in an airtight container in the refrigerator.

ingredients

4 cups vegetable stock
2 tablespoons butter
1 large onion, chopped
2 cloves garlic, crushed
2 cups arborio or short-
  grain rice
2 x 14 oz cans chopped
  tomatoes
½ cup shredded Cheddar
½ cup chopped fresh
  herbs (oregano, basil,
  parsley and chives)

preparation: 15 minutes
cooking: 35 minutes
serves: 4

1 Place the stock in a saucepan and bring to a boil. Reduce the heat and keep at a low simmer.

2 Melt the butter in a saucepan. Add the onion and garlic and cook over medium heat for 1–2 minutes, or until soft. Add the rice and stir for 1 minute, or until well coated.

3 Add ½ cup stock and cook, stirring constantly, over medium heat until all the stock has been absorbed. Continue adding the stock, ½ cup at a time, stirring constantly over low heat for 20–25 minutes, allowing the stock to be completely absorbed after each addition.

4 When all the stock has been absorbed and the rice is almost cooked, stir in the tomatoes. Cook for another 2–3 minutes, or until the rice is tender and creamy in texture. Stir in the cheese and herbs and season with salt and freshly ground black pepper. Serve immediately with grated Parmesan or extra Cheddar, if desired.

nutrition per serve
Protein 15 g; Fat 10 g; Carbohydrate 90 g; Dietary Fiber 6 g; Cholesterol 30 mg; 510 calories

handy tip...

It is important to make sure that the stock is really hot before gradually adding to the rice—this allows it to be absorbed faster and will not cool the risotto down. Leftover, cold risotto can be shaped into patties, coated with egg and bread crumbs and fried in oil.

ingredients

8 cups vegetable stock

⅓ cup butter

1 onion, finely chopped

8 oz butternut squash,
   cut into cubes

2 carrots, cut into cubes

2 cups arborio rice

¾ cup freshly grated
   Romano cheese

¼ teaspoon ground nutmeg

preparation: 15 minutes
cooking: 40 minutes
serves: 4

1 Place the vegetable stock in a saucepan and bring to a boil.

Reduce the heat and keep at a low simmer.

2 Heat ¼ cup of the butter in a large saucepan. Add the onion and cook for 3–5 minutes, or until soft. Add the squash and carrots, and cook for 10 minutes, or until the vegetables are tender.

3 Add the rice to the vegetables and cook for 1 minute, stirring constantly. Add enough hot stock to cover the rice and stir well. Reduce the heat and add more stock as it is absorbed, stirring constantly. Continue adding the stock ½ cup at a time, and cooking for 25 minutes, or until the rice is tender and creamy in texture. (You may not need to use all the stock.)

4 Remove from the heat. Add the cheese, nutmeg and remaining butter. Season to taste with salt and freshly ground black pepper. Cover and allow to stand for 5 minutes before serving.

nutrition per serve
Protein 18 g; Fat 9.5 g; Carbohydrate 93 g; Dietary Fiber 6.5 g; Cholesterol 20 mg; 530 calories

hint

Romano is a hard, grating cheese similar to Parmesan. For a creamier risotto, mash the carrot and squash before adding the rice.

ingredients

¼ cup peanut oil

2 eggs, beaten

1½ cups finely diced, cooked ham

3 oz cooked shrimp, finely chopped

4 cups cold cooked rice

¼ cup frozen peas

¼ cup light soy sauce

6 green onions, thinly sliced on the diagonal

preparation: 10 minutes
cooking: 5 minutes
serves: 4–6

1 Heat a wok until very hot, add 1 tablespoon of the peanut oil and swirl to coat the side. Add the eggs and start to scramble. When almost cooked, remove from the wok and set aside. Heat the remaining oil in the wok, then add the ham and shrimp, tossing to heat through evenly.

2 Add the rice and peas, toss and stir-fry for 3 minutes, or until the rice grains separate. Add the scrambled eggs, sprinkle with the soy sauce and toss to coat the rice. Add the green onions, stir-fry for 2 minutes and serve.

nutrition per serve (6)
Protein 17 g; Fat 14 g; Carbohydrate 41 g; Dietary Fiber 2.5 g; Cholesterol 105 mg; 358 calories

handy tip...

Cook the rice in a large saucepan of boiling water for 10–15 minutes, or until tender. Drain well, spread out on a flat tray, cover and refrigerate until ready to use. This recipe is great for using up leftover cooked rice.

ingredients

1 lb 6 oz butternut squash, peeled
2 tablespoons olive oil
1 lb ricotta
1/3 cup pine nuts, toasted
3/4 cup firmly packed fresh basil
1/3 cup grated Parmesan
4 oz fresh lasagne sheets (see hint)
1 1/4 cups shredded Mozzarella

preparation: 15 minutes
cooking: 1 hour 25 minutes
serves: 4

1 Preheat the oven to 350°F. Lightly grease a baking pan. Cut the squash into 1/2 in slices and arrange in a single layer in the pan. Brush with oil and cook for 1 hour, or until softened, turning halfway through cooking.

2 Place the ricotta, pine nuts, basil and Parmesan in a bowl and mix together well.

3 Lightly grease an 8 in square baking dish. Cook the lasagne sheets according to the package instructions, or until tender. Cover the base of the dish with a single layer of the pasta sheets. Spread with a layer of the ricotta mixture and top with another layer of pasta.

4 Arrange the squash evenly over the pasta sheets with as few gaps as possible. Season to taste with salt and freshly ground black pepper and top with a final layer of pasta sheets. Sprinkle with the shredded Mozzarella and bake for 20–25 minutes, or until the cheese is golden. Rest for 10 minutes, then cut into squares and serve.

nutrition per serve
Protein 37 g; Fat 46 g; Carbohydrate 35 g; Dietary Fiber 4.5 g; Cholesterol 97 mg; 700 calories

hint

If the pasta has no cooking instructions, cook the sheets one at a time in a large saucepan of boiling water for 3 minutes, or until tender. If fresh lasagne sheets are not available, use dried sheets and adjust the cooking time accordingly.

blue cheese sauce

Place 7 oz crumbled creamy blue cheese (or to taste) in a large skillet with 1¼ cups whipping cream. Stir over low heat until the cheese melts, then bring to a boil. Boil for 5 minutes, or until the sauce is thick enough to coat the back of a wooden spoon.

serves 4

From left to right: Blue cheese sauce; Speedy bolognese; Simple browned butter and herb sauce; Rich sweet pepper, olive and tomato sauce; White wine and mushroom sauce; Creamy bacon and mushroom sauce.

speedy bolognese

Heat 1 tablespoon oil in a large skillet. Add 1 finely chopped onion and 2 crushed cloves garlic, and cook over medium heat for 3 minutes, or until golden. Add 1 lb lean ground beef and cook for 10 minutes, or until browned. Break up any lumps with a wooden spoon. Drain any excess fat, then add 1¾ cups bottled pasta sauce, ½ cup red wine, 1 tablespoon balsamic vinegar and 1 teaspoon dried mixed herbs. Bring to a boil, then reduce the heat and simmer for 10 minutes, or until the sauce is slightly thickened.

serves 4

simple browned butter and herb sauce

Melt ¾ cup butter in a large skillet and cook over medium heat for 3 minutes, or until the butter turns a nutty brown color. Be careful— if done too quickly the butter will burn and become bitter. Add ¼ cup chopped fresh mixed herbs (such as sage, chives, parsley) and stir gently.

serves 4

rich sweet pepper, olive and tomato sauce

Heat 1 tablespoon oil in a skillet. Add 1 crushed clove garlic and 1 finely chopped onion and cook over medium heat for 3 minutes, or until golden. Add ¾ cup chopped marinated charbroiled sweet red peppers and cook for 2 minutes. Stir in 1¾ cups tomato pasta sauce and ½ cup Kalamata olives, then bring to a boil. Cook for 10 minutes, or until the sauce reduces and thickens slightly. Stir in 2 tablespoons slivered basil. Season with salt and freshly ground black pepper before serving.

serves 4

white wine and mushroom sauce

Heat in a skillet 1 tablespoon oil and 2 tablespoons butter, then add 2 crushed cloves garlic and cook over medium heat for 1 minute. Add 1 lb mixed mushrooms (eg. enoki, oyster, Swiss brown, button) and fry until golden brown. Stir in 1 tablespoon tomato paste and ½ cup white wine. Bring to a boil, then reduce the heat and simmer for 3 minutes. Stir in 1 tablespoon finely chopped fresh parsley before serving.

serves 4

creamy bacon and mushroom sauce

Heat 1 tablespoon oil in a large skillet. Add 4 slices chopped bacon, 2 crushed cloves garlic and 3 chopped green onions and cook over medium heat for 2 minutes, or until golden. Add about 3 cups sliced button mushrooms and cook for 5 minutes, or until soft and browned. Stir in 1 tablespoon brandy and 2 cups whipping cream, bring to a boil and cook for 9 minutes, or until sauce is thick and coats the back of a spoon.

serves 4

ingredients

1 lb rissoni pasta
2 tablespoons butter
¼ cup olive oil
4 onions, sliced
⅓ cup mascarpone cheese
6 oz blue cheese
2 cups slivered spinach
    leaves

preparation: 15 minutes
cooking: 35 minutes
serves: 4

1 Cook the rissoni in a large saucepan of boiling water according to the package instructions. Drain and return to the pan.

2 Meanwhile, heat the butter and olive oil in a large skillet. Add the sliced onions and cook over low heat for 20–30 minutes, or until golden brown and caramelized. Remove from the pan with a slotted spoon and drain on paper towels.

3 Place the mascarpone, blue cheese and onions in a bowl and mix together well.

4 Add the spinach and the cheese and onion mixture to the rissoni and toss well. Season to taste with salt and freshly ground black pepper before serving.

nutrition per serve
Protein 30 g; Fat 45 g; Carbohydrate 95 g; Dietary Fiber 9 g; Cholesterol 90 mg; 895 calories

handy tip...

Blue vein is a soft cheese made from cow's milk, with veins of blue-green mold culture criss-crossing the interior. It is a sharp and strong-flavored cheese with a crumbly texture. Varieties include Gorgonzola and Stilton.

ingredients

1 lb linguine
2 cups whipping cream
1⅓ cups frozen peas
1 clove garlic, crushed
pinch of nutmeg
½ barbecued chicken
7 oz sliced ham,
    cut into strips
¾ cup loosely packed
    fresh flat-leaf parsley,
    finely chopped

preparation: 15 minutes
cooking: 15 minutes
serves: 4

1 Cook the linguine in a large saucepan of boiling water according to the package instructions. Drain and keep warm.

2 Meanwhile, pour the cream into a large skillet and bring to a boil. Reduce the heat, add the peas, garlic and nutmeg and simmer for 3 minutes. Season to taste.

3 Remove the skin and bones from the chicken and cut the flesh into bite-size pieces. Add the chicken, ham and parsley to the cream and bring to a boil. Reduce the heat and simmer until the sauce has thickened slightly.

4 Add the linguine to the cream sauce. Toss to coat, then transfer to a serving bowl. Top with grated Parmesan, if desired, and serve with a fresh green salad.

nutrition per serve
Protein 50 g; Fat 65 g; Carbohydrate 70 g; Dietary Fiber 7.5 g; Cholesterol 320 mg; 1055 calories

hint

Linguine is a long flat pasta that is about the width of spaghetti. Other types of flat pasta can be used in this recipe—try fettuccine, pappardelle or tagliatelle.

ingredients

1 lb fresh tortellini
1/4 cup butter
7 oz small mushrooms,
  finely sliced
1 clove garlic, crushed
1 1/4 cups whipping cream
pinch of nutmeg
2 teaspoons finely grated
  lemon rind
1/4 cup grated Parmesan

preparation: 10 minutes
cooking: 10 minutes
serves: 4

1 Cook the tortellini in a large saucepan of boiling water according to the package instructions. Drain and keep warm.

2 Meanwhile, melt the butter in a saucepan. Add the mushrooms and cook over medium heat for 5 minutes, or until browned and tender.

3 Add the garlic, cream, nutmeg, lemon rind and freshly ground black pepper. Bring to a boil and cook until the sauce is thick enough to coat the back of a spoon. Stir in the Parmesan and cook gently for 3 minutes.

4 Place the cooked tortellini in a warm serving dish. Add the sauce and stir gently to combine well. Serve immediately.

nutrition per serve
Protein 17 g; Fat 16 g; Carbohydrate 88 g; Dietary Fiber 7 g; Cholesterol 45 mg; 575 calories

handy tip...

Tortellini are small rings of pasta, usually stuffed with finely chopped seasoned meat—they can also be filled with spinach and ricotta for a complete vegetarian meal. Tortellini is often served with a cream or tomato sauce.

ingredients

1 lb fresh egg noodles
¼ cup olive oil
1 clove garlic, crushed
4 green onions, sliced
1 lb 8 oz raw shrimp,
    shelled and deveined
1 cup fresh cilantro
    leaves
2 tablespoons finely
    chopped preserved
    lemon *(see hint)*
1 teaspoon harissa

preparation: 15 minutes
cooking: 10 minutes
serves: 4

1 Cook the egg noodles in a large saucepan of boiling water according to the package instructions. Drain and keep warm.

2 Heat the oil in a wok or large skillet over high heat. When hot, add the garlic, green onions and shrimp. Stir-fry until the shrimp just turn pink.

3 Add the cooked egg noodles, cilantro leaves, preserved lemon and harissa, and stir-fry until the noodles are hot. Serve at once.

nutrition per serve
Protein 50 g; Fat 15 g; Carbohydrate 35 g; Dietary Fiber 5 g; Cholesterol 280 mg; 480 calories

hint

To use preserved lemons, wash well under cold water. Remove the flesh and only use the rind.
Harissa is a fiery condiment for meats, couscous and soups. It's also used as a marinade for chicken, lamb or fish.

nutrition per serve
Protein 32 g; Fat 64 g; Carbohydrate
73 g; Dietary Fiber 5 g; Cholesterol
182 mg; 995 calories

ingredients

14 oz pappardelle
1/4 cup unsalted butter
1 1/4 cups whipping cream
2 cups freshly grated
   Parmesan
1 tablespoon olive oil
1 small fresh red chile,
   cut into fine shreds
2–3 drops chili oil
1/2 teaspoon paprika

preparation: 10 minutes
cooking: 12 minutes
serves: 4

1 Cook the pappardelle in a large saucepan of boiling water according to the package instructions. Drain.

2 Melt the butter in a saucepan (do not allow it to brown). Add the cream and Parmesan and heat gently for 4–5 minutes.

3 In another saucepan, heat the olive oil. Add the chile, chili oil and paprika. Cook for 1–2 minutes. Add the pasta and toss well.

4 Place the pasta into a heated serving dish. Pour on the cream sauce and serve immediately.

handy tip...

It is advisable to protect your hands with plastic gloves when preparing fresh chiles. Try using scissors to chop, instead of a knife—it makes the job much easier.

ingredients

8 oz fresh thick egg
noodles

2 red sweet bell peppers,
seeded

2 green sweet bell
peppers, seeded

1 large carrot, cut into
fine strips

3 green onions, finely
chopped

1/3 cup olive oil

2 tablespoons lemon juice

1 tablespoon finely
chopped fresh mint

preparation: 15 minutes +
10 minutes standing +
overnight refrigeration
cooking: 20 minutes
serves: 4

1 Cook the noodles in a large saucepan of boiling water according to the package instructions. Drain and cool.

2 Cut the red and green peppers into quarters. Place them on a foil-lined broiler rack, skin-side up. Cook under a medium broiler for 20 minutes, or until the skin blackens and blisters. Remove from the broiler, cover with a clean, damp dish towel and rest for 10 minutes.

3 Carefully remove the skins from the peppers and cut the flesh into 1/2 in wide strips. Place the peppers in a bowl with the noodles, carrot and green onions and toss together well.

4 Place the oil, lemon juice and mint in a small bowl and whisk together. Pour over the salad and mix well. Cover and refrigerate for several hours or overnight. Toss again just before serving.

nutrition per serve
Protein 10 g; Fat 20 g; Carbohydrate 50 g; Dietary Fiber 3.5 g; Cholesterol 11 mg; 425 calories

hint

Drained, canned pimientos may be used in this recipe if desired, but the full roasted flavor will not be obtained.

vegetables & salads

ingredients

6 plum tomatoes
5 bocconcini
²/₃ cup loosely packed
  fresh basil

Dressing
¼ cup extra virgin olive oil
2 tablespoons balsamic
  vinegar

preparation: 15 minutes
cooking: none
serves: 4

1 Cut the tomatoes lengthwise into 3–4 slices, discarding the thin outside slices, which won't lie flat. Slice the bocconcini lengthwise into 3–4 slices.

2 Arrange some tomato slices on a serving plate, place a bocconcini slice on top of each tomato and scatter with some of the basil leaves. Continue arranging until all the tomatoes, bocconcini and basil have been used. Season with salt and freshly ground black pepper.

3 To make the dressing, place the oil and vinegar in a small bowl and whisk together well. Drizzle over the salad.

nutrition per serve
Protein 10 g; Fat 25 g; Carbohydrate 3 g; Dietary Fiber 2 g; Cholesterol 25 mg; 255 calories

handy tip...

Try this salad with a pesto dressing: Process ½ cup firmly packed fresh basil, 1 tablespoon pine nuts, ¼ cup grated Parmesan and 1 crushed garlic clove in a food processor until finely chopped. With the motor running, add ¼ cup olive oil and 1 tablespoon lemon juice in a steady stream and process until smooth.

ingredients

½ cup plain yogurt

½ cup whole-egg mayonnaise

⅓ cup creamy or mild blue cheese

2 tablespoons whipping cream

1 lb button mushrooms

2 celery sticks, sliced

1 cup firmly packed arugula leaves

2 tablespoons chopped walnuts

preparation: 15 minutes
cooking: none
serves: 4

1 To make the dressing, place the yogurt, mayonnaise, cheese and cream in a food processor and process until smooth. Season.

2 Wipe the mushrooms with a damp paper towel, cut in half and place in a large bowl with the celery. Add the dressing and toss gently to combine.

3 Arrange the arugula leaves in a large serving dish and spoon in the mushroom and celery mixture. Sprinkle with the chopped walnuts.

nutrition per serve
Protein 10 g; Fat 25 g; Carbohydrate 10 g; Dietary Fiber 4 g; Cholesterol 45 mg; 310 calories

hint

If you would like to marinate some mushrooms, try these marinated garlic mushrooms. Place 1 lb button mushrooms, 3 crushed cloves garlic, 1 tablespoon Dijon mustard, 1 tablespoon lemon juice and 1 cup olive oil in a bowl and mix to combine. Allow to marinate for 3 hours before serving.

ingredients

6 tomatoes, cut into thin wedges

1 red onion, cut into thin rings

2 short thin cucumbers, sliced

1 cup Kalamata olives

7 oz feta cheese

¼ cup extra virgin olive oil

dried oregano, to sprinkle

preparation: 15 minutes
cooking: none
serves: 6–8

1 Place the tomatoes, onion rings, sliced cucumbers and Kalamata olives in a large bowl and mix together. Season with salt and freshly ground black pepper.

2 Break the feta up into large pieces with your fingers and scatter over the top of the salad. Drizzle with the olive oil and sprinkle with some dried oregano.

nutrition per serve (8)
Protein 6.5 g; Fat 14 g; Carbohydrate 4 g; Dietary Fiber 2.5 g; Cholesterol 17 mg; 170 calories

handy tip...

Feta is a sheep's milk cheese with a sharp salty flavor. There are many different varieties available.
If you are looking to add a little more flavor to the salad, use marinated feta and use the oil that it has been marinating in for the dressing.

nutrition per serve
Protein 2.5 g; Fat 26 g; Carbohydrate 0.5 g; Dietary Fiber 1.7 g; Cholesterol 0 mg; 242 calories

ingredients

2 cups baby spinach leaves

1 oak leaf lettuce

2 avocados, thinly sliced

1/4 cup olive oil

2 tablespoons sesame seeds

1 tablespoon lemon juice

2 teaspoons coarse grain mustard

preparation: 15 minutes
cooking: 2 minutes
serves: 8

1 Wash and dry the spinach and lettuce. Tear into bite-size pieces and place in a serving bowl. Scatter the avocados over the leaves.

2 Heat 1 tablespoon oil in a small saucepan. Add the sesame seeds and cook over low heat until they just start to turn golden. Remove from the heat immediately. Set aside and cool for a minute or so.

3 Add the lemon juice to the saucepan with the mustard and remaining oil and stir to warm through. Pour over the salad and toss gently.

hint

This dish is best prepared just before serving.
You can replace the sesame seeds with pepita or sunflower seeds or a mix of both. You could also try roasted pine nuts or chopped peanuts.

ingredients

1 cup bulghur (cracked wheat)

½ cup olive oil

1 cup chopped fresh flat-leaf parsley

1 cup chopped fresh mint

¾ cup finely chopped green onions

4 plum tomatoes, chopped

½ cup lemon juice

2 cloves garlic, crushed

preparation: 15 minutes + 30 minutes refrigeration

cooking: none

serves: 8

1 Place the bulghur in a bowl and pour in 1 cup boiling water. Mix in 2 teaspoons of the oil, then set aside for 10 minutes. Stir again and cool.

2 Add the parsley, mint, green onions and tomatoes to the bulghur and mix well. Place the lemon juice, garlic and remaining oil in a small bowl and whisk together well. Add to the bulghur and mix together gently. Season to taste with salt and freshly ground black pepper. Cover and chill for 30 minutes before serving.

nutrition per **serve**
Protein 3 g; **Fat 15 g; Carbo**hydrate 15 g; Dietary **Fiber 5 g; Cholesterol** 0 mg; 210 calories

handy tip...

Bulghur is also sold as burghul or cracked wheat. For a different taste, couscous can be used instead of bulghur in this recipe.

ingredients

10 oz sweet potato,
    peeled
2 slender eggplants
    (about 11 oz each)
oil, for deep-frying
¼ teaspoon ground chili
    powder
1 teaspoon chicken salt
¼ teaspoon ground
    coriander

preparation: 5 minutes
cooking: 10 minutes
serves: 4–6

1 Cut the sweet potato and the eggplants lengthwise into long, thin strips, similar in size. Place the vegetables into a large bowl.

2 Fill a deep heavy-based saucepan one-third full of oil. Heat the oil to 375°F, or until a cube of bread dropped in the oil browns in 10 seconds. Cook the sweet potato and eggplants in batches over high heat for 5 minutes, or until golden and crisp. Carefully remove the chips from the oil with tongs or a slotted spoon. Drain chips on paper towels.

3 Place the chili powder, chicken salt and coriander in a small bowl and mix well. Sprinkle the mixture over the hot chips, toss until well coated and serve immediately.

nutrition per serve (6)
Protein 1.5 g; Fat 6.5 g; Carbohydrate 8.5 g; Dietary Fiber 2 g; Cholesterol 0 mg; 100 calories

hint

Cook the chips just before serving.
Try using other vegetables such as beets, carrots, potatoes and zucchini.

ingredients

Dressing
⅓ cup olive oil
2 tablespoons balsamic
   vinegar
2 tablespoons chopped
   fresh rosemary
3 cloves garlic, crushed

2 large red bell peppers
2 large sweet potatoes
6 zucchini, halved
4 large button mushrooms

preparation: 15 minutes
cooking: 15 minutes
serves: 4

1 To make the dressing, place the oil, balsamic vinegar, rosemary and garlic in a small bowl. Season with salt and freshly ground black pepper and whisk together well.

2 Remove seeds and membrane from the sweet peppers, then cut the flesh into thick strips. Cut the sweet potatoes into slices. Place bell peppers, sweet potatoes, zucchini and mushrooms on a cold, lightly oiled broiler rack and brush with the dressing. Cook under a hot broiler (or on a barbecue) for 15 minutes, turning occasionally, or until all the vegetables are tender and light golden. Brush the remaining dressing over the vegetables during cooking. Serve warm with mashed potatoes, if desired.

nutrition per serve
Protein 3 g; Fat 20 g; Carbohydrate
13 g; Dietary Fiber 3 g; Cholesterol
0 mg; 240 calories

handy tip...

For a faster version of this recipe, use your favorite bottled dressing to brush on the vegetables instead of making your own.

ingredients

2 large potatoes, cubed
5 large parsnips, cubed
2 tablespoons butter
1 tablespoon milk
2 tablespoons sour cream
chopped fresh chives,
    to garnish

preparation: 10 minutes
cooking: 20 minutes
serves: 4–6

1 Bring a large saucepan of lightly salted water to a boil. Add the potatoes and parsnips and cook for 20 minutes, or until soft. Drain well.

2 Transfer the potatoes and parsnips to a bowl, add the butter, milk and sour cream and mash until smooth and fluffy. Season with salt and pepper. Sprinkle with the chives and serve immediately.

nutrition per serve (6)
Protein 5 g; Fat 7 g; Carbohydrate 30 g; Dietary Fiber 5 g; Cholesterol 25 mg; 190 calories

hint

For this recipe, use an all-purpose floury potato that mashes well. Creamy mash works well with other fresh herbs, such as parsley.

ingredients

2 tablespoons olive oil

2 cloves garlic, sliced

1 lb 4 oz large button
   mushrooms, halved

2 tablespoons chopped
   fresh marjoram

2 tablespoons tomato paste

8 oz cherry tomatoes,
   halved

1 tablespoon chopped
   fresh oregano leaves

preparation: 15 minutes
cooking: 15 minutes
serves: 4 as a side dish

1 Heat the oil in a saucepan, add the garlic and stir over moderate heat for 1 minute. Do not brown.

2 Add the mushrooms and cook, stirring, for 5 minutes, or until light golden brown.

3 Stir in the marjoram, tomato paste and cherry tomatoes and cook over low heat for 5 minutes, or until the mushrooms are soft. Sprinkle with oregano leaves and season with cracked black pepper.

nutrition per serve
Protein 6 g; Fat 10 g; Carbohydrate 4.5 g; Dietary Fiber 5.3 g; Cholesterol 0 mg; 133 calories

handy tip...

This dish can be made up to 2 days ahead and is delicious served hot or cold. This 'saucy' dish can be served with mashed potatoes or soft polenta.

ingredients

1 lb 8 oz sweet potatoes, chopped
3 tablespoons butter
1 clove garlic, crushed
2 teaspoons grated fresh ginger
1½ tablespoons chopped fresh cilantro leaves
2 teaspoons soy sauce
fresh cilantro sprigs, to garnish

preparation: 15 minutes
cooking: 20 minutes
serves: 4

1 Bring a large saucepan of lightly salted water to a boil. Add the sweet potatoes and cook for 10–15 minutes, or until tender. Drain well.

2 Chop and melt the butter in a small saucepan, add the garlic and ginger and cook over low heat, stirring, for 1 minute, or until fragrant.

3 Mash the sweet potatoes until almost smooth. Stir in the garlic mixture, cilantro and soy sauce. Garnish with sprigs of cilantro and serve immediately.

nutrition per serve
Protein 4 g; Fat 9.5 g; Carbohydrate 27 g; Dietary Fiber 3.5 g; Cholesterol 30 mg; 205 calories

hint

Sweet potato is sweeter than regular potato, with a texture between potato and butternut squash. This mash goes well with pork, chicken, beef or lamb.

ingredients

4 fennel bulbs,
    cut into wedges
1 clove garlic, crushed
1/2 lemon, sliced
2 tablespoons olive oil
1/4 cup butter, melted
1/4 cup grated pecorino
    pepato cheese

preparation: 15 minutes
cooking: 25 minutes
serves: 4

1 Place the fennel in a saucepan with the garlic, lemon, olive oil and 1 teaspoon salt. Pour in enough water to cover the fennel and bring to a boil. Reduce the heat, then simmer for 20 minutes, or until just tender. Drain well.

2 Place the fennel in a shallow heatproof dish, then drizzle with the melted butter. Sprinkle with the cheese. Season to taste with salt and freshly ground black pepper.

3 Place under a hot broiler until the cheese has browned and melted. Serve immediately.

nutrition per serve
Protein 5.5 g; Fat 24 g; Carbohydrate 6 g; Dietary Fiber 5 g; Cholesterol 45 mg; 265 calories

handy tip...

Pecorino pepato is a hard cheese (made from sheep's milk) which is studded with black peppercorns and has a mild peppery flavor. If it is not available, use Parmesan or Romano instead.

ingredients

2 lb 4 oz potatoes,
  cut into 3/4 in cubes
1/3 cup olive oil
2 slices bacon, chopped
1 onion, chopped
2 green onions, sliced
1 tablespoon fresh thyme,
  finely chopped
1 clove garlic, crushed

preparation: 15 minutes
cooking: 35 minutes
serves: 4

1 Bring a large saucepan of water to a boil. Add the potatoes and cook for 5 minutes, or until just tender. Drain well and dry on a clean dish towel.

2 Heat the oil in a large non-stick skillet. Add the bacon, onion and green onions and cook for 5 minutes. Add the potatoes and cook over low heat, shaking the pan occasionally, for 20 minutes, or until tender. Turn frequently to prevent sticking. Partially cover the pan halfway through cooking. The steam will help cook the potatoes.

3 Add the thyme and garlic, and season to taste with salt and pepper in the last few minutes of cooking. Increase the heat to crisp the potatoes, if necessary.

nutrition per serve
Protein 10 g; Fat 20 g; Carbohydrate 35 g; Dietary Fiber 4.7 g; Cholesterol 9.5 mg; 365 calories

hint

The potatoes can be cooked ahead of time and reheated in a lightly oiled skillet.
Use fresh rosemary instead of thyme, if desired.

ingredients

4 slices white bread, crusts
    removed, cut into cubes
3 slices bacon,
    coarsely chopped
1 romaine lettuce
½ cup whole-egg
    mayonnaise
4 canned anchovy fillets,
    finely chopped
1 clove garlic, chopped
1 tablespoon lemon juice
½ cup shaved Parmesan

preparation: 15 minutes
cooking: 15 minutes
serves: 4

1 Preheat the oven to 425°F. Spread the bread cubes evenly on a baking sheet and bake for 15 minutes, or until light golden brown. Fry the bacon in a skillet until crisp, then drain on paper towels. Tear the lettuce leaves into bite-size pieces.

2 To make the dressing, place the mayonnaise, anchovies, garlic and lemon juice in a small bowl and mix together well.

3 Place the lettuce, bread cubes, Parmesan and bacon in a serving bowl, add the dressing and toss until combined. Serve immediately.

nutrition per serve
Protein 15 g; Fat 17 g; Carbohydrate 21 g; Dietary Fiber 2.5 g; Cholesterol 40 mg; 295 calories

handy tip...

The bread cubes can be baked a day in advance, then stored in an airtight container. The dressing can also be made a day in advance and stored in an airtight container in the refrigerator. Assemble the salad just before serving.

ingredients

4 slices bacon
3 lb small, waxy,
    red-skinned potatoes
4 green onions, finely
    sliced
¼ cup chopped fresh
    flat-leaf parsley

Dressing
½ cup extra virgin
    olive oil
1 tablespoon Dijon
    mustard
⅓ cup white wine vinegar

preparation: 15 minutes
cooking: 20 minutes
serves: 6–8

1 Cook the slices of bacon under a hot broiler until crisp. Chop into small pieces.

2 Bring a large saucepan of lightly salted water to a boil. Add the potatoes, reduce the heat and simmer for 10 minutes, or until just tender, trying not to let the skins break away too much. Drain and cool slightly.

3 To make the dressing, place the oil, mustard and vinegar in a bowl and whisk together until well blended.

4 When cool enough to handle, cut the potatoes into quarters and place in a large bowl with the green onions, chopped parsley and half the bacon pieces. Season to taste with salt and freshly ground black pepper. Pour half the dressing over the salad and then toss gently to coat the potatoes and bacon.

5 Transfer to a serving bowl, drizzle with the remaining dressing and sprinkle with the remaining bacon pieces.

nutrition per serve (8)
Protein 8 g; Fat 20 g; Carbohydrate 25 g; Dietary Fiber 3 g; Cholesterol 10 mg; 325 calories

hint

Waxy potatoes have a high moisture content and are ideal for salads. Make sure you use extra virgin olive oil for the dressing — its fruitiness adds so much flavor.

ingredients

15 canned anchovy fillets
⅓ cup butter
2 large onions, thinly sliced
5 potatoes, cut into
   matchsticks
2 cups whipping cream

preparation: 15 minutes
cooking: 1 hour 5 minutes
serves: 4

1 Preheat the oven to 400°F. Place the anchovy fillets in a bowl of water or milk and soak for 5 minutes to reduce their saltiness. Rinse and drain well.

2 Melt half the butter in a skillet and cook the onions over medium heat for 5 minutes, or until golden. Chop the remaining butter into small cubes.

3 Arrange half the potato matchsticks over the base of a shallow baking dish, top with the anchovies and onions, then with the remaining potatoes.

4 Pour half the cream over the potatoes and scatter the butter cubes on top. Bake for 20 minutes, or until golden. Pour the remaining cream over the top and bake for another 40 minutes, or until the potatoes are tender.

nutrition per serve
Protein 11 g; Fat 70 g; Carbohydrate 30 g; Dietary Fiber 4 g; Cholesterol 240 mg; 800 calories

handy tip...

A traditional Swedish dish, thought to have tempted a religious man from his vow to give up earthly pleasures of the flesh. Often served at the end of a party when it is supposed to tempt guests to stay longer.

ingredients

2 tablespoons butter
1 onion, sliced into
   thin rings
1 lb 8 oz waxy or
   all-purpose potatoes,
   thinly sliced
1½ cups whipping cream
1 cup shredded Cheddar

preparation: 15 minutes
cooking: 45 minutes
serves: 4–6

1 Preheat the oven to 350°F. Heat the butter in a skillet, add the onion and cook for 5 minutes, or until soft and translucent.

2 Place the potato slices, onion rings, whipping cream and half the cheese in a large bowl. Season with salt and pepper and mix together well.

3 Spread the potato mixture into a greased 4-cup baking dish and flatten down with clean hands. Sprinkle the remaining cheese over the top, then bake for 40 minutes, or until the potatoes are tender, the cheese has melted and the top is golden brown.

nutrition per serve (6)
Protein 9 g; Fat 40 g; Carbohydrate 19 g; Dietary Fiber 2.5 g; Cholesterol 120 mg; 435 calories

hint

A gratin is any dish topped with cheese and/or bread crumbs and cooked until browned. There are many versions of gratin, some are creamy, others less so.
If you prefer a lighter texture, you could use some vegetable or chicken stock in place of the cream. Waxy or all-purpose potatoes are the best varieties to use because they hold their shape better when slow-cooked. This gratin is also delicious made with half potato and half sweet potato.

asparagus and snow pea salad

ingredients

5 oz asparagus
2 tablespoons peanut oil
1 tablespoon sesame oil
1 tablespoon red wine
    vinegar
½ teaspoon sugar
7 oz snow peas
1 tablespoon sesame
    seeds

preparation: 15 minutes
cooking: 3 minutes
serves: 4–6

1 Cut the asparagus in half diagonally. Place in a saucepan of boiling water for 1 minute, then drain and plunge into iced water. Drain well.

2 To make the dressing, place the peanut and sesame oils, vinegar and sugar in a small bowl and whisk together well. Place the asparagus and snow peas in a serving bowl. Pour on the dressing and toss well.

3 Place the sesame seeds in a dry skillet. Cook over medium heat for 1–2 minutes, or until light golden brown. Sprinkle over the salad and serve immediately.

nutrition per serve (6)
Protein 3.5 g; Fat 8.5 g; Carbohydrate 3.5 g; Dietary Fiber 2.5 g; Cholesterol 0 mg; 100 calories

handy tip...

The vegetables can be prepared up to four hours in advance and the dressing can be added up to one hour in advance.
Any spring vegetables are suitable for this recipe—try sugar snap peas, zucchini and peas.

ingredients

8 oz cherry tomatoes, halved

4 bocconcini, quartered

1 clove garlic, crushed

1 tablespoon olive oil

9½ in oval focaccia

⅓ cup purchased pizza sauce

2 teaspoons fresh oregano leaves

1 teaspoon fresh rosemary sprigs

preparation: 15 minutes
cooking: 20 minutes
serves: 2

1 Preheat the oven to 425°F. Place the tomatoes, bocconcini, garlic and oil in a bowl and mix well.

2 Place the focaccia on a baking sheet, spread with the pizza sauce and bake for 5 minutes. Top with the tomato and bocconcini mixture. Season to taste with salt and pepper. Bake for 20 minutes, or until the focaccia is crunchy and the cheese has melted. Sprinkle with the oregano and rosemary. Cut into wedges and serve.

nutrition per serve
Protein 18 g; Fat 22 g; Carbohydrate 26 g; Dietary Fiber 4 g; Cholesterol 32 mg; 372 calories

hint

Any prepared pizza base is suitable for this recipe, fresh or frozen. If you are looking for a healthy alternative, try rounds of Lebanese flat bread.

ingredients

2 carrots, sliced
    diagonally
2 tablespoons butter
2 teaspoons honey
chopped fresh chives,
    to serve

preparation: 5 minutes
cooking: 15 minutes
serves: 4

1 Steam the carrots in a saucepan for 5–10 minutes, or until tender.

2 Place the butter and honey in a small saucepan and stir over low heat until melted.

3 Pour the butter and honey mixture over the carrots and toss to combine. Sprinkle the chives over the top and serve hot.

nutrition per serve
Protein 1 g; Fat 5 g; Carbohydrate 4 g; Dietary Fiber 2 g; Cholesterol 20 mg; 75 calories

handy tip...

To make this in the microwave, place 1 tablespoon water and the carrots in a microwave-safe bowl. Cover and cook on High (100%) for 6–8 minutes. Drain. Cook the butter and honey in a microwave-safe bowl on High (100%) for 45 seconds, or until melted. Pour over the carrots, toss to coat and sprinkle with chives.

ingredients

¹/₃ cup butter
³/₄ cup whole-egg mayonnaise
2 tablespoons prepared horseradish cream
1 small onion, grated
¹/₄ teaspoon dry mustard
pinch of paprika
1 large head fresh broccoli
1 tablespoon lemon juice

preparation: 5 minutes + chilling
cooking: 10 minutes
serves: 6

1 Put ¹/₄ cup butter in a small saucepan and stir over low heat until melted. Place in a bowl with the mayonnaise, horseradish, onion, mustard and paprika and mix together well. Season to taste with salt and black pepper. Chill.

2 Cut the broccoli into florets and bring a saucepan of water to a boil. Drop the florets into the boiling water and cook for 6–8 minutes. Refresh under cold running water and drain well.

3 Return the broccoli to the pan, add the lemon juice and remaining butter. Serve drizzled with the horseradish sauce.

nutrition per serve
Protein 2 g; Fat 22 g; Carbohydrate 8 g; Dietary Fiber 1.5 g; Cholesterol 45 mg; 232 calories

hint

For a delicious, tangy sauce that's lower in calories, substitute ¹/₂ cup plain low-fat yogurt for ¹/₂ cup of the whole-egg mayonnaise.

ingredients

2 tablespoons butter

3 green onions, finely chopped

2 slices bacon, chopped

1 lb Brussels sprouts

2 tablespoons slivered almonds

preparation: 10 minutes
cooking: 15 minutes
serves: 4

1 Melt the butter in a small saucepan. Add the green onions and bacon and cook over medium heat for 5 minutes, or until green onions are soft but not brown.

2 Remove the outer leaves from the Brussels sprouts and trim the bases if necessary. Place the sprouts in a saucepan of salted boiling water. Cook, covered, for 5 minutes, or until just tender. Drain. Place in a shallow 5-cup baking dish.

3 Scatter the green onions and bacon over the sprouts and season with freshly ground black pepper. Sprinkle with the slivered almonds. Cook under a hot broiler for 5–7 minutes, or until the sprouts are hot and the almonds are golden. Serve immediately.

nutrition per serve
Protein 9.5 g; Fat 10 g; Carbohydrate 3.5 g; Dietary Fiber 5.5 g; Cholesterol 30 mg; 144 calories

handy tip...

Small Brussels sprouts have the best flavor. Although the name suggests that sprouts originated in Belgium, the Belgians themselves believe they were brought to their country by the Romans.

ingredients

1 lb cauliflower, cut into florets

2 tablespoons butter

2 tablespoons all-purpose flour

1 1/4 cups warm milk

1 teaspoon Dijon mustard

1/2 cup grated Parmesan

3/4 cup shredded Cheddar

2 tablespoons fresh, soft bread crumbs

preparation: 15 minutes
cooking: 20 minutes
serves: 4

1 Grease a 6-cup shallow baking dish. Cook the cauliflower in a saucepan of lightly salted boiling water until just tender. Drain, then place in the prepared dish and keep warm.

2 Melt the butter in a saucepan. Add flour and cook for 1 minute, or until golden and bubbling. Remove from heat, then whisk in milk and mustard. Return to heat and bring to a boil, stirring constantly. Cook, stirring, over low heat for 2 minutes. Remove from heat. Add Parmesan and 1/2 cup of the Cheddar and stir until melted. Season to taste with salt and pepper and pour cheese sauce over the cauliflower.

3 Combine the bread crumbs and remaining Cheddar and sprinkle over the cheese sauce. Cook under a hot broiler until the top is browned and bubbling.

nutrition per serve
Protein 17 g; Fat 20 g; Carbohydrate 15 g; Dietary Fiber 2.5 g; Cholesterol 64 mg; 315 calories

hint

For a slightly different and simple creamy mustard sauce, combine 1/2 cup mayonnaise, 1 cup whipping cream and 1 tablespoon coarse grain mustard. Pour over the cauliflower, sprinkle with shredded cheese and broil until golden brown.

ingredients

10½ oz can cannellini
    beans, drained
2 tablespoons lemon juice
¼ cup olive oil
1 clove garlic, crushed
5 oz fresh green beans

preparation: 15 minutes
cooking: 5 minutes
serves: 6

1 Place the cannellini beans in a food processor. Using the pulse action, process for 1 minute, or until the mixture is smooth.

2 Place the lemon juice, oil and garlic in a small jar. Screw the top on tightly and shake vigorously for 1 minute, or until combined. Add 2 teaspoons of the dressing to the bean purée and process briefly to combine. Refrigerate, covered, until required.

3 Trim the green beans. Place in a saucepan and cover with water. Bring to a boil and cook for 3 minutes, or until tender. Plunge into cold water, then drain. Pat dry with paper towels. Place the beans in a bowl and toss with the remaining dressing. To serve, pile the green beans on serving plates, then spoon the bean purée over. Serve with lamb chops, if desired.

nutrition per serve
Protein 4 g; Fat 10 g; Carbohydrate 6 g; Dietary Fiber 4 g; Cholesterol 0 mg; 130 calories

handy tip...

The cannellini bean purée can be made one day ahead and stored in the refrigerator. Cook the green beans just before serving.

nutrition per serve (6)
Protein 3 g; Fat 30 g; Carbohydrate
1 g; Dietary Fiber 1 g; Cholesterol
200 mg; 270 calories

ingredients

4 egg yolks
¾ cup butter, melted
2 tablespoons lemon juice
10 oz fresh asparagus

preparation: 10 minutes
cooking: 10 minutes
serves: 4–6

1 Place the egg yolks in a food processor and process for about 20 seconds. With the motor running, pour the melted butter in a thin, steady stream into the food processor and process until thick and creamy. Add the lemon juice and ½ teaspoon cracked black pepper and season with salt.

2 Cut any thick, woody ends from the asparagus and discard. Place the asparagus in a saucepan of boiling water and cook for 2–3 minutes, or until bright green and tender. Drain quickly.

3 Place the asparagus on serving plates and spoon the hollandaise sauce over the top. Serve immediately.

hint

The hollandaise can be kept warm in a bowl over a saucepan of simmering water while the asparagus cooks. Do not overheat it, however, or the sauce will separate.

ingredients

2 cups vegetable stock
1 lb 8 oz butternut squash,
    cut into ¾ in cubes
2 onions, chopped
2 cloves garlic, halved
¼ teaspoon ground
    nutmeg
¼ cup whipping cream

preparation: 15 minutes
cooking: 20 minutes
serves: 4

1 Put the vegetable stock and 2 cups water into a large saucepan and bring to a boil over high heat. Add the squash, onions and garlic to the stock and return to a boil. Reduce the heat slightly and cook for 15 minutes, or until the squash is soft.

2 Drain the vegetables through a colander, reserving the liquid. Purée the squash mixture in a blender until smooth (you may need to add some of the reserved liquid). Return the squash purée to the pan and stir through enough of the reserved liquid for it to reach the desired consistency. Add the nutmeg and season to taste.

3 Divide among four warm bowls. Pour a little cream into each bowl to create a swirl pattern on the top. Serve with warm crusty bread.

nutrition per serve
Protein 5 g; Fat 6.5 g; Carbohydrate 15 g; Dietary Fiber 3.5 g; Cholesterol 17 mg; 145 calories

handy tip...

You can vary the flavor of this soup to suit your own taste. To make a sweeter, nuttier soup, roast the squash pieces in a 425°F oven until tender. Blend with ¼ cup roasted cashews and swirl in some sour cream. For a slightly spicy soup, add 2 teaspoons curry powder when cooking the onion.

ingredients

12 ripe plum tomatoes
1 tablespoon olive oil
1 large onion, finely
chopped
3 cloves garlic, crushed
6 cups vegetable stock
4 fresh thyme sprigs
1/4 cup tomato paste
2 tablespoons slivered
fresh basil

preparation: 15 minutes
cooking: 20 minutes
serves: 4

1 Score a cross in the base of each tomato, place in a heatproof bowl and cover with boiling water. Let stand for 30 seconds then transfer to a bowl of cold water. Peel the skin away from the cross and coarsely chop the tomatoes.

2 Heat the oil in a saucepan and add the onion and garlic. Cook over medium heat for 3 minutes, or until the onion is soft. Meanwhile, place the stock in a separate saucepan and bring to a boil.

3 Add the tomatoes and thyme to the onion mixture. Cover and cook for 4 minutes, or until the tomatoes soften slightly. Add the stock and tomato paste and bring to a boil. Reduce the heat and simmer, covered, for 10 minutes, or until the onion and tomatoes are soft. Remove the thyme sprigs.

4 Transfer the soup to a blender or food processor and blend in batches until smooth. Reheat gently, and stir in the slivered basil. Season to taste with salt and freshly ground black pepper. Divide the soup among four soup bowls and garnish with the fresh thyme sprigs. Serve with herb bread.

nutrition per serve
Protein 3.5 g; Fat 5 g; Carbohydrate 8.5 g; Dietary Fiber 8.5 g; Cholesterol 0 mg; 95 calories

hint

If ripe tomatoes are not available, use a 28 oz can peeled tomatoes and reduce the stock to 4 cups. If the soup is lacking flavor, add a little sugar when seasoning.

ingredients

4 leeks, trimmed and cut
 into 4 lengthwise
2 tablespoons butter
3 floury potatoes,
 chopped
3 cups vegetable stock
1 cup milk
¼ teaspoon ground
 nutmeg
¼ cup whipping cream,
 to garnish
green onions, chopped,
 to garnish

preparation: 15 minutes
cooking: 30 minutes
serves: 4

1 Wash the leeks thoroughly in cold water, then cut into small chunks. Heat the butter in a large saucepan. Add the leeks and cook for 3–4 minutes, stirring frequently, until softened. Add the potatoes and stock. Bring slowly to a boil, then reduce the heat and simmer for 20 minutes, or until the vegetables are tender.

2 Cool the mixture slightly, then transfer to a blender or food processor and purée in batches. Return to the pan, stir in the milk and nutmeg, and season well with salt and cracked black pepper. Reheat gently and serve garnished with a swirl of cream and a scattering of green onions.

nutrition per serve
Protein 4 g; Fat 15 g; Carbohydrate 20 g; Dietary Fiber 4 g; Cholesterol 48 mg; 240 calories

handy tip...

Leek and potato soup is also known as Vichyssoise and is delicious served hot or cold. Old floury potatoes such as Idaho will give you the best results for this dish.

ingredients

2 tablespoons oil

1/3 cup Tikka Masala curry paste

12 oz waxy potatoes, cut into 3/4 in cubes

12 oz butternut squash, cut into 3/4 in cubes

14 oz can chopped tomatoes

1 cup frozen peas

10 oz firm tofu, cubed

1/2 cup toasted cashews, chopped

preparation: 10 minutes
cooking: 45 minutes
serves: 4

1 Heat the oil in a saucepan. Add the paste and cook over low heat for 2 minutes, or until fragrant.

2 Add the potatoes and squash and stir until well combined, then add the tomatoes and 1 cup water. Bring to a boil, then reduce the heat and simmer, partially covered, for 30 minutes, or until the vegetables are tender.

3 Add the peas and tofu and cook for another 5 minutes. Scatter the cashews over and serve with rice.

nutrition per serve
Protein 15 g; Fat 23 g; Carbohydrate 25 g; Dietary Fiber 7 g; Cholesterol 1 mg; 390 calories

hint

Any vegetables can be used in this recipe—carrots, spinach, cauliflower, zucchini and sweet bell peppers would be delicious. Any curry paste is suitable, though you may only need to use 1–2 tablespoons as Tikka Masala is very mild.

ingredients

1¼ cups red lentils
2 tablespoons ghee
1 onion, finely chopped
2 cloves garlic, crushed
1 tablespoon grated fresh
   ginger
1 teaspoon garam masala
1 teaspoon ground
   turmeric
2 tablespoons chopped
   fresh mint

preparation: 15 minutes
cooking: 20 minutes
serves: 4–6

1 Place the lentils in a large bowl and cover with cold water. Let stand 5 minutes, then remove any scum and drain well.

2 Melt the ghee in a saucepan. Add the onion and cook over medium heat for 3 minutes, or until soft and golden. Add the garlic, ginger and spices and cook until fragrant.

3 Add the lentils and 2 cups water and bring to the boil. Reduce the heat and simmer for 15 minutes, or until nearly all the liquid has been absorbed and the dhal is thick. Stir in the chopped mint and serve with plenty of naan bread.

nutrition per serve (6)
Protein 13 g; Fat 6.5 g; Carbohydrate 20 g; Dietary Fiber 7 g; Cholesterol 15 mg; 190 calories

handy tip...

This Indian dish has a consistency similar to porridge and can be eaten on its own, served with boiled rice or Indian breads, or as an accompaniment to a meat dish.

ingredients

2 tablespoons butter

1 leek, finely sliced

12 oz can asparagus cuts, drained

2 tablespoons chopped sun-dried tomatoes

5 eggs

½ cup whipping cream

preparation: 10 minutes
cooking: 35 minutes
serves: 4

1 Preheat the oven to 350°F. Lightly grease a 9 in pie plate or quiche dish.

2 Melt the butter in a skillet. Add the leek and cook, stirring, over medium heat for 2 minutes, or until softened. Drain on paper towels.

3 Place the leek, asparagus and sun-dried tomatoes in a bowl and stir together well. Spread the mixture evenly into the prepared dish. Whisk together the eggs and cream, and season to taste with salt and freshly ground black pepper. Pour over the vegetables and bake for 30 minutes, or until golden brown.

nutrition per serve
Protein 11 g; Fat 25 g; Carbohydrate 3 g; Dietary Fiber 2 g; Cholesterol 287 mg; 285 calories

hint

Sun-dried tomatoes are available from supermarkets and delicatessens.
If preferred, this recipe can be adapted to make individual frittatas. Divide the mixture among a 12-cup non-stick muffin pan and bake in a 350°F oven for 20–25 minutes, or until set.

chunky minestrone

Heat 1 tablespoon oil in a large saucepan. Add 1 chopped onion and cook over medium heat for 3 minutes, or until golden. Add 2 cups mixed frozen vegetables, 14 oz can drained kidney beans, 14 oz can chopped tomatoes and 4 cups chicken stock. Bring to a boil, then add 1 cup macaroni. Cook for 30 minutes, or until the macaroni is tender. Season well with salt and pepper and serve topped with grated Parmesan.

serves 4

From left to right: Chunky minestrone; Spicy sausage pasta sauce; Hearty lamb and bean stew; Speedy fish provençale; In-a flash cannelloni; Mussels in tomato and white wine.

spicy sausage pasta sauce

Heat 1 tablespoon oil in a large skillet. Add 2 crushed cloves garlic and 1 chopped onion. Cook over medium heat for 3 minutes, or until golden. Add 10 oz chopped sliced Hungarian salami or pepperoni and cook for 3 minutes, or until browned. Stir in a 14 oz can peeled tomatoes and ½ cup red wine. Bring to a boil. Boil for 10 minutes, or until slightly thickened. Add a few drops of Tabasco sauce and season with salt and freshly ground black pepper. Stir in 1 tablespoon finely slivered basil before serving.

serves 6

hearty lamb and bean stew

Preheat the oven to 350°F. Heat 1 tablespoon oil in a large flameproof casserole and cook 2 lb 4 oz lamb shoulder arm chops in batches until browned on both sides. Add 1 red onion cut into wedges, 1 cup white wine, 10 oz can cannellini beans, 28 oz can chopped tomatoes and 1 bay leaf. Bake, covered, for 1 hour 30 minutes, or until the lamb is tender and starting to fall off the bone.

serves 4–6

speedy fish provençale

Melt 2 tablespoons butter in a large skillet. Add 1 onion cut into wedges and 1 chopped red sweet bell pepper. Cook over medium heat for 3 minutes, or until soft. Add a 14 oz can chopped tomatoes, 1 bouquet garni (1 bay leaf, sprig of thyme and 3 sprigs of parsley tied together with string) and bring to a boil. Add 1 tablespoon chopped fresh oregano and 1 lb 10 oz cubed firm boneless white fish fillets, then simmer, covered, for 10 minutes, or until the fish is tender. Season to taste and serve with rice.

serves 4

in-a-flash cannelloni

Preheat the oven to 400°F. Cut 3 fresh lasagne sheets into rectangles large enough to enclose a small skinless beef or pork sausage and wrap 10 sausages. Place the cannelloni in a lightly greased ovenproof dish. Pour in two 14 oz cans chopped tomatoes, spread 1¼ cups sour cream over the top and sprinkle with 1 cup grated Parmesan. Bake for 45 minutes, or until golden and bubbling.

serves 3–4

mussels in tomato and white wine

Heat 1 tablespoon oil in a large saucepan. Add 2 crushed cloves garlic and 1 chopped onion and cook for 3 minutes, or until golden. Add a 14 oz can chopped tomatoes, ½ cup white wine, a pinch of saffron and 1 cup fish stock. Bring to a boil, reduce the heat and simmer for 10 minutes, or until slightly thickened. Scrub 1 lb mussels and remove the hairy beards—discard any mussels that are open. Add mussels to the pan. Cook, covered, for 5–10 minutes, or until all the mussels have opened—discard any that do not open. Sprinkle with 2 tablespoons chopped fresh parsley and serve with crusty French bread.

serves 4

snacks

ingredients

1 small baguette
(about 12 in long)
¼ cup olive oil
1 clove garlic, crushed
1 tablespoon tomato paste
1 tablespoon mashed
canned anchovy fillets
3 oz bocconcini, sliced
fresh basil leaves, to serve

preparation: 15 minutes
cooking: 10 minutes
makes: 20

1 Preheat the oven to 350°F. Cut the baguette into ¾ in slices. Place the slices in a single layer on a baking sheet. Bake for 5 minutes, or until just crisp and dry.

2 Place the olive oil and garlic in a small bowl, mix together and brush onto the bread. Place the tomato paste and mashed anchovies in a small bowl and mix together, then spread on the bread. Top with the bocconcini slices.

3 Return the bread slices to the oven for 3 minutes, or until the cheese has melted. Garnish each slice with a basil leaf before serving.

nutrition per crostini
Protein 2 g; Fat 4 g; Carbohydrate 2 g; Dietary Fiber 0 g; Cholesterol 4 mg; 53 calories

handy tip...

Bocconcini is fresh mozzarella and comes in small round balls stored in whey. If bocconcini is not available, use shredded mozzarella.
For a vegetarian alternative, omit the anchovies and assemble as instructed.

ingredients

8 oz mixed nuts (almonds, Brazil nuts, peanuts, walnuts)
4 oz pepitas *(see hint)*
4 oz sunflower seeds
4 oz cashew nuts
4 oz macadamia nuts
½ cup tamari

preparation: 5 minutes + 10 minutes standing
cooking: 25 minutes
serves: 10–12

1 Preheat the oven to 275°F. Lightly grease two large baking sheets.

2 Place the mixed nuts, pepitas, sunflower seeds, cashew nuts and macadamia nuts in a large bowl. Pour the tamari over the nuts and seeds and toss together well, coating them evenly in the tamari. Stand for 10 minutes.

3 Spread the nut and seed mixture evenly over the prepared baking sheets and bake for 20–25 minutes, or until dry roasted. Let the mixture cool completely before serving.

nutrition per serve (12)
Protein 11.5 g; Fat 36 g; Carbohydrate 4 g; Dietary Fiber 5 g; Cholesterol 0 mg; 383 calories

hint

Pepitas are peeled pumpkin seeds—they are available at most supermarkets and health food stores.
The nut mixture may be stored in an airtight container for up to 2 weeks. However, once stored, it may become soft. If it does, lay the nuts out flat on a baking sheet and bake in a 300°F oven for 5–10 minutes.

ingredients

2 baguettes
(about 14 in long)
olive oil
4 ripe tomatoes, finely
chopped
½ cup slivered fresh
basil
1 clove garlic, crushed
2 tablespoons extra virgin
olive oil

preparation: 10 minutes
cooking: 15 minutes
makes: 30

1 Cut the baguettes into ½ in slices and brush with olive oil. Place each slice under a hot broiler or on a baking sheet in a 400°F oven, until golden on both sides, turning as needed.

2 Place the tomatoes, basil, garlic and extra virgin olive oil in a bowl and mix together. Season well with salt and pepper. Top the toasted bread slices with the tomato mixture and serve.

nutrition per bruschetta
Protein 0.5 g; Fat 2.5 g; Carbohydrate 3 g; Dietary Fiber 0.5 g; Cholesterol 0 mg; 40 calories

handy tip...

Try these topping variations. Olive, mozzarella and tomato: Combine 1½ cups chopped pitted marinated Kalamata olives, ⅔ cup diced mozzarella, 1 diced tomato. Spoon on the toasted bread. Tapenade and Parmesan: Spread the bruschetta with olive tapenade and top with shaved Parmesan.

ingredients

1 tablespoon olive oil
4½ cups finely chopped
  mushrooms
2 cloves garlic, crushed
1 tablespoon chopped
  fresh parsley
¾ cup thick Greek-style
  yogurt
¾ cup sour cream
2 green onions, chopped
1 tablespoon lemon juice,
  or to taste

preparation: 15 minutes
cooking: 8 minutes
serves: 8

1 Heat the oil in a skillet. Add the mushrooms and ½ teaspoon salt and cook over medium heat for 8 minutes, or until very soft and all the liquid has evaporated. Allow the mixture to cool.

2 Place the mushrooms, garlic, parsley, yogurt, sour cream, green onions and lemon juice in a bowl and mix together well. Season to taste with salt and freshly ground black pepper. Serve with crackers or savoury toasts.

nutrition per serve
Protein 14 g; Fat 50 g; Carbohydrate 11 g; Dietary Fiber 6 g; Cholesterol 136 mg; 552 calories

hint

Use older button mushrooms in this recipe as they have a stronger flavor.
This dip can be made 2–3 days ahead. Store in an airtight container in the refrigerator. Return to room temperature before serving.

ingredients

2 flour tortillas
1/3 cup taco sauce
1 cup shredded
    barbecued chicken
1 cup shredded Cheddar
    or jack cheese
2 green onions, finely
    chopped
sour cream, to serve
paprika, to serve

preparation: 15 minutes
cooking: 5 minutes
serves: 2

1 Heat a skillet and place one tortilla in the base. Spread lightly with taco sauce and cook over medium heat for 2–3 minutes, or until heated through.

2 Arrange the shredded chicken evenly over the tortilla, then sprinkle with the shredded cheese and green onions. Place the remaining tortilla on top and cook for 2 minutes, or until light brown.

3 Place a plate over the pan, turn the quesadilla out, then slide it back into the pan with the cooked tortilla on top. Cook the other side until the cheese has melted and the quesadilla is heated through. Remove from the pan. Cut the quesadilla into wedges and serve with a dollop of sour cream and a sprinkling of paprika.

nutrition per serve
Protein 50 g; Fat 27 g; Carbohydrate 43 g; Dietary Fiber 3 g; Cholesterol 144 mg; 614 calories

handy tip...

Tortillas are thin, round flatbreads made from wheat flour or cornmeal. For a spicy quesadilla, add 1–2 thinly sliced jalapeño chiles.
Shredded beef or mashed, refried beans can also be used instead of the chicken.

ingredients

Tartare sauce
1 cup whole-egg
   mayonnaise
1½ tablespoons pickled
   capers, finely chopped
2 gherkins, finely chopped

1 lb 10 oz firm white fish
   fillets, boned
2 eggs
½ cup all-purpose flour
1½ cups dry
   bread crumbs
light olive oil, for deep-frying

preparation: 15 minutes
cooking: 10 minutes
serves: 4

1 To make the tartare sauce, place the mayonnaise, capers and gherkins in a bowl and mix well. Cover and set aside.

2 Cut the fish fillets into strips (4 x 1¼ in). Place the eggs and 1 tablespoon water in a shallow dish and lightly beat together.

3 Dip each fish strip into the flour and shake off the excess. Dip into the egg mixture, then coat in the bread crumbs, pressing the crumbs on firmly with your fingers.

4 Fill a deep heavy-based saucepan one-third full of oil. Heat the oil to 350°F, or until a bread cube dropped in browns in 15 seconds. Deep-fry the fish fingers in two batches, for 3–5 minutes each batch, or until golden brown all over and cooked through. Drain the fish fingers on paper towels and serve immediately with the tartare sauce.

nutrition per serve
Protein 50 g; Fat 39 g; Carbohydrate 40 g; Dietary Fiber 2 g; Cholesterol 250 mg; 710 calories

hint

Fish is valued for its low calorie and cholesterol counts, and also its high protein content. Fresh fish deteriorates quickly and should be stored in the refrigerator and used within 2–3 days. Fresh fish can also be frozen in a single layer. However, defrost completely overnight in the refrigerator before using.

ingredients

4 boneless, skinned
   chicken breast halves
   (about 7 oz each),
   trimmed
flour, to coat
2 eggs, lightly beaten
cornflake crumbs, to coat
½ cup whole-egg
   mayonnaise
1 tablespoon each coarse
   grain and Dijon mustard
1 tablespoon honey
oil, for deep-frying

preparation: 15 minutes +
   15 minutes refrigeration
cooking: 16 minutes
serves: 4

1 Cut each breast into bite-size pieces, then pat dry with paper towels. Coat each piece of chicken in the flour, shaking off any excess, dip in the egg and coat with the cornflake crumbs. Cover and refrigerate for 15 minutes.

2 Place the mayonnaise, mustards, honey and ¼ cup water in a bowl and mix together well.

3 Fill a deep heavy-based saucepan one-third full of oil. Heat the oil to 350°F, or until a cube of bread dropped into the oil browns in 15 seconds. Cook the chicken in 3–4 batches for 4 minutes each batch, or until golden brown all over and cooked through. Drain on paper towels and serve hot with the honey mustard sauce.

nutrition per serve
Protein 50 g; Fat 25 g; Carbohydrate 20 g; Dietary Fiber 0.5 g; Cholesterol 200 mg; 510 calories

handy tip...

Use plain dry bread crumbs instead of cornflake crumbs, if desired.
The chicken pieces can be crumbed ahead of time and frozen. Thaw completely before deep-frying.

ingredients

1 avocado, mashed
½ small red onion, finely
    chopped
1 tablespoon lemon juice
2 plum tomatoes,
    diced
7 oz package corn chips
10 oz jar tomato salsa
15 oz can red kidney
    beans, rinsed and
    drained
1 cup shredded Cheddar
    or jack cheese

preparation: 10 minutes
cooking: 8 minutes
serves: 4

1 Place the avocado, onion, lemon juice and tomatoes in a small bowl and mix together well.

2 Preheat the oven to 350°F. Arrange the corn chips on a large ovenproof serving platter.

3 Place the salsa and kidney beans in a small saucepan and stir over medium heat until warmed through. Pour the bean mixture over the corn chips and scatter the cheese over the top. Bake for 5 minutes, or until the cheese has melted and is golden.

4 Top with the avocado mixture and serve with sour cream, if desired. Serve immediately.

nutrition per serve
Protein 15 g; Fat 40 g; Carbohydrate 30 g; Dietary Fiber 8 g; Cholesterol 30 mg; 515 calories

hint

For a 'meaty' version, add 11 oz lean ground beef to a skillet in batches, breaking up any lumps with a fork. Remove from the pan. Fry 1 chopped onion for 2–3 minutes, then return the beef to the pan. Stir in the jar of tomato salsa, and kidney beans if desired, and simmer for 5–10 minutes. Pour over the corn chips, scatter with cheese and bake.

ingredients

4 large potatoes
1/3 cup sour cream
1/2 cup shredded Cheddar
3 1/2 oz can tuna, drained
4 1/2 oz can corn kernels,
    drained
2 tablespoons chopped
    fresh chives

preparation: 15 minutes
cooking: 1 hour 30 minutes
serves: 4

1 Preheat the oven to 375°F. Wash and scrub the potatoes clean. Pat dry with paper towels and pierce the skin all over with a fork or skewer.

2 Place the potatoes directly on the oven shelf. Bake for 1 hour 15 minutes, or until cooked through.

3 Cut a lid off the top of each potato and spoon out the flesh, leaving a thick shell. Place the flesh in a bowl and mash with a potato masher. Add the sour cream, cheese, tuna, corn and chives and season well with salt and freshly ground black pepper. Mix until coarsely combined.

4 Place the potato shells on a baking sheet. Divide the mixture evenly among the potatoes, piling the mixture high. Replace the lids at an angle and return to the oven. Bake for another 15 minutes and serve hot.

nutrition per serve
Protein 14 g; Fat 15 g; Carbohydrate 26 g; Dietary Fiber 3.5 g; Cholesterol 57 mg; 300 calories

handy tip...

For a different kind of baked potato topping, try hummus and tabbouleh—put a spoonful of hummus into a baked potato and top with tabbouleh. For an extra creamy potato, add a spoonful of sour cream as well.

ingredients

2 tablespoons olive oil

2 slender eggplants,
quartered lengthwise

1 large red bell pepper,
cut into ½ in strips

4 large lavosh breads

1 cup purchased hummus

1 red onion, finely
chopped

2 tablespoons chopped
fresh flat-leaf parsley

1 large tomato, chopped

preparation: 15 minutes +
cooling time
cooking: 8 minutes
serves: 4

1 Heat the oil in a large skillet. Add the eggplants and red pepper and cook for 6–8 minutes, or until tender. Drain well on paper towels. Allow to cool, then coarsely chop.

2 Lay the lavosh breads on a clean flat surface. Spread with the hummus, then sprinkle evenly with the onion and parsley. On the lower half of the long side of the lavosh, arrange the eggplant, red bell pepper and tomato, and season. Roll each bread up firmly from the long side. Cut each roll in half diagonally and serve.

nutrition per serve
Protein 17 g; Fat 20 g; Carbohydrate 67 g; Dietary Fiber 10 g; Cholesterol 0 mg; 523 calories

hint

Wrap-ups can be made 1 hour ahead. Wrap each roll firmly in plastic wrap and refrigerate before cutting. This recipe is also delicious with marinated vegetables from delicatessens. Lavosh is also known as Armenian cracker bread.

ingredients

Spicy ketchup
2 tablespoons butter
1 small onion, finely
    chopped
1 teaspoon curry
    powder
½ lemon
⅔ cup ketchup
2 teaspoons soft brown
    sugar

4 all-beef frankfurters
4 hot dog buns

preparation: 15 minutes
cooking: 15 minutes
serves: 4

1 Preheat the oven to 350°F.

2 To make the spicy ketchup, melt the butter in a small saucepan over medium heat. Add the onion and curry powder and cook for 3 minutes, or until the onion is softened. Add ½ teaspoon grated lemon rind, 1 tablespoon lemon juice, the ketchup, sugar and 2 tablespoons water. Simmer for 2 minutes, or until heated through.

3 Bring a saucepan of water to a boil. Reduce the heat to simmer. Add the frankfurters and cook for 3 minutes, or until heated through.

4 Place the buns in the oven for 5 minutes, or until warmed. Cut lengthwise, leaving one side attached. Drain the frankfurters well. Place a frankfurter in the hot bun and serve with spicy ketchup.

nutrition per serve
Protein 17 g; Fat 20 g; Carbohydrate 60 g; Dietary Fiber 5.5 g; Cholesterol 48 mg; 483 calories

handy tip...

Use mini dinner rolls and cocktail franks to make small hot dogs. These are great for kids' parties or to have with drinks.

ingredients

4 English muffins,
split in half

1/3 cup tomato paste

1 cup firmly packed
shredded Cheddar

16 thin slices salami,
cut into strips

1/2 green sweet bell
pepper, finely
chopped

12 pitted black olives,
sliced

preparation: 10 minutes
cooking: 10 minutes
serves: 4

1 Place the muffins, cut-side down, on a baking sheet and broil under a moderately hot broiler until lightly toasted.

2 Spread the cut side of the muffins with the tomato paste and season to taste with salt and freshly ground black pepper. Top with the cheese, salami, green pepper and olives.

3 Return the muffins to the broiler for 3–5 minutes, or until the cheese has melted.

nutrition per serve
Protein 20 g; Fat 18 g; Carbohydrate 33 g; Dietary Fiber 3.5 g; Cholesterol 48 mg; 378 calories

hint

For a different topping, try ham and pineapple. Replace the salami and olives with 8 slices cooked ham and 1 cup drained canned pineapple chunks.

ingredients

2 lb 4 oz ground fresh
   chicken
1 cup fresh, soft
   bread crumbs
4 green onions, sliced
1 tablespoon ground
   coriander
1 cup chopped cilantro
   leaves
¼ cup sweet chili sauce
1–2 tablespoons lemon
   juice
oil, for frying

preparation: 15 minutes
cooking: 40 minutes
serves: 6

1 Preheat the oven to 400°F. Place the chicken and bread crumbs in a bowl and mix together well.

2 Add the green onions, ground coriander, fresh cilantro, chili sauce and lemon juice and mix together well. Using damp hands, shape the mixture into evenly sized balls that are small enough to eat with your fingers.

3 Heat the oil in a deep skillet, and shallow-fry the chicken balls in batches over high heat until browned all over. Place them on a baking sheet and bake for 5 minutes, or until cooked through.

nutrition per serve
Protein 40 g; Fat 8 g; Carbohydrate 10 g; Dietary Fiber 1 g; Cholesterol 85 mg; 275 calories

handy tip...

This mixture can be shaped into burger patties. For this size, bake for 10–15 minutes, or until the mixture is cooked through.
This mixture is suitable for ground beef and also makes a delicious filling for puff pastry sausage rolls.

2 tablespoons hazelnuts, roasted

14 oz can artichoke hearts, drained

1 clove garlic, chopped

¼ cup finely grated Parmesan

¼ cup extra virgin olive oil

2 tablespoons finely chopped fresh flat-leaf parsley

preparation: 15 minutes
cooking: none
serves: 6

1 Place the hazelnuts in a food processor and process until finely chopped. Add the artichoke hearts, garlic and Parmesan. Process until smooth. With the motor running, add the oil in a thin stream.

2 Stir in the parsley and spoon into a serving dish. Serve with herb and garlic pita chips, pretzels or lavosh (soft Armenian cracker bread).

nutrition per serve
Protein 4 g; Fat 15 g; Carbohydrate 1 g; Dietary Fiber 2.5 g; Cholesterol 4 mg; 155 calories

hint

To add extra flavor to the dip, use marinated artichokes instead of canned, and reserve the marinade. Substitute the extra virgin olive oil for the reserved marinade.

1 lb boneless white fish
 fillets
1 nori (seaweed) sheet
1 tablespoon tempura flour

Tempura batter
1 cup iced water
2 cups tempura flour
oil, for deep-frying

preparation: 10 minutes
cooking: 20 minutes
makes: 24

1 Cut the fish into 24 bite-size pieces and set aside. Using scissors, cut the nori into tiny squares and combine on a plate with the tempura flour.

2 To make the batter, quickly mix the iced water with the tempura flour. Do not overmix—it should be slightly lumpy. If it is too thick, add more water. Fill a heavy-based saucepan one-third full of oil and heat to 350°F. The oil is ready when ¼ teaspoon of batter dropped into the oil keeps its shape, sizzles and rises to the top. Make sure the oil stays at the same temperature and does not get too hot. The fish should cook through as well as brown.

3 Dip the fish in batches into the nori and flour, then in the batter. Deep-fry the fish until golden, then drain on crumpled paper towels. Season with salt and keep warm in a 250°F oven.

nutrition per piece
Protein 5 g; Fat 2 g; Carbohydrate 7.5 g; Dietary Fiber 0.5 g; Cholesterol 14 mg; 72 calories

handy tip...

This very light, thin batter is made with iced water to make sure that it puffs up as soon as it hits the oil. Tempura flour is available at Asian supermarkets. If unavailable, substitute with 1½ cups all-purpose flour and ½ cup rice flour. This batter recipe is also suitable for chicken or vegetable pieces.

ingredients

2 lb 4 oz sweet potatoes, unpeeled
2 tablespoons vegetable oil
chili powder, to taste
1¼ cups sour cream
2 tablespoons sweet chili sauce
2 green onions, finely chopped
1 tablespoon chopped fresh cilantro leaves

preparation: 10 minutes
cooking: 50 minutes
serves: 4

1 Preheat the oven to 375°F. Scrub the sweet potatoes well and pat dry with paper towels. Cut the potatoes into 3–4 in wedges. Place in a bowl with the oil and toss gently to coat.

2 Place the wedges in a single layer on a large baking sheet and sprinkle lightly with chili powder and salt. Bake for 40–50 minutes, or until tender and lightly browned on the edges.

3 To make the dipping sauce, place the sour cream, sweet chili sauce, green onions and cilantro in a bowl, mix together and season. Cover and refrigerate.

4 Serve the hot wedges with the dipping sauce.

nutrition per serve
Protein 7 g; Fat 40 g; Carbohydrate 40 g; Dietary Fiber 5 g; Cholesterol 98 mg; 539 calories

hint

Wedges can also be made using plain potatoes. Floury potatoes such as Idaho are the best to use.
Scrub 6 large potatoes, cut each into about ten wedges and soak in cold water for 10 minutes. Preheat the oven to 400°F. Drain the wedges on paper towels and toss in 2 tablespoons olive oil. Place in a shallow baking dish in a single layer and bake for 40–50 minutes, or until golden and crisp, turning occasionally. Drain on paper towels and season. Sprinkle with finely grated Parmesan.

quick feta and spinach freeform pie

Preheat the oven to 350°F. Combine 10 oz thawed frozen spinach, drained well, 5 chopped green onions, 2 lightly beaten eggs, 1⅓ cups crumbled feta and ¾ cup cream-style cottage cheese in a bowl. Line a 9 in pie plate with a sheet of phyllo pastry, brush lightly with melted butter and keep layering another nine layers with melted butter. Spoon in the filling and fold the pastry over loosely, but do not cover all the filling in the center. Bake for 35–40 minutes, or until the pastry is golden brown.

serves 4–6

olive and tomato tart

Preheat the oven to 400°F. Place an 8 in prepared short pastry tart shell on a baking sheet and bake for 10 minutes, or until golden brown. Heat 1 tablespoon oil in a skillet, add 1¾ cups canned chopped tomatoes, 2 teaspoons chopped fresh thyme and 1 teaspoon sugar. Bring to a boil and cook over high heat for 15 minutes, or until very thick. Stir in ¼ cup grated Parmesan. Spoon the mixture into the tart shell, top with 8 canned anchovy fillets and ⅔ cup pitted Kalamata olives, and then bake for 15 minutes.

serves 4

prosciutto-wrapped chicken breasts

Preheat the oven to 350°F. Wrap 4 lightly pounded, boneless, skinned chicken breast halves with 4–6 wafer-thin slices of prosciutto and a sprig of rosemary. Heat 1 tablespoon oil in a large skillet and cook the breasts in batches, for 5–7 minutes on each side, or until browned. Transfer to a baking sheet and bake for 15 minutes, or until tender. Serve with bottled tomato relish.

serves 4

broiled kasseri on bruschetta

Cut 10 oz Kasseri cheese into thick slices and place in a shallow glass dish. Add 2 tablespoons extra virgin olive oil, 2 crushed cloves garlic and 2 tablespoons balsamic vinegar, then cover and marinate in the refrigerator for 30 minutes. Drain the cheese and reserve the marinade. Place the cheese on a baking sheet and cook under a hot broiler for 3 minutes on each side, or until golden brown. Cut a French baguette into thick slices on the diagonal and toast under the broiler until golden on both sides, then top with a slice of Kasseri. Combine 2 chopped plum tomatoes, 2 tablespoons drained baby capers and 1 finely chopped red onion. Spoon on top of the cheese and drizzle with the reserved marinade.

makes 15

speedy caesar salad

Tear 1 romaine lettuce into large bite-size pieces and place in a large salad bowl. Add 1½ cups grated Parmesan, 4 quartered hard-cooked eggs, 1 cup purchased croutons, 6 chopped canned anchovy fillets and 6 slices bacon cooked until crisp, then broken into large pieces. Toss gently, then drizzle with 1 cup bottled caesar salad dressing.

serves 4

simple salami and bocconcini pizza

Preheat the oven to 425°F. Spread 2 tablespoons tomato paste over a 12 in purchased pizza base and top with ¼ cup thinly sliced spicy salami, 3 oz thinly sliced drained baby bocconcini and 5 oz halved cherry tomatoes. Sprinkle with ¼ cup grated fresh Parmesan and bake for 30 minutes, or until crisp and bubbling. Sprinkle with finely slivered basil just before serving.

serves 4

From left to right: Quick feta and spinach freeform pie; Olive and tomato tart; Prosciutto-wrapped chicken breasts; Broiled Kasseri on bruschetta; Speedy Caesar salad; Simple salami and bocconcini pizza.

ingredients

Herbed aïoli
1 cup whole-egg
    mayonnaise
2 cloves garlic, crushed
2 tablespoons chopped
    fresh mixed herbs
    (chives, parsley and
    tarragon)

4 large onions
1 cup all-purpose flour
1 egg, lightly beaten
1 cup milk
olive oil, for deep-frying

preparation: 15 minutes
cooking: 10 minutes
serves: 4

1 To make the herbed aïoli, place the mayonnaise, garlic and herbs in a bowl and mix together well. Season with salt and freshly ground black pepper. Cover and set aside.

2 Cut ³/₄ in from the ends of each onion and discard. Cut the onions into ¹/₃ in thick slices and separate into rings (use the smaller center rings for another purpose).

3 Sift the flour into a bowl and make a well in the center. Combine the egg and the milk and gradually add to the flour, stirring to make a smooth batter. Season the batter well with salt and freshly ground black pepper. Heat a large, deep saucepan one-third full with oil to 350°F, or until a cube of bread dropped in the oil browns in 15 seconds.

4 Dip the onion rings separately into the batter and drain off any excess. Deep-fry in the hot oil in batches for 2 minutes each batch, or until golden brown, turning once. Drain on paper towels and serve with the herbed aïoli.

nutrition per serve
Protein 10 g; Fat 33 g; Carbohydrate 45 g; Dietary Fiber 4 g; Cholesterol 72 mg; 512 calories

handy tip...

Onion rings make a great alternative to French fries. Aïoli is a garlic mayonnaise from France. In Marseilles it is said that aïoli should contain at least two garlic cloves per serving. It is used over fish, meat and cold boiled potatoes, and it is also added to soup.

1 Preheat the oven to 350°F. Wipe clean the mushrooms, and trim the stems level with the caps. Brush the rounded side of the mushrooms with the oil and arrange rounded-side down on a baking sheet.

2 Squeeze any excess liquid from the cooked spinach and coarsely chop the leaves. Place the spinach in a bowl and add the ricotta and basil. Season with salt and freshly ground black pepper and mix together well. Divide the filling among the mushrooms, and sprinkle with the pine nuts and grated Parmesan.

3 Bake for 15–20 minutes, or until the mushrooms are tender and the cheese begins to brown. Serve immediately.

nutrition per serve
Protein 8 g; Fat 15 g; Carbohydrate 1 g; Dietary Fiber 2.5 g; Cholesterol 12 mg; 180 calories

hint

Ricotta is a smooth, moist, white cheese with a bland, sweet flavor. It is traditionally made from whey. Skim or full-cream milk is sometimes added, giving the cheese a creamier consistency and a fuller flavor. It is suitable for sweet and savory dishes.

ingredients

4 slices bread
1½ oz can anchovy fillets
    in oil, drained
2 teaspoons lemon juice
¼ cup butter, softened
3 eggs, lightly beaten
½ cup whipping cream
1 tablespoon finely
    chopped fresh parsley
pinch of cayenne pepper

preparation: 15 minutes
cooking: 25 minutes
serves: 4

1 Preheat the oven to 350°F. Remove the crusts from the bread and cut the bread diagonally in half. Arrange the triangles on an ungreased baking sheet and bake for 20 minutes, or until crisp and golden. Remove from the oven and allow to cool.

2 Place the anchovies and lemon juice in a bowl and mash with a fork to make a paste. Gradually blend in all but 1 teaspoon butter and stir until smooth.

3 Spread the anchovy mixture on the toasted triangles. Arrange 2 triangles on each serving plate.

4 Place the eggs, cream, parsley and cayenne pepper in a bowl and whisk together well. Heat the remaining butter in a saucepan. Add the egg mixture and stir with a wooden spoon over low heat for 4 minutes, or until just cooked. Spoon the mixture over the anchovy toasts. Serve immediately.

nutrition per serve
Protein 11 g; Fat 30 g; Carbohydrate 14 g; Dietary Fiber 1 g; Cholesterol 225 mg; 375 calories

handy tip...

The egg mixture for this dish may also be cooked over boiling water in a double boiler for a smoother, creamier texture. This will take longer than the 4 minutes specified in this recipe. Cook the eggs just before serving. If the strong, salty taste of anchovies does not appeal, sardines may be substituted.

nutrition per tart
Protein 2 g; Fat 5.75 g; Carbohydrate
5 g; Dietary Fiber 0.5 g; Cholesterol
9 mg; 80 calories

ingredients

2 sheets frozen puff pastry

10 oz goats cheese, sliced

2 cooking apples, unpeeled

2 tablespoons extra virgin olive oil

1 tablespoon chopped fresh lemon thyme

preparation: 10 minutes
cooking: 25 minutes
makes: 32

1 Preheat the oven to 425°F. While the pastry is still frozen, cut each sheet into four squares and then each square into quarters. Place the pastry pieces slightly apart on a lightly greased baking sheet. Set aside for a few minutes to thaw and then lay the cheese over the center of each square of pastry, leaving a small border.

2 Core the apples and slice them thinly. Overlap several slices on the pastry, making sure the cheese is covered completely. Lightly brush the apples with oil and sprinkle with lemon thyme and a little salt and pepper to taste.

3 Bake the tarts for 20–25 minutes, or until the pastry is cooked through and golden brown at the edges. Serve immediately.

hint

The pastry can be topped with cheese, covered and refrigerated overnight. Top with the apple just before cooking. Sliced pear can also be used instead of the apple.

ingredients

1 lb potatoes, cut into
1/2 in cubes

1 carrot, cut into 1/2 in
cubes

1 parsnip, cut into 1/2 in
cubes

1 1/2 cups chopped
cabbage

1/2 cup frozen peas

1 tablespoon chopped
fresh chives

3 tablespoons butter

preparation: 15 minutes
cooking: 30 minutes
serves: 4

1 Bring a large saucepan of lightly salted water to a boil. Add the potatoes, carrot and parsnip and return to a boil. Reduce the heat, cover and simmer for 8 minutes, or until almost tender. Add the cabbage and peas, return to a boil and cook, covered, for 3 minutes. Drain the vegetables very well, then mash coarsely with a potato masher. Add the chives and season with salt and pepper.

2 Melt the butter in a large skillet, then add 4 lightly greased egg rings. Spoon half the vegetable mixture into the rings and press down firmly. Cook over medium heat for 4–5 minutes on each side, or until lightly browned. Remove carefully from the egg rings and repeat with the remaining mixture. Serve hot with toast.

nutrition per serve
Protein 5.5 g; Fat 9.5 g; Carbohydrate 23 g; Dietary Fiber 6 g; Cholesterol 30 mg; 205 calories

handy tip...

'Bubble and Squeak' is a great way to use up leftover roasted or cooked vegetables. Add some pieces of crispy bacon to the mashed vegetables, if desired.

ingredients

4 flour tortillas
2 tablespoons butter
1 teaspoon olive oil
1 chorizo sausage, peeled
    and finely chopped
2 tablespoons butter
5 eggs, lightly beaten
1/4 cup milk
1 tablespoon chopped
    fresh cilantro, to garnish

preparation: 15 minutes
cooking: 10 minutes
makes: 28

1 To make the tostadas, preheat the oven to 400°F. Line two baking sheets with parchment paper. Cut the tortillas into 28 rounds with a 2½ in cutter and place on the baking sheets. Melt the butter and brush the tortilla rounds with it. Bake for 5–6 minutes, or until golden and crisp, taking care not to burn. Transfer to a serving platter.

2 Meanwhile, heat the oil in a small saucepan and cook the chorizo until crispy. Drain on paper towels. Wipe out the pan with paper towels and gently melt the butter. Combine the eggs and milk in a small bowl, add to the pan and cook gently over low heat, stirring constantly, for 4 minutes, or until soft and creamy.

3 Remove from the heat and spoon the mixture into a warm bowl. (This is to stop the eggs from cooking further.) Fold in the chorizo and season to taste with salt and freshly ground pepper. Pile 2–3 teaspoons of the egg and chorizo mixture onto each tostada. Scatter with the fresh cilantro and serve immediately.

nutrition per tostada
Protein 3 g; Fat 3.5 g; Carbohydrate 7.5 g; Dietary Fiber 0.5 g; Cholesterol 40 mg; 72 calories

hint

You can cook the tostadas ahead of time. Just before serving, wrap them in foil and warm them in the oven for a few minutes. You will have to cook the eggs and chorizo at the last minute.

desserts

ingredients

3 oranges
7 oz (about 1²/3 cups)
   raspberries
7 oz (about 1¹/3 cups)
   blueberries
¹/3 cup superfine sugar
mascarpone cheese,
   to serve

preparation: 20 minutes +
   30 minutes refrigeration
cooking: 10 minutes
serves: 4–6

1 Cut a ¾ in-wide slice from the ends of each orange. Remove the rind in wide strips, including the pith and white membrane. Remove the pith from the rind with a sharp knife. Cut the rind into thin strips.

2 Separate the orange segments by carefully cutting between the membrane and the flesh. Place the orange segments and the berries in a bowl, sprinkle with half the sugar and toss lightly. Cover and refrigerate for 30 minutes.

3 Place the remaining sugar and ¹/3 cup water in a saucepan. Stir over low heat, without boiling, until the sugar has dissolved. Bring to a boil, then reduce the heat and add the orange rind. Simmer for 2 minutes, or until the rind is tender. Cool. Reserve 1 tablespoon of the syrupy rind.

4 Pour the syrup over the berry mixture and gently mix together.

Spoon into serving goblets and garnish with the reserved rind and large dollops of mascarpone.

nutrition per serve (6)
Protein 1 g; Fat 0 g; Carbohydrate 24 g; Dietary Fiber 3.5 g; Cholesterol 0 mg; 100 calories

handy tip...

The fruit can be combined with syrup and refrigerated for up to 4 hours.
For liqueur fruits, add ¼ cup Cointreau, or your favorite liqueur, to the fruits. Cover and refrigerate for at least 30 minutes to marinate. Serve with mascarpone or whipped cream.

ingredients

14 oz package frozen
    mango *(see hint)*
½ cup superfine sugar
¼ cup mango or apricot
    nectar
1¼ cups whipping cream
mango slices, to garnish
fresh mint sprigs,
    to garnish

preparation: 10 minutes +
    freezing
cooking: none
serves: 6

1 Defrost the mango until it is soft enough to mash but still icy. Place the mango in a large bowl and add the sugar and mango nectar.

Stir for 1–2 minutes, or until the sugar has dissolved.

2 Beat the cream in a bowl until stiff peaks form. Gently fold the cream into the mango mixture.

3 Spoon the mixture into a shallow plastic container, cover and freeze for 1 hour 30 minutes, or until half-frozen. Quickly spoon the mixture into a food processor. Process for 30 seconds, or until the ice cream mixture is smooth. Return to the container, cover and freeze completely.

4 Remove the ice cream from the freezer for 15 minutes before serving, to allow it to soften a little. Serve the ice cream in scoops and garnish with the mango slices and sprigs of mint.

nutrition per serve
Protein 1.5 g; Fat 22 g; Carbohydrate 32 g; Dietary Fiber 1 g; Cholesterol 68 mg; 320 calories

hint

When available, use fresh mangoes. Purée the flesh of 3–4 large mangoes in a food processor. The ice cream should be frozen for at least eight hours before serving and can be kept frozen for up to three weeks.

ingredients

15 oz can peach halves

15 oz can apricot halves

1/3 cup Cointreau

2 tablespoons soft brown
sugar

1 cup (about 8 oz)
mascarpone cheese

preparation: 5 minutes
cooking: 8 minutes
serves: 6

1 Drain the peach and apricot halves and reserve the syrup. Place the apricots and peaches in a baking dish and pour half the reserved syrup over.

2 Sprinkle the fruit with Cointreau, then the sugar. Cook under a medium broiler for 5 minutes, or until the fruit is soft and a golden glaze has formed on top.

3 Serve immediately with a dollop of mascarpone and dust with ground nutmeg, if desired.

nutrition per serve
Protein 5 g; Fat 14 g; Carbohydrate 20 g; Dietary Fiber 2.5 g; Cholesterol 40 mg; 245 calories

handy tip...

Any liqueur or sweet wine can be used for this recipe, such as Grand Marnier. Use fresh peeled and stoned peaches and apricots when available.

ingredients

¼ cup honey

2 large green apples,
    peeled, cored and
    cut into eighths

2 large firm ripe pears,
    peeled, cored and
    cut into eighths

8 purchased waffles

2 x 7 oz tubs honey-
    flavored yogurt

preparation: 15 minutes
cooking: 10 minutes
serves: 4

1 Place the honey and 1 cup water in a large saucepan and bring to a boil. Add the fruit, then reduce the heat, cover and simmer, stirring occasionally, for 8 minutes, or until tender.

2 To serve, warm the waffles in the oven or microwave according to the package instructions.

3 Place two waffles on each plate. Spoon some apple and pear mixture on the waffles, then pour on the cooking syrup. Top with a dollop of honey-flavored yogurt and serve immediately.

nutrition per serve
Protein 5 g; Fat 4.5 g; Carbohydrate 45 g; Dietary Fiber 2.5 g; Cholesterol 15 mg; 300 calories

hint

Waffles are sold in the freezer cabinet and can be reheated in a toaster. For a special occasion, purchase fresh Belgian waffles from the deli section and reheat by warming in the oven.

ingredients

1¼ cups whipping cream
10 oz package frozen
   raspberries, thawed
18 small meringue shells
2 x 1 oz flaky chocolate
   bars, coarsely broken

preparation: 15 minutes
cooking: none
serves: 6

1 Place the cream in a large bowl and, using an electric mixer, beat until soft peaks form. Fold the raspberries into the cream until just combined.

2 Divide the meringue shells among the serving plates. Spoon the raspberry cream into the shells and sprinkle with the chocolate shards. Serve immediately.

nutrition per serve
Protein 4 g; Fat 26 g; Carbohydrate 78 g; Dietary Fiber 3 g; Cholesterol 68 mg; 544 calories

handy tip...

For a banana and passion fruit version, fold 2 sliced bananas and the pulp of 2 passion fruit into the cream. Garnish with extra passion fruit. You can also use chopped, fresh strawberries or drained canned fruit. Prepared meringue shells are available from bakeries and good supermarkets.

ingredients

Strawberry sauce
10 oz fresh or thawed
   frozen strawberries
½ cup strawberry jam

2 eggs
2 tablespoons oil
⅓ cup superfine sugar
1¾ cups self-rising flour,
   sifted
oil, for deep-frying
¾ cup superfine sugar,
   extra, to coat

preparation: 15 minutes
cooking: 6 minutes
serves: 4–6

1 To make the sauce, place the strawberries and the jam in a food processor and process until smooth.

2 Place the eggs, oil, sugar and 3 tablespoons water in a bowl and mix together until smooth. Stir in the flour and mix to a soft dough. Roll 2 teaspoons of the mixture into a ball with floured hands. Repeat with the remaining mixture.

3 Fill a deep, heavy-based saucepan one-third full of oil and heat to 375°F, or until a cube of bread dropped into the oil browns in 10 seconds. Cook doughnut balls in three batches for 1–2 minutes each batch, or until cooked through and lightly browned all over. While still hot, roll in the extra sugar. Serve immediately with the strawberry sauce, and if desired, ice cream and fresh strawberries.

nutrition per serve (6)
Protein 6.5 g; Fat 15 g; Carbohydrate 90 g; Dietary Fiber 3 g; Cholesterol 60 mg; 510 calories

hint

Use a good-quality vegetable oil for deep-frying the doughnuts. Do not use olive or grapeseed oil because the flavor will overpower the doughnuts.

ingredients

2 cups self-rising flour, sifted

1/2 cup butter, coarsely chopped

2 tablespoons superfine sugar

3 tablespoons milk

2/3 cup raspberry jam

1 tablespoon milk, extra

preparation: 20 minutes
cooking: 35 minutes
serves: 4

1 Preheat the oven to 350°F. Line a baking sheet with parchment paper. Sift the flour into a large mixing bowl and add the butter. Rub the butter into the flour with your fingertips until the mixture resembles fine bread crumbs. Stir in the sugar.

2 Add the milk and 3 tablespoons water, and stir with a flat-bladed knife to form a dough. Turn out on a lightly floured surface and gather together to form a smooth dough.

3 On a large sheet of parchment paper, roll out the dough into a rectangle (13 x 9 in) about 1/4 in thick. Spread with the raspberry jam, leaving a 1/4 in border around the edge.

4 Roll up lengthwise like a jelly roll and place on the baking sheet seam-side down. Brush with the extra milk and bake for 35 minutes, or until golden and cooked through. Allow to stand for a few minutes, then cut into thick slices using a serrated knife. Serve warm with custard or whipped cream.

nutrition per serve
Protein 7 g; Fat 25 g; Carbohydrate 73 g; Dietary Fiber 3 g; Cholesterol 80 mg; 555 calories

handy tip...

Any flavored jam can be used for this recipe. Apricot, fruits of the forest, rhubarb and ginger, or lime marmalade are all delicious substitutes.

ingredients

1½ cups strongly brewed espresso coffee

¾ cup Kahlua or Tia Maria

2 cups mascarpone cheese

2 tablespoons superfine sugar

½ cup whipping cream, lightly whipped

8 oz thin ladyfinger biscuits

¼ cup cocoa powder

preparation: 15 minutes + overnight chilling

cooking: none

serves: 8

1 Place the coffee and ½ cup of the Kahlua in a shallow dish and stir together. Set aside.

2 Place the mascarpone, sugar and remaining Kahlua in a large bowl and mix together well. Gently fold in the whipped cream.

3 Quickly dip half the ladyfinger biscuits into the coffee mixture (it is important to do this quickly so they do not take up too much liquid and go soggy), and place them in a single layer on the bottom of an 8-cup ceramic dish.

4 Spread half of the mascarpone mixture over the ladyfingers and dust liberally with half of the cocoa, using a fine sieve. Dunk the remaining ladyfingers in the coffee and lay them on top, then spread with the remaining mascarpone mixture. Dust with the remaining cocoa, then cover and refrigerate overnight.

nutrition per serve
Protein 9 g; Fat 26 g; Carbohydrate 64 g; Dietary Fiber 1 g; Cholesterol 82 mg; 512 calories

hint

Tiramisu means 'pick-me-up' in Italian. Sometimes referred to as Italian trifle, tiramisu actually has a much lighter texture than trifle.

If you would prefer this as an alcohol-free dessert, you can omit the Kahlua or Tia Maria and use ¾ cup more coffee to make up for the missing liquid.

ingredients

1 egg, lightly beaten
3 tablespoons cornstarch
2 tablespoons sugar
1 cup milk
½ cup whipping cream
4 bananas, thickly sliced
  on the diagonal
2 tablespoons shredded
  coconut, toasted
½ teaspoon ground
  cinnamon

preparation: 15 minutes
cooking: 5 minutes
serves: 4

1 Place the egg, cornstarch, sugar, milk and cream in the top insert of a double boiler and whisk until the mixture is smooth.

2 Place the insert over simmering water without touching the water. Stir constantly for 5 minutes, or until the custard has thickened slightly and coats the back of a wooden spoon.

3 Divide the banana pieces among four serving dishes and drizzle with the custard. Sprinkle with the toasted coconut and ground cinnamon. Garnish with fresh mint, if desired, and serve immediately.

nutrition per serve
Protein 6.5 g; Fat 15 g; Carbohydrate 42 g; Dietary Fiber 3.5 g; Cholesterol 95 mg; 355 calories

handy tip...

This will keep for up to 2 days in the refrigerator, if the banana is stirred into the custard.
For variety, the custard can be flavored with a few drops of almond or vanilla extract.

ingredients

2 cups superfine sugar
5 large peaches
3/4 cup Champagne
2 egg whites

preparation: 15 minutes +
    freezing
cooking: 20 minutes
serves: 6

1 Place the sugar and 4 cups water in a large saucepan. Stir over medium heat without boiling until the sugar has dissolved. Bring to a boil, add the peaches and simmer for 20 minutes. Remove the peaches from the saucepan with a slotted spoon and cool them completely. Reserve 1 cup of the poaching liquid.

2 Remove the skin and stones from the peaches, and cut the flesh into chunks. Place in a food processor and process until smooth. Add the reserved liquid and Champagne and process briefly until combined.

3 Pour the mixture into a shallow metal tray and freeze for 6 hours, or until just firm. Transfer mixture to a large bowl and beat with an electric mixer until smooth.

4 Place the egg whites in a separate bowl and beat, using cleaned beaters, until soft peaks form. Gently fold the egg whites into the sorbet mixture. Return the mixture to the metal tray and freeze until firm. Serve the sorbet in scoops, with sliced fresh peaches and dessert wafers, if desired.

nutrition per serve
Protein 2 g; Fat 0 g; Carbohydrate 88 g; Dietary Fiber 1 g; Cholesterol 0 mg; 365 calories

hint

Don't be tempted to use cheap Champagne or sparkling wine in this recipe—the difference will be noticeable. Use a wine of the same quality you would choose to drink. Other soft stone fruits, such as nectarines or plums, can be used in this sorbet if you prefer.

8 oz (about 1²/₃ cups)
  strawberries, halved
1 banana, peeled and
  thickly sliced
2 kiwi fruit, peeled,
  halved and sliced
8 oz package
  marshmallows
2 apples, cored and
  cut into ³/₄ in cubes

Fondue
8 oz semi-sweet chocolate
  chips
¹/₂ cup heavy whipping
  cream
2–3 teaspoons orange-
  flavored liqueur

preparation: 15 minutes
cooking: 8 minutes
serves: 6

1 Thread the halved strawberries, banana slices, kiwi fruit slices, marshmallows and cubed apples alternately onto skewers.

2 To make the fondue, place the chocolate and cream in the top insert of a double boiler. Place the insert over simmering water without touching the water. Stir mixture until melted and smooth. Remove from the heat.

3 Add the liqueur to the chocolate mixture, then transfer the fondue to a warmed serving bowl. Serve warm with the fruit skewers.

nutrition per serve
Protein 5 g; Fat 24 g; Carbohydrate 54 g; Dietary Fiber 4 g; Cholesterol 30 mg; 450 calories

handy tip...

The fondue can be prepared several hours in advance. Reheat gently before serving. White chocolate fondue can easily be made—just use white chocolate instead of the semi-sweet chocolate. You may need to add a little more cream if it is too thick.

ingredients

2 x 6 oz cans passion fruit
    in syrup
10 oz silken tofu, chopped
2²/₃ cups buttermilk
2 tablespoons superfine
    sugar
1 teaspoon vanilla extract
2 tablespoons plain
    gelatin powder
¾ cup fresh passion fruit
    pulp
8 strawberries, to garnish

preparation: 10 minutes +
    overnight refrigeration
cooking: none
serves: 8

1 Push the passion fruit in syrup through a sieve. Discard the seeds. Combine the strained syrup with the tofu, buttermilk, sugar and vanilla in a blender. Blend for 90 seconds on high, to mix thoroughly. Leave in the blender.

2 Put ⅓ cup water in a small bowl and put the bowl in a slightly larger bowl of boiling water. Sprinkle the gelatin powder onto the water in the small bowl and stir until dissolved. Allow to cool.

3 Place eight ¾-cup capacity dariole molds in a baking dish. Add the gelatin to the blender and mix on high for 1 minute. Pour into the molds, cover the dish with plastic wrap and refrigerate overnight.

4 When ready to serve, carefully run a spatula around the edge of each mold and dip the bases into hot water for 2 seconds to make removal easier. Place each on a plate and spoon the fresh passion fruit pulp around the bases. Garnish with fresh strawberries cut into halves.

nutrition per serve
Protein 8 g; Fat 2.5 g; Carbohydrate 10 g; Dietary Fiber 10 g; Cholesterol 3 mg; 110 calories

hint

It is important to thoroughly dissolve the gelatin (the liquid will be clear and golden). Don't be tempted to add the gelatin to the passion fruit mixture while it is still warm or it will become lumpy.

ingredients

10 oz (about 2 cups)
  fresh or frozen
  blueberries
½ cup port or muscat
1 cinnamon stick,
  broken in half
½ cup superfine sugar
1 tablespoon brandy
1 pint good-quality vanilla
  ice cream

preparation: 15 minutes
cooking: 8 minutes
serves: 4

1 Place the blueberries, port and both halves of the cinnamon stick in a small saucepan. Add the sugar to taste (this will vary depending on the tartness of the berries). Simmer very gently over low heat for 5–8 minutes, or until the berries are tender. Remove from the heat and add the brandy. Allow to cool slightly.

2 Place scoops of ice cream into serving dishes. Top with the simmered blueberries and any juices. Serve with whipped cream, if desired.

nutrition per serve
Protein 5.5 g; Fat 14 g; Carbohydrate 70 g; Dietary Fiber 1.5 g; Cholesterol 35 mg; 450 calories

handy tip...

The syrup can be served hot or cold over the ice cream. If allowed to cool, the berries will macerate in the port and absorb more flavor.

ingredients

8 oz (about 1½ cups) semi-sweet chocolate chips
3 eggs
¼ cup superfine sugar
2 teaspoons dark rum
1 cup whipping cream, softly whipped

preparation: 15 minutes + 2 hours chilling
cooking: 5 minutes
serves: 4

1 Place the chocolate in the top insert of a double boiler. Place the insert over simmering water without touching the water. Stir occasionally until the chocolate is melted. Remove from the heat and cool.

2 Place the eggs and sugar in a bowl and beat with an electric mixer for 5 minutes, or until thick, pale and increased in volume.

3 Add the melted chocolate and rum and beat together until well combined. Gently fold in the cream until the mixture is just combined.

4 Spoon the mousse into four 1-cup capacity dessert glasses. Refrigerate for 2 hours, or until set. Decorate with chocolate leaves, if desired.

nutrition per serve
Protein 9 g; Fat 50 g; Carbohydrate 60 g; Dietary Fiber 1 g; Cholesterol 220 mg; 685 calories

hint

The chocolate must be cooled before you add the cream or the mixture will go lumpy. If you are melting chocolate in the microwave, chop it into pieces. Stir to test frequently during heating to make sure it melts completely, because chocolate will hold its shape when microwaved.

ingredients

8 oz strawberries, hulled
    and halved
7 oz blueberries
15 oz can pitted Bing
    cherries, strained,
    reserving ½ cup juice
½ teaspoon cornstarch
1 tablespoon confectioners'
    sugar, sifted

Topping
⅓ cup butter
¼ cup golden syrup
2 cups rolled or
    old-fashioned oats

preparation: 10 minutes
cooking: 15 minutes
serves: 6

1 Preheat the oven to 350°F. Place the fruit in a baking dish and mix together well. Place the cornstarch with the reserved cherry juice in a small bowl and blend together until smooth. Pour over the fruit, then sprinkle the confectioners' sugar over the top.

2 To make the topping, place the butter and golden syrup in a small saucepan and stir over low heat until melted. Remove from the heat and stir in the rolled oats.

3 Spoon the topping evenly over the berries. Bake for 15 minutes, or until the topping is golden and crunchy. Delicious served hot with whipped cream or ice cream.

nutrition per serve
Protein 5 g; Fat 15 g; Carbohydrate 52 g; Dietary Fiber 5 g; Cholesterol 38 mg; 365 calories

handy tip...

Golden syrup is available in some gourmet markets. If not, substitute with dark corn syrup or honey. Try muesli as an alternative to rolled oats.

strawberry sorbet

ingredients

1 lb (about 3½ cups)
 fresh strawberries
1 cup superfine sugar

preparation: 15 minutes +
 freezing
cooking: 5 minutes
serves: 2

1 Place the strawberries in a food processor or blender and purée until smooth—you will need 2 cups of purée.

2 Place the sugar and 1 cup water in a saucepan and stir over low heat until the sugar has dissolved. Remove from the heat and allow to cool.

3 Add the strawberry purée to the cooled sugar syrup, mix together well and pour into a metal freezer tray. Freeze for 3–4 hours, or until the mixture begins to set around the edges.

4 Place the mixture in a bowl and beat with an electric mixer until smooth. Return to the metal tray and refreeze until set. Serve with fresh strawberries and whipped cream, if desired.

nutrition per serve
Protein 8.5 g; Fat 0 g; Carbohydrate 264 g; Dietary Fiber 11 g; Cholesterol 0 mg; 1052 calories

hint

It is important to freeze the sorbet in a shallow metal tray—it will freeze more quickly and evenly. The process of freezing, beating and refreezing will give you smaller ice crystals.

ingredients

1½ cups sugar
1 tablespoon finely
  shredded fresh ginger
1 stem fresh lemon grass,
  bruised *(see handy tip)*
4 firm ripe bosc pears,
  peeled, halved and
  cored
lemon sorbet, to serve
mint leaves, to garnish

preparation: 10 minutes
cooking: 20 minutes
serves: 4

1 Place 2 cups water in a saucepan and bring to a boil. Add sugar and stir together until it has completely dissolved. Add the ginger and lemon grass, bring to a boil, then reduce the heat and simmer for 5 minutes.

2 Gently lower the pear halves into the syrup and poach over low heat for 10 minutes, or until tender, turning occasionally. Remove the lemon grass.

3 Divide the pears among the serving dishes and spoon on a little syrup. Serve warm with the lemon sorbet and garnish with the mint.

nutrition per serve
Protein 0.5 g; Fat 0 g; Carbohydrate 112 g; Dietary Fiber 3.5 g; Cholesterol 0 mg; 430 calories

handy tip...

Bruising the stem of lemon grass develops its full flavor. Cut the stem into 2 in lengths. Using the back of a chef's knife, firmly press down on the stem to crush the coarse outer skin. Lemon grass is available from Asian markets.

ingredients

½ cup flaked almonds

8 oz package mini jelly rolls

⅓ cup medium dry sherry

2 fresh mangoes or 2 fresh peaches, chopped

2½ cups ready-made dairy custard

1¼ cups whipping cream

preparation: 15 minutes
cooking: 8 minutes
serves: 6

1 Preheat the oven to 350°F. Scatter the flaked almonds over a baking sheet and toast in the oven for 6–8 minutes, or until golden. Cut the mini jelly rolls into ½ in thick slices and place half of them on the base of a 10-cup glass serving bowl.

2 Sprinkle with half the sherry, then add half the mangoes. Top with half the custard. Repeat the layers, finishing with the custard, then refrigerate until cold.

3 Whip the cream until stiff peaks form, then spread over the custard. Scatter with the toasted almonds and serve.

nutrition per serve
Protein 9 g; Fat 27 g; Carbohydrate 45 g; Dietary Fiber 1.5 g; Cholesterol 130 mg; 460 calories

hint

If possible, use fresh fruit. If you can't buy fresh fruit, use a 14 oz can of drained mango or peach slices.
This trifle doesn't have Jello. If you would like to add it, prepare it according to the package instructions and allow it to set. Cut into pieces and layer it in the trifle.

ingredients

3 large mangoes, peeled
¾ cup whipping cream
2 tablespoons soft brown
   sugar
1 tablespoon superfine
   sugar

preparation: 15 minutes
cooking: 5 minutes
serves: 6

1 Cut the mangoes into thin slices and arrange in six ¾-cup capacity ramekins or soufflé dishes. Pour the cream evenly into each dish, then sprinkle with the sugars.

2 Place under a hot broiler for 5 minutes, or until the sugar has caramelized and the mangoes are warm. Serve immediately, with a wafer biscuit or tuille.

nutrition per serve
Protein 1.5 g; Fat 13 g; Carbohydrate 20 g; Dietary Fiber 1 g; Cholesterol 42 mg; 200 calories

handy tip...

Make this dish just before serving.
This recipe can also be made using bananas or peaches.
For a richer dessert, add a few drops of Grand Marnier to the cream.

ingredients

5 oz (about 1 cup) mixed nuts (almonds, brazil nuts, cashews, hazelnuts, pecans)

⅓ cup superfine sugar

2 tablespoons whipping cream

1 cup mascarpone cheese

2 tablespoons soft brown sugar

½ cup whipping cream, extra

1 teaspoon vanilla extract

1 prepared, baked short pastry tart shell

preparation: 20 minutes
cooking: 8 minutes
serves: 4

1 Preheat the oven to 350°F. Spread the mixed nuts on a baking sheet and roast in the oven for 5 minutes, or until light golden brown. Allow to cool.

2 Meanwhile, place the superfine sugar in a small saucepan and stir over medium heat for 2–3 minutes, or until the sugar dissolves and turns golden. Remove from the heat and stir in the cream—be careful as it will spit a little. Stir until smooth and well combined. Allow to cool.

3 Place the mascarpone, brown sugar, extra cream and vanilla in a bowl and beat with an electric mixer until combined—be careful not to overmix or it will curdle.

4 Spoon the mixture evenly into the pastry shell. Arrange the nuts evenly over the surface. Drizzle the toffee sauce over the nuts in a zigzag pattern. Chill until ready to serve.

nutrition per serve
Protein 14 g; Fat 73 g; Carbohydrate 56 g; Dietary Fiber 4 g; Cholesterol 129 mg; 919 calories

hint

The toffee sauce has to cool before you drizzle it over the nuts, otherwise it will melt the mascarpone filling. The sauce should have a thick consistency suitable to drizzle.

nutrition per serve
Protein 8.5 g; Fat 20 g; Carbohydrate
30 g; Dietary Fiber 0 g; Cholesterol
190 mg; 326 calories

ingredients

3 eggs
½ cup soft brown sugar
1½ cups milk
½ cup whipping cream
1 teaspoon vanilla extract
ground nutmeg, for
    dusting

preparation: 5 minutes
cooking: 35 minutes
serves: 4

1 Preheat the oven to 350°F. Grease a 4-cup baking dish with a small amount of oil or butter.

2 Place the eggs, sugar, milk, cream and vanilla in a bowl and whisk together for 1 minute. Pour the custard mixture into the prepared dish.

3 Place the dish in a shallow baking pan and pour enough hot water into the pan to come halfway up the side. Sprinkle the nutmeg over the top of the custard and bake for 15 minutes. Reduce the heat to 300°F and then bake for another 20 minutes, or until the custard is set and a sharp knife comes out clean when inserted in the center. Remove the dish from the water immediately. Serve the custard warm or cold with fresh or canned fruit.

handy tip...

The mixture can be prepared several hours in advance. If serving warm, cook just before serving. If serving cold, the custard can be cooked a day in advance, and stored, covered, in the refrigerator.

ingredients

¾ cup self-rising flour
1 tablespoon cocoa
  powder
½ cup superfine sugar
1 egg, lightly beaten
¼ cup milk
¼ cup butter, melted
⅓ cup soft brown sugar
1 tablespoon cocoa
  powder, extra

preparation: 10 minutes
cooking: 20 minutes
serves: 4

1 Preheat the oven to 350°F. Grease four ½-cup capacity baking cups or soufflé dishes.

2 Sift the flour and cocoa into a bowl and stir in the superfine sugar. Add the combined egg, milk and butter and stir together well.

3 Divide the mixture evenly among the dishes. Sprinkle with the combined brown sugar and extra cocoa. Carefully pour ¼ cup boiling water into each dish, then place on a baking sheet. Bake for 15–20 minutes, or until a skewer comes out clean when inserted in the center of the cakes. Dust with confectioners' sugar, if desired, then serve immediately with cream or ice cream.

nutrition per serve
Protein 6 g; Fat 16 g; Carbohydrate 65 g; Dietary Fiber 1.25 g; Cholesterol 85 mg; 413 calories

hint

When testing whether the cakes are ready, insert the skewer at an angle. This way there is a larger area checked for doneness.

black forest dessert

Drain a 15 oz can Bing cherries. Cut a 1 lb purchased round or loaf chocolate cake into three equal layers using a serrated knife. Whip 1¼ cups whipping cream to soft peaks. Brush the bottom cake layer with 2 tablespoons cherry jam. Top with half the cherries and half the whipped cream, then repeat the layers, finishing with the cake. Dust with confectioners' sugar and serve with chocolate ice cream.

serves 6

two-fruit strudel

Preheat the oven to 425°F. Place a drained 15 oz can diced peaches and pears (or use fruit cocktail), ½ teaspoon ground cinnamon, 2 tablespoons soft brown sugar and 1 teaspoon vanilla extract in a bowl. Spoon the mixture onto the edge of 1 thawed sheet of ready-rolled puff pastry. Fold in the edges and roll into a strudel shape. Trim the ends to prevent the filling from falling out. Place on a non-stick baking sheet, brush with 1 lightly beaten egg and sprinkle with raw sugar. Bake for 20 minutes, or until crisp and golden brown.

serves 4

mango and almond trifle

Line the base of an 8-cup glass serving bowl with a single layer of ladyfinger biscuits, then drizzle with ¼ cup sherry. Top with a 15 oz can drained mango slices and 1 cup ready-made dairy custard. Top with another single layer of ladyfinger biscuits, another 15 oz can drained mango slices, 2 tablespoons sherry, 1 cup custard and 1¼ cups whipping cream, whipped. Refrigerate overnight. Just before serving, coarsely chop 1 cup toasted flaked almonds and sprinkle over the cream.

serves 6–8

pear galette

Preheat the oven to 400°F. Cut 2 thawed sheets of ready-rolled puff pastry into quarters. Drain a 28 oz can pear halves and pat the pears dry with paper towels. Cut the pears into thin slices, taking care not to cut all the way through at the stem end—this allows the pear to fan out and maintain its shape. Place the pear, core-side down, on the pastry and gently fan out the slices. Following the pear shape, cut around the pear, leaving a ¾ in border. Brush the pastry lightly with beaten egg and sprinkle the pear with brown sugar. Place on a non-stick baking sheet and bake for 15–20 minutes, or until the pastry is puffed and golden. Serve hot with vanilla ice cream.

makes 8

raspberry and blackberry jelly

Drain a 15 oz can raspberries and a 15 oz can blackberries, reserving ½ cup of the juice. Combine the reserved juice with enough hot water to make up a 3 oz package of raspberry Jello crystals, according to the instructions. Stir the liquid until the Jello crystals have dissolved. Divide the berries among 4–6 champagne glasses, pour in the liquid and chill until set.

serves 4–6

blackberries and plums with streusel topping

Preheat the oven to 350°F. Drain a 28 oz can plums. Cut the plums in half and remove the stones. Place in a 6-cup baking dish with a 15 oz can drained blackberries. Place ¾ cup all-purpose flour, 1 cup dry shredded coconut, ¼ cup soft brown sugar, ¼ cup old-fashioned rolled oats and ¼ cup melted butter in a bowl and mix together well. Sprinkle over the top of the fruit and bake for 15–20 minutes, or until golden.

serves 4

From left to right: Black forest dessert; Two-fruit strudel; Mango and almond trifle; Pear galette; Raspberry and blackberry jelly; Blackberries and plums with streusel topping.

nutrition per serve
Protein 5 g; Fat 20 g; Carbohydrate
95 g; Dietary Fiber 1 g; Cholesterol
97 mg; 555 calories

ingredients

1 cup self-rising flour
3 tablespoons cold butter, chopped
1 egg
1 tablespoon milk
1 cup sugar
3 tablespoons butter, extra
2 tablespoons golden syrup (*see tip, page 238*)
¼ cup lemon juice

preparation: 15 minutes
cooking: 30 minutes
serves: 4

1 Sift the flour into a bowl and add a pinch of salt. Rub the butter into the flour with your fingertips until the mixture resembles fine bread crumbs, and make a well in the center. Stir the combined egg and milk into the flour mixture to make a soft dough.

2 To make the syrup, place 2 cups water in a large saucepan. Add the sugar, butter, golden syrup and lemon juice. Stir over medium heat until combined and the sugar has dissolved.

3 Bring to a boil, then gently drop large spoonfuls of the dough into the syrup. Reduce the heat and simmer, covered, for 20 minutes, or until a knife inserted into a dumpling comes out clean.

4 Divide the dumplings among the serving bowls, spoon the syrup over, and serve with whipped cream.

handy tip...

For a richer sauce, use brown sugar instead of white sugar. For spiced dumplings, add ½ teaspoon each of ground cinnamon, nutmeg and cloves to the dry ingredients.

ingredients

⅓ cup butter
1⅔ cups plain sweet
  wafers, finely crushed
  (see hint)
1 lb cream cheese, at
  room temperature
⅔ cup superfine sugar
2 eggs, lightly beaten
½ teaspoon finely grated
  lemon rind
1 tablespoon lemon juice

preparation: 15 minutes +
  overnight refrigeration
cooking: 25 minutes
serves: 6–8

1 Preheat the oven to 300°F. Grease an 8 in springform, and line the base with parchment paper.

2 Melt the butter in a saucepan. Place the wafer crumbs in a bowl, add the butter and mix until combined. Press the mixture firmly and evenly into the base and side of the prepared pan. Place in the freezer while preparing the filling. (It is not necessary to press the crumbs to the top of the pan, because the mixture does not quite fill the pan.)

3 Place the cream cheese and sugar in a large bowl and beat with an electric mixer until smooth. Gradually add the eggs and beat until mixed together well. Stir in the lemon rind and juice.

4 Pour into the prepared pan and smooth the surface. Bake for 25 minutes. Turn the oven off, leave the door open slightly and allow the cheesecake to cool in the oven. Refrigerate overnight.

nutrition per serve (8)
Protein 8 g; Fat 35 g; Carbohydrate 38 g; Dietary Fiber 0.5 g; Cholesterol 140 mg; 505 calories

hint

Wafers are quickly and easily crushed in a food processor. Alternatively, place them into two clean plastic bags and crush them with a rolling pin.
Add extra flavor to the crust by folding in some toasted and chopped macadamia nuts.

ingredients

4 eggs, separated
½ cup superfine sugar
1⅓ cups fresh ricotta
¼ cup finely chopped
   pistachio nuts
1 teaspoon grated lemon
   rind
2 tablespoons lemon juice
1 tablespoon vanilla sugar
   (see handy tip)
7 oz (about 1⅔ cups)
   fresh or frozen
   raspberries

preparation: 15 minutes
cooking: 25 minutes
serves: 4

1 Preheat the oven to 350°F. Grease four 1-cup capacity ramekins or soufflé dishes.

2 Place the egg yolks and sugar in a bowl and beat with an electric mixer until thick and pale. Add the ricotta, pistachio nuts, lemon rind and juice and mix together well.

3 In a separate bowl, beat the egg whites with clean beaters until stiff peaks form. Beat in the vanilla sugar. Fold into the ricotta mixture, stirring gently until just combined.

4 Divide the raspberries among the ramekins and spoon the ricotta filling over the top. Place on a baking sheet and bake for 20–25 minutes, or until puffed and lightly browned. Dust with confectioners' sugar.

nutrition per serve
Protein 18 g; Fat 19 g; Carbohydrate 40 g; Dietary Fiber 4 g; Cholesterol 222 mg; 405 calories

handy tip...

You can buy vanilla sugar at the supermarket or, if you prefer, make your own. Split a whole vanilla bean in half lengthwise and place in a jar of superfine sugar (about 2 lb). Leave for at least 4 days before using.
Any berries can be used in this recipe—mango is also delicious.

nutrition per serve
Protein 3.5 g; Fat 8 g; Carbohydrate
30 g; Dietary Fiber 6 g; Cholesterol
20 mg; 210 calories

ingredients

1 lb 4 oz fresh rhubarb

2 strips lemon rind

1 tablespoon honey,
   or to taste

2 firm, ripe pears

½ cup rolled old-fashioned
   oats

¼ cup wholewheat flour

⅓ cup soft brown sugar

¼ cup butter

preparation: 15 minutes
cooking: 25 minutes
serves: 6

1 Preheat the oven to 350°F. Trim the fresh rhubarb, wash and cut it into 2½ in pieces. Place in a saucepan with the lemon rind and 1 tablespoon water. Cook, covered, over low heat for 10 minutes, or until tender. Cool slightly. Stir in the honey, then remove the lemon rind.

2 Peel, core and cut the pears into ¾ in cubes and combine with the rhubarb. Spoon into a 5-cup baking dish and smooth the surface.

3 To make the topping, place the oats, flour and brown sugar in a bowl and mix together well. Add the butter and rub in with your fingertips until the mixture resembles bread crumbs. Spread evenly over the fruit. Bake for 15 minutes, or until cooked and golden. Serve warm with whipped cream or custard.

hint

The amount of honey added to the rhubarb will depend on how sweet the fruit is. Sugar can be used instead of honey, if preferred.
Most fruits are suitable for making crumble except citrus fruits such as lemon, lime and grapefruit. Try apple and berry, pear and apricot, or peach, nectarine and apple.

ingredients

28 oz can pitted cherries, very well drained
1/2 cup self-rising flour, sifted
1/3 cup superfine sugar
2 eggs, lightly beaten
1 cup milk
2 tablespoons butter, melted
confectioners' sugar, for dusting

preparation: 15 minutes
cooking: 40 minutes
serves: 6–8

1 Preheat the oven to 350°F. Grease a shallow, 9 in glass or ceramic pie plate with a little oil or butter. Spread the cherries into the dish in a single layer.

2 Sift the flour and sugar into a bowl and make a well in the center. Pour in the combined eggs, milk and butter gradually and whisk until just combined—do not overbeat.

3 Pour the batter over the cherries and bake for 40 minutes. Dust generously with confectioners' sugar and serve immediately.

nutrition per serve (8)
Protein 4 g; Fat 5 g; Carbohydrate 38 g; Dietary Fiber 2 g; Cholesterol 57 mg; 210 calories

handy tip...

A clafoutis (pronounced 'clafootee') is a classic French batter pudding. It is traditionally made with cherries, but berries such as blueberries, blackberries, raspberries, or small, well-flavored strawberries can be used instead if you prefer. A delicious version can also be made using slices of poached pear.

nutrition per serve
Protein 9 g; Fat 15 g; Carbohydrate 60 g; Dietary Fiber 0 g; Cholesterol 165 mg; 390 calories

ingredients

2 tablespoons butter, softened
3/4 cup superfine sugar
1 teaspoon grated lemon rind
3 eggs, separated
1/4 cup all-purpose flour
1/2 cup lemon juice
1 1/2 cups warm milk
confectioners' sugar, to dust

preparation: 10 minutes
cooking: 45 minutes
serves: 4

1 Preheat the oven to 350°F. Grease a 6-cup baking dish. Place the butter, sugar, rind and egg yolks in a bowl, and then beat with an electric mixer until light and creamy.

2 Fold in the sifted flour in two batches, alternately with the lemon juice and milk. Place the egg whites in a separate clean, dry bowl and beat with cleaned beaters until soft peaks form. Pour the lemon mixture down the inside of the bowl of the beaten egg whites and fold the whites gently into the mixture.

3 Pour the combined mixture into the prepared dish and put the dish in a baking pan. Pour in enough warm water to come halfway up the sides of the dish. Bake for 40 minutes, or until puffed and golden. Dust with confectioners' sugar and serve with ice cream.

hint

Try using limes or oranges for a different citrus flavor. It is essential that this dessert is served immediately. If it is left to sit, the sauce will absorb into the cake and it will be dry and gluggy.

ingredients

1 cup sugar

Custard
4 cups milk, warmed
½ cup sugar
6 eggs
1½ teaspoons vanilla
    extract

preparation: 15 minutes +
    refrigeration
cooking: 40 minutes
serves: 8

1 Preheat the oven to 350°F. Grease eight ½-cup capacity ramekins or soufflé dishes.

2 Place the sugar and ¼ cup water in a saucepan. Stir over low heat until the sugar dissolves. Bring to a boil, then reduce the heat and simmer for 6 minutes, or until the mixture turns golden brown. Remove from the heat. Pour a little of the hot mixture into each ramekin and swirl to cover the base. Set aside.

3 To make the custard, place the milk and sugar in a saucepan and stir gently over low heat until the sugar has dissolved. Place the eggs and vanilla in a bowl and whisk together for 2 minutes, then stir in the warm milk. Strain the custard mixture into a pitcher or a glass measure and pour into the ramekins.

4 Place the ramekins in a baking pan, then pour in enough hot water to come halfway up the sides. Bake for 30 minutes, or until the custard is set and a knife comes out clean when inserted. Allow to cool, then refrigerate for at least 6 hours.

5 To unmold, run a knife around the edge of each custard and gently invert onto a serving plate. Shake gently, if necessary, to remove. Serve with whipped cream, fresh fruit and wafers, if desired.

nutrition per serve
Protein 9 g; Fat 8.5 g; Carbohydrate 53 g; Dietary Fiber 0 g; Cholesterol 150 mg; 314 calories

handy tip...

This can be made 1 day ahead and stored in the refrigerator.
To avoid a burnt flavor in step 2, remove the pan containing the caramel from the heat just before it reaches the desired color. The mixture will darken further even after cooking has finished.
The custard for Crème Caramel may be flavored with spices such as cardamom, cinnamon and nutmeg; with lemon or orange rind; or with your favorite spirit or liqueur.

ingredients

⅓ cup superfine sugar
rind of 1 orange
1 tablespoon plain gelatin
powder
2½ cups pink Champagne
10 oz (about 1½ cups)
mixed berries, fresh
or frozen

preparation: 15 minutes +
cooling + refrigeration
cooking: 5 minutes
serves: 4–6

1 Place the sugar, orange rind and 1⅓ cups water in a saucepan. Bring to a boil, stirring over low heat until the sugar dissolves. When dissolved, remove the pan from the heat and allow to cool for 1 hour.

2 Strain the rind out of the syrup. Place about ¼ cup syrup in a small heatproof bowl, sprinkle the gelatin in an even layer over the top and allow to go spongy. Bring a saucepan filled with about 1½ in water to a boil. When it boils, remove from the heat and carefully lower the gelatin bowl into the water (it should come up halfway), then stir until dissolved. Cool slightly, add to the rest of the syrup and mix. Add the Champagne, then pour a little of the gelatin into the base of a 5-cup loaf pan and refrigerate until set. Don't leave too long or the next layer will not stick.

3 Arrange the fruit in the pan, pour in a little more gelatin to cover the fruit, set in the refrigerator, then pour the rest of the gelatin in and set completely. (Setting in layers will make sure of a smooth surface on top and stop the fruit floating.)

4 To unmold, wipe the pan with a cloth dipped in hot water then invert the terrine onto a plate. Bring to room temperature before serving—it should not be stiff and should sag very slightly. Serve with cream or ice cream, if desired.

nutrition per serve (6)
Protein 2 g; Fat 2 g; Carbohydrate 17 g; Dietary Fiber 1.5 g; Cholesterol 0 mg; 137 calories

hint

If you wish to use gelatin sheets, put 6 sheets in a bowl of cold water and let stand until floppy. Remove the gelatin, squeeze out any excess water. Add the gelatin to the hot sugar syrup and stir until thoroughly dissolved.

4 oz (about 1 cup) fresh or
  frozen raspberries
4 oz (about 1 cup) fresh or
  frozen blueberries
2 tablespoons orange-
  flavored liqueur
8 brandy snap baskets
8 small scoops strawberry
  swirl ice cream
mint leaves, to garnish

preparation: 20 minutes
cooking: none
serves: 8

1 Place the raspberries and blueberries in a bowl, pour in the orange-flavored liqueur and stir gently to combine.

2 Place each brandy snap basket on a serving plate. Place one small scoop of ice cream in one half of each basket. Add the mixed berries to the other half of the basket. Serve the baskets decorated with a few mint leaves.

nutrition per serve
Protein 2.5 g; Fat 11 g; Carbohydrate 35 g; Dietary Fiber 1.5 g; Cholesterol 32 mg; 255 calories

handy tip...

Brandy snap baskets are available at supermarkets or delicatessens.
For a delicious variation, try spooning the berries into purchased meringue shells instead of the brandy snaps.

ingredients

¾ cup butter, coarsely
    chopped
3 cups coarse fresh
    bread crumbs
¾ cup firmly packed soft
    brown sugar
½ teaspoon ground
    nutmeg
28 oz can peaches,
    drained, chopped
¾ cup slivered almonds

preparation: 20 minutes
cooking: 50 minutes
serves: 4

1 Preheat the oven to 350°F. Grease a 5-cup soufflé dish.

2 In a large skillet, melt ⅔ cup of the butter, add the bread crumbs and toss over medium heat until the bread crumbs are golden brown. Place the sugar and nutmeg in a bowl and mix together well.

3 Place one third of the bread crumb mixture over the base of the prepared dish and top with half of the peaches, a third of the sugar mixture and half of the almonds. Repeat with a second layer of each and top with a final layer of bread crumbs. Use the back of a spoon to firmly press the mixture down.

Sprinkle with the remaining sugar and dot with the remaining butter. Bake for 35–40 minutes, or until golden brown.

nutrition per serve
Protein 15 g; Fat 48 g; Carbohydrate 105 g; Dietary Fiber 7.5 g; Cholesterol 110 mg; 895 calories

hint

Any canned fruit is suitable for this recipe. For example, mix canned apples with ½ teaspoon of ground cinnamon and 1 teaspoon vanilla. You could also substitute the almonds with ground hazelnuts, for a slightly different flavor.

praline ice cream terrine with mango coulis

Line the base and sides of a 7½ x 4 in loaf pan with parchment paper. Firmly press 2 quarts softened French vanilla ice cream into the pan. Smooth the surface and tap gently to release any air pockets. Freeze for 1–2 hours, or until firm. In a non-stick skillet, heat 1 cup sugar, stirring over low heat until dissolved. Bring to a boil and cook until it has turned a light golden color. Add ¼ cup slivered almonds, then pour onto a foil-lined baking sheet and allow to harden. Process half the praline in a food processor until crushed, and break the remaining praline into large pieces. Place a well-drained 28 oz can mango slices, 1 tablespoon confectioners' sugar and 1 tablespoon Cointreau in a blender and process until smooth. Remove the ice cream from the pan and sprinkle the crushed praline over it. Slice the ice cream to serve and garnish with praline pieces and mango coulis.

serves 4–6

banana and caramel parfait

Place 4 teaspoons butter, ½ cup soft brown sugar and ½ cup whipping cream in a small saucepan and stir over low heat for 5 minutes, or until the sugar has dissolved. Simmer for 2 minutes. Set aside and allow to cool slightly. Divide 1 thinly sliced banana evenly between two large parfait glasses. Top each banana layer with ¼ cup ready-made custard, a scoop of vanilla ice cream and some caramel sauce. Repeat the layers. Serve with wafers.

serves 2

blueberry ice cream pie

Line the base of an 8 in round springform pan with parchment paper. Process 8 oz plain sweet wafers in a food processor until crumbly. Add ½ cup melted butter and mix well. Press firmly into the base and side of the pan. Sprinkle 1⅔ cups fresh or frozen blueberries or blackberries over the base. Dollop 2 quarts of softened berry swirl ice cream carefully over the berries until the base is covered, then smooth the surface. Tap the pan lightly to remove any air pockets. Freeze for 1–2 hours, or until firm. Melt ⅔ cup semi-sweet chocolate chips and pipe or drizzle over the top to decorate.

serves 6

pecan freezer pie

Finely crush 8 oz sweet wafers in a food processor. Add ¾ cup melted butter and ½ teaspoon ground cinnamon and stir together well. Press the crumb mix into the base of an 8 in round fluted tart pan and chill. Soften 1 quart pecan caramel ice cream until just spreadable, then evenly spread over the pie base and return to the freezer. Press ½ cup whole pecans around the edge and return to the freezer until firm. Drizzle with ½ cup bottled caramel fudge topping and serve immediately.

serves 6

christmas ice cream pudding

Place 1 tablespoon brandy, ¾ cup dried mixed fruit and ½ teaspoon ground cinnamon in a bowl and leave to stand for 15 minutes. Add 2 quarts softened vanilla ice cream and mix well. Spoon the mixture into six 1-cup dariole molds or ramekins. Freeze for 1 hour, or until firm. Turn out ice cream from the molds using a warm cloth, place on a baking sheet, and return to the freezer for 5–10 minutes. Melt ⅔ cup semi-sweet chocolate chips and drizzle over each pudding. Return to the freezer for 5–10 minutes. Melt ⅔ cup chopped white chocolate and drizzle over the dark chocolate. Return the puddings to the freezer for 10 minutes to set firm before serving. Top each with half a red and half a green glacé cherry.

serves 6

bombe alaska

Preheat the oven to 450°F. Drain a 16 oz can sliced pineapple and reserve the juice. Cut a 10 oz jelly roll into six, ½ in thick slices. Place the slices onto a baking sheet and brush lightly with the reserved juice. Top the jelly roll slices with a slice of pineapple and a scoop of raspberry or strawberry ice cream, then place in the freezer while you make the meringue. Place 2 egg whites in a clean, dry bowl and whisk until soft peaks form. Gradually add ⅓ cup superfine sugar. Beat until glossy and stiff peaks form. Spread the meringue roughly over the ice cream then bake for 2–3 minutes, or until light golden brown on the outside. Serve immediately.

serves 8

From left to right: Praline ice cream terrine with mango coulis; Banana and caramel parfait; Blueberry ice cream pie; Christmas ice cream pudding; Pecan freezer pie; Bombe Alaska.

ingredients

1/4 cup short-grain rice

1 2/3 cups milk

2 tablespoons superfine
   sugar

3/4 cup whipping cream

1/4 teaspoon vanilla
   extract

1/4 teaspoon grated
   nutmeg

1 bay leaf

preparation: 10 minutes
cooking: 2 hours
serves: 4

1 Preheat the oven to 300°F. Grease a 4-cup baking dish.

2 Place the rice, milk, sugar, cream and vanilla extract in a bowl and mix together. Pour into the greased dish. Dust the surface with the grated nutmeg and float the bay leaf on top.

3 Bake for 2 hours, by which time the rice should have absorbed most of the milk and will have become creamy in texture with a brown skin on top. Remove the bay leaf before serving and serve hot, if desired.

nutrition per serve
Protein 5 g; Fat 24 g; Carbohydrate 25 g; Dietary Fiber 0 g; Cholesterol 77 mg; 330 calories

handy tip...

Alternatively, try adding a couple of tablespoons of golden raisins. Add grated lemon or orange rind to give the pudding a citrus flavor. Rice pudding is delicious served hot or cold.
For a low-fat version, use skim milk.

ingredients

2 cups all-purpose flour
3 eggs, lightly beaten
1 cup milk
¼ cup butter, melted

Sauce
3 tablespoons butter
¼ cup sifted cocoa
    powder
1 cup soft brown sugar
1¼ cups whipping cream

preparation: 5 minutes +
    30 minutes standing
cooking: 20 minutes
serves: 4

1 Sift the flour into a large bowl and make a well in the center. Add the combined eggs, milk and ¾ cup water and whisk together to make a smooth batter. Stir in the melted butter. Pour the mixture into a glass measure and set aside for 30 minutes.

2 Heat an 8 in crêpe pan or non-stick skillet and grease lightly with butter. When the pan is hot, pour in ¼ cup of the mixture and tilt the pan to coat. Drain out any excess batter. When the edges begin to curl, gently turn the crêpe over with a flexible metal spatula. Cook until light brown on both sides, and slide onto a plate. If not serving immediately, keep the crêpes warm in a preheated oven. Cook the remaining batter and stack the crêpes on top of each other with a piece of parchment paper between each one.

3 To make the sauce, place the butter, cocoa and sugar in a saucepan and mix well. Add the cream and stir over low heat until it comes to a boil.

4 To serve, fold three crêpes into quarters and put them on a plate. Pour a generous amount of the sauce over the top and add a scoop of vanilla ice cream.

nutrition per serve
Protein 18 g; Fat 60 g; Carbohydrate 99 g; Dietary Fiber 3 g; Cholesterol 300 mg; 1005 calories

hint

This dessert can be made ahead of time. The sauce will keep well in the refrigerator for up to a week and the crêpes can be made ahead and frozen. Store the crêpes in between layers of parchment paper. Defrost and reheat in the oven.

ingredients

²/₃ cup self-rising flour
2 eggs
½ cup milk
¼ cup butter
⅓ cup soft brown sugar
1 tablespoon grated
    orange rind
¼ cup orange juice
3 bananas, sliced

preparation: 15 minutes
cooking: 15 minutes
serves: 4

1 Sift the flour into a bowl and make a well in the center. Place the eggs, milk and ¼ cup water in a small bowl and whisk until combined, then gradually add to the flour. Stir until the liquid is mixed together well and the batter is free of lumps.

2 Pour 2–3 tablespoons of batter onto a lightly greased 8 in crêpe pan, swirling evenly over the base. Cook over medium heat for 1 minute, or until the underside is golden. Turn the crêpe over and cook the other side. Transfer to a plate, cover with a clean dish towel and keep warm. Repeat with the remaining batter, greasing the pan when necessary. You will need 8 crêpes for this recipe.

3 Heat the butter in a saucepan, add the brown sugar and stir over low heat until the sugar has dissolved and the mixture is bubbling. Add the rind and juice and bring to a boil. Reduce the heat and simmer for 2 minutes. Add the bananas and simmer for another minute. Divide the mixture among the 8 crêpes. Fold the crêpes into quarters to enclose, arrange on serving plates and serve.

nutrition per serve
Protein 8 g; Fat 16 g; Carbohydrate 54 g; Dietary Fiber 3 g; Cholesterol 133 mg; 390 calories

handy tip...

The batter can be made several hours ahead. Cover the bowl with plastic wrap and refrigerate. Cook the crêpes just before serving. Alternatively, the crêpes can be cooked several hours ahead. Place on a baking sheet and cover with aluminum foil. Just before serving, place the crêpes in a 350°F oven for 10 minutes, or until warmed through.

ingredients

1 sheet frozen ready-rolled
 puff pastry
¼ cup bottled apple sauce
3 medium green apples
4 teaspoons butter, melted
2 tablespoons soft brown
 sugar
¼ teaspoon ground
 cinnamon

preparation: 15 minutes
cooking: 25 minutes
serves: 6

1 Preheat the oven to 350°F. Lightly grease a baking sheet with a little oil or butter.

2 Lay out the pastry on a work surface. Using a plate as a guide, cut a 9 in circle from the pastry and place on the prepared sheet. Spread the apple sauce over the pastry, leaving a ¾ in border around the pastry edge.

3 Peel, core and quarter the apples. Slice thinly and arrange decoratively over the apple sauce, fanning out from the center of the pastry. Brush the melted butter over the apples, then sprinkle with the sugar and cinnamon.

4 Bake for 25 minutes, or until the edge of the pastry is golden brown. Serve hot, with whipped cream, custard or vanilla ice cream, if desired.

nutrition per serve
Protein 2 g; Fat 9 g; Carbohydrate 27 g; Dietary Fiber 2 g; Cholesterol 16 mg; 194 calories

hint

This dish is best made just before serving. Granny Smith apples are excellent for cooking as they soften without losing their shape. Canned fruit is not suitable for this recipe.

ingredients

8 oz cream cheese, softened
1 tablespoon lemon juice
¼ cup superfine sugar
⅓ cup golden raisins
¼ cup all-purpose flour, sifted
2 sheets frozen ready-rolled puff pastry
2 tablespoons milk
1 tablespoon superfine sugar, extra

preparation: 15 minutes
cooking: 25 minutes
serves: 6

1 Preheat the oven to 350°F. Lightly grease a baking sheet.

2 Place the cream cheese, lemon juice and sugar in a bowl and beat with an electric mixer until smooth. Add the raisins and flour and stir with a wooden spoon.

3 Place half the cheese mixture along one side of one of the pastry sheets, about 2 in in from the edge. Roll up the pastry like a jelly roll and press the ends together to seal. Repeat with the remaining mixture and pastry sheet.

4 Place the rolls on the prepared baking sheet. Lightly brush the rolls with the milk and sprinkle with the extra sugar. Bake for 25 minutes, or until golden brown.

nutrition per serve
Protein 7.5 g; Fat 27 g; Carbohydrate 43 g; Dietary Fiber 1 g; Cholesterol 55 mg; 440 calories

handy tip...

For something different, try a berry, white chocolate and cream cheese strudel. Instead of the raisins, fold in 1⅔ cups fresh raspberries and ¼ cup coarsely shredded white chocolate.

ingredients

2 large bosc pears
(about 1 lb 4 oz)
⅓ cup dry white wine
¼ cup superfine sugar
1 cup milk
3 eggs
2 teaspoons vanilla extract
⅔ cup all-purpose flour
confectioners' sugar,
to dust

preparation: 15 minutes +
1 hour marinating
cooking: 50 minutes
serves: 4–6

1 Peel and core the pears, and cut them into 12 slices each. Place in a large bowl and pour in the combined wine and sugar. Gently stir, then set aside for 1 hour. (Do not leave for any longer or the pears will turn brown.)

2 Preheat the oven to 350°F. Grease a shallow, round 5-cup ovenproof dish. Drain the pears and reserve the syrup. Spread the pear slices evenly over the base of the dish.

3 Pour the syrup into the bowl of a food processor. With the motor running, add the milk, eggs, vanilla extract and flour. Process until smooth, then pour the mixture over the pears. Bake for 50 minutes, or until the tart is puffed and golden on top. Sprinkle the sifted confectioners' sugar liberally over the top. Serve hot or warm with cream or ice cream, if desired.

nutrition per serve (6)
Protein 6 g; Fat 4 g; Carbohydrate 35 g; Dietary Fiber 3 g; Cholesterol 95 mg; 205 calories

hint

Apples can be used instead of the pears—firm apples such as Granny Smith or Golden Delicious are best for cooking.

ingredients

1/3 cup semi-sweet
    chocolate chips
1/4 cup butter, softened
4 egg yolks
1 1/4 cups whipping cream
2 teaspoons vanilla
2 tablespoons whisky
1/4 cup dark cocoa,
    for dusting

preparation: 10 minutes +
    3 hours freezing
cooking: none
serves: 6

1 Line an 8 1/2 x 4 1/2 x 2 1/2 in loaf pan with plastic wrap.

2 Place the chocolate in a heatproof bowl and stand over a saucepan of simmering water. Melt the chocolate gently, then allow to cool.

3 Place the butter and egg yolks in a small bowl and beat with an electric mixer until thick and creamy, then beat in the cooled chocolate mixture.

4 Place the cream and vanilla in a separate bowl and beat with an electric mixer until soft peaks form. Fold in the whisky. Fold the cream and chocolate mixtures together until they are just combined.

5 Pour the mixture into the prepared pan and freeze for 2–3 hours, or until firm. Remove from the freezer, unmold and carefully peel away the plastic wrap. Smooth out the wrinkles on the surface of the loaf with a flexible metal spatula. Place on a serving plate and dust with cocoa. Cut into slices and serve with extra cream and dessert wafers, if desired.

nutrition per serve
Protein 4 g; Fat 37 g; Carbohydrate 8 g; Dietary Fiber 0.5 g; Cholesterol 215 mg; 385 calories

handy tip...

This dish should be served immediately. If not, return it to the freezer until you are ready.
The whisky can be replaced by a coffee liqueur.

ingredients

2 sheets frozen short or
    puff pastry
1 sheet frozen puff pastry
2 x 26 oz cans apple pie
    filling
pinch of ground cloves
½ teaspoon finely grated
    lemon rind
2 teaspoons milk
2 teaspoons sugar

preparation: 15 minutes
cooking: 40 minutes
serves: 4

1 Thaw all the sheets of pastry. Preheat the oven to 400°F. Grease an 8 in round, deep pie dish and line with two sheets of pastry, trimming the overhanging edges. Line the pastry shell with a piece of crumpled parchment paper that is large enough to cover the base and side, and pour in some pie weights or uncooked rice. Bake for 10 minutes. Remove the paper and weights, and bake for a further 10 minutes, or until the base is dry and light golden.

2 Place the apple filling, ground cloves and lemon rind in a bowl and mix together. Spoon the apple mixture into the hot pastry shell.

3 Cover the top of the pie with the sheet of puff pastry and use a sharp knife to trim off any excess pastry. Cut a hole in the center to allow the steam to escape, and decorate with any leftover pastry.

4 Glaze the pastry with the milk and sprinkle with the sugar. Bake for 20 minutes, or until the pastry is golden brown. Serve warm or cold, with whipped cream or ice cream.

nutrition per serve
Protein 8 g; Fat 33 g; Carbohydrate 93 g; Dietary Fiber 4.5 g; Cholesterol 36 mg; 687 calories

hint

For an apple and blackberry pie, substitute 10 oz of the canned apple pie filling with frozen or canned blackberries. Drain the canned berries well before adding to the apples.

ingredients

4 egg yolks
¼ cup superfine sugar
½ cup Marsala, sherry or
   sweet white wine
14 oz (about 2 cups)
   mixed berries (eg.
   raspberries, blackberries,
   mulberries, strawberries)

preparation: 15 minutes
cooking: 5 minutes
serves: 4–6

1 Place the egg yolks, sugar and Marsala in a large heatproof bowl and rest the bowl over a pan of barely simmering water. Beat with an electric mixer for 5 minutes, or until thick, light and foamy.

2 Divide the mixed berries among the serving dishes, pour the sabayon over the berries and serve immediately.

nutrition per serve (6)
Protein 3 g; Fat 3 g; Carbohydrate 16 g; Dietary Fiber 2 g; Cholesterol 120 mg; 125 calories

handy tip...

Sabayon should be made just before serving time, as the sabayon mixture will separate if it is left to stand. This dish can be broiled until golden brown and served hot.

ingredients

¼ cup butter
½ cup soft brown sugar
2 tablespoons lemon juice
1 tablespoon orange
     liqueur
4 firm, ripe bananas,
     sliced in half lengthwise

preparation: 5 minutes
cooking: 10 minutes
serves: 4

1 Melt the butter in a skillet. Add the sugar and mix together well. Simmer for 3 minutes, or until golden and bubbly.

2 Add the lemon juice and orange liqueur and stir gently. Add the bananas to the sauce and simmer for 5 minutes, or until the sauce thickens. Spoon the sauce occasionally over the bananas to baste them.

3 Serve the bananas and sauce with ice cream or with waffles and whipped cream, if desired.

nutrition per serve
Protein 2.5 g; Fat 12 g; Carbohydrate 55 g; Dietary Fiber 3 g; Cholesterol 38 mg; 340 calories

hint

This recipe also makes a delicious crêpe filling if you chop the bananas instead of halving them.
Try stacking the crêpes between layers of bananas and sauce. Sprinkle with demerara sugar and flash under a broiler until caramelized.

cakes & bakes

ingredients

2/3 cup unsalted butter
3/4 cup superfine sugar
2 eggs, lightly beaten
1 teaspoon vanilla extract
2 cups self-rising flour,
   sifted
1/2 cup milk

Lemon glacé icing
1 cup confectioners'
   sugar, sifted
3–4 teaspoons lemon
   juice

preparation: 20 minutes
cooking: 45 minutes
serves: 6–8

1 Preheat the oven to 350°F. Grease the base and sides of a 3 in deep, 8 in round cake pan or springform pan. Line the base with parchment paper.

2 Place 1/2 cup of the butter and all the superfine sugar in a large bowl and beat together with an electric mixer until light and creamy. Add the eggs gradually, beating thoroughly after each addition. Then add the vanilla extract and beat until combined. Fold in all the flour alternately with the milk. Stir until just combined and the mixture is almost smooth.

3 Spoon the cake mixture into the prepared pan and smooth the surface. Bake for 45 minutes, or until a skewer comes out clean when inserted into the center of the cake. Cool the cake in the cake pan for 10 minutes before turning it out onto a wire rack to cool completely.

4 To make the lemon glacé frosting, melt the remaining butter in the top of a double boiler. Stir in confectioners' sugar and enough lemon juice to make a firm paste. Place the insert over simmering water, stirring constantly until the icing is smooth and glossy—do not overheat or it will be dull and grainy. Remove from the heat. Pour the icing over the cake and spread out using a flexible metal spatula.

nutrition per serve (8)
Protein 4.9 g; Fat 16 g; Carbohydrate 61 g; Dietary Fiber 1 g; Cholesterol 90 mg; 400 calories

handy tip...

Unfrosted, the cake can be stored in an airtight container for 1 week or in the freezer for up to 3 months.
Sugar helps in incorporating air into fat, so it is important to use the appropriate sugar for the recipe. Superfine sugar is ideal for butter cakes—the finer the crystals, the more numerous the air cells and the lighter the finished cake.

ingredients

1 cup superfine sugar
1¾ cups self-rising flour
⅔ cup cocoa powder
1 teaspoon baking soda
¼ cup vegetable oil
2 eggs
¾ cup sour cream

preparation: 15 minutes
cooking: 40 minutes
serves: 6–8

1 Preheat the oven to 350°F. Lightly grease a deep 8 in baba or ring cake pan with a small amount of butter or oil.

2 Place the sugar, flour, cocoa, baking soda, oil, eggs, sour cream and ⅔ cup water in a food processor. Process in short bursts until the mixture is well combined and smooth in texture.

3 Spoon mixture evenly into the pan. Bake for 35–40 minutes, or until a skewer comes out clean when inserted in the center of the cake. Cool in the pan for 10 minutes before turning onto a wire rack to cool completely. Serve with whipped cream and fresh berries, if desired, or drizzle with a rich chocolate icing (see hint).

nutrition per serve (8)
Protein 4 g; Fat 13 g; Carbohydrate 24 g; Dietary Fiber 0.5 g; Cholesterol 40 mg; 229 calories

hint

To make a rich chocolate icing, place ¼ cup butter, ⅔ cup semi-sweet chocolate chips and 1 tablespoon whipping cream in the top of a double boiler. Place over simmering water and stir until the butter and chocolate have melted and the mixture is smooth. Cool slightly until the mixture is cool enough to pour.

ingredients

½ cup all-purpose flour
½ cup self-rising flour
4 eggs, separated
⅔ cup superfine sugar
½ cup strawberry jam
½ cup whipping cream,
    whipped
confectioners' sugar,
    to dust

preparation: 15 minutes
cooking: 20 minutes
serves: 8

1 Preheat the oven to 350°F. Grease two round 8 in cake pans and line the base of each pan with parchment paper.

2 Sift the flours together three times onto parchment paper. Place the egg whites in a large clean, dry bowl. Beat with an electric mixer until firm peaks form. Add the sugar gradually, beating constantly until the sugar has dissolved and the mixture is thick and glossy.

3 Add the egg yolks and beat for another 20 seconds. Fold the mixture into the flour quickly and lightly.

4 Pour mixture into the prepared pans and spread evenly. Bake for 20 minutes, or until light golden and springy to touch. Cool in the pans for 5 minutes before turning onto wire racks to cool completely.

5 Spread the strawberry jam evenly onto one of the layers, then spoon the cream over the jam. Top with the second layer, and dust with sifted confectioners' sugar before serving.

nutrition per serve
Protein 6.5 g; Fat 10.5 g; Carbohydrate 27 g; Dietary Fiber 0.9 g; Cholesterol 156 mg; 226 calories

handy tip...

The secret to making a perfect sponge cake lies in the folding technique. Work quickly yet gently to incorporate the flour. A beating action will cause loss of volume in the egg mixture and will result in a flat, heavy cake.
Unfilled sponge cakes can be frozen for up to one month—though make sure you freeze them in separate freezer bags. Thaw sponge cakes at room temperature (for about 20 minutes). A filled sponge cake is best served immediately.

ingredients

½ cup butter

½ cup superfine sugar

3 eggs, lightly beaten

1¼ cups self-rising flour

1 tablespoon caraway seeds

2 tablespoons milk

confectioners' sugar, to dust

preparation: 15 minutes
cooking: 40 minutes
serves: 6–8

1 Preheat the oven to 350°F. Grease an 8 in round cake or springform pan and line the base with parchment paper.

2 Place butter and sugar in a bowl and beat with an electric mixer until light and creamy. Add eggs gradually, beating thoroughly after each addition. Sift the flour and gently fold in the flour and caraway seeds alternately with the milk.

3 Spoon the mixture into the pan and smooth the surface. Bake for 40 minutes, or until a skewer comes out clean when inserted in the center of the cake. Cool in the pan for 20 minutes before turning onto a wire rack to cool completely. Dust with confectioners' sugar.

nutrition per serve (8)
Protein 7 g; Fat 24 g; Carbohydrate 43 g; Dietary Fiber 1 g; Cholesterol 72 mg; 408 calories

hint

Seed cake is a traditional English cake made to celebrate the end of spring sowing of the crop.
This cake will store well for up to one week in an airtight container, or up to three months in the freezer.

ingredients

1½ cups dried fruit
medley *(see handy tip)*
½ cup golden raisins
1 cup whole bran cereal
½ cup soft brown sugar
1½ cups milk
1½ cups self-rising flour,
sifted
whole blanched almonds,
to decorate

preparation: 15 minutes +
15 minutes soaking
cooking: 50 minutes
serves: 6–8

1 Preheat the oven to 350°F. Lightly grease a 9 x 5 x 3 in loaf pan. Line the base of the pan with parchment paper.

2 Place the fruit medley, raisins, bran cereal, sugar and milk in a bowl and mix together well. Allow to soak for at least 15 minutes.

3 Add the flour to the mixture and mix together well. Spoon into the prepared pan, smooth the surface and decorate with the almonds. Bake for 45–50 minutes, or until a skewer comes out clean when inserted in the center of the loaf. Cool in the pan for 5 minutes, then turn onto a wire rack to cool completely. Serve plain, sliced with butter or toasted.

nutrition per serve (8)
Protein 7.5 g; Fat 3 g; Carbohydrate 52.5 g; Dietary Fiber 10.5 g; Cholesterol 6 mg; 263 calories

handy tip...

Use any combination of dried fruits—apricots, pears, apples, peaches and golden raisins. Make sure you finely chop the fruit before soaking. This loaf is delicious toasted and served for breakfast.

ingredients

1½ cups self-rising flour
½ cup all-purpose flour
¾ cup unsalted butter
⅔ cup superfine sugar
3 eggs, lightly beaten
⅓ cup milk
1 cup canned apple pie
    filling
2 tablespoons golden syrup
    (*see tip, page 238*)

preparation: 20 minutes
cooking: 1 hour 5 minutes
serves: 8–10

1 Preheat the oven to 350°F. Grease a 9 in round springform pan. Line the base of the pan with parchment paper.

2 Sift the flours into a large mixing bowl and make a well in the center.

3 Place the butter and sugar in a small saucepan and stir over low heat for 5 minutes, or until the sugar has dissolved. Remove from the heat. Place the eggs and milk in a bowl and whisk together well.

4 Add the butter and egg mixtures to the flour and stir with a wooden spoon until just combined—do not overbeat.

5 Pour half the mixture into the prepared pan. Smooth the surface. Top with the pie filling and drizzle with the golden syrup. Spoon in the remaining cake mixture and smooth the surface. Bake for 50–60 minutes, or until a skewer comes out clean when inserted in the center of the cake. Dust with confectioners' sugar and serve with cream.

nutrition per serve (10)
Protein 4.5 g; Fat 17 g; Carbohydrate 44 g; Dietary Fiber 1 g; Cholesterol 102 mg; 346 calories

hint

Use 1 cup of freshly cooked apples instead of the pie filling, if desired, and add a clove or a pinch of cinnamon for extra flavor. Canned chopped peaches, pears or fruit salad can be used to replace the apples. Drain well before using.

3 cups all-purpose
   flour
4 teaspoons baking
   powder
1 cup soft brown sugar
1/2 cup butter, melted
2 eggs, lightly beaten
1 cup milk
1 1/3 cups fresh or thawed
   frozen blueberries

preparation: 20 minutes
cooking: 20 minutes
makes: 12 muffins

1 Preheat the oven to 425°F. Grease a twelve cup (1/2-cup capacity) muffin pan.

2 Sift the flour and baking powder into a large bowl. Stir in the sugar and make a well in the center. Add the combined melted butter, eggs and milk all at once, and fold until just combined. (Do not overmix, the batter should look quite lumpy.)

3 Gently fold in the blueberries, then spoon the batter into the muffin cups. Bake for 20 minutes, or until golden brown. Cool on a wire rack.

nutrition per muffin
Protein 7 g; Fat 12 g; Carbohydrate 40 g; Dietary Fiber 1.5 g; Cholesterol 65 mg; 300 calories

handy tip...

If using frozen blueberries, drain the liquid once they have thawed.
To make chocolate chip muffins, replace the blueberries with semi-sweet chocolate chips.

ingredients

⅓ cup butter

½ cup superfine sugar

1 egg, lightly beaten

¾ cup self-rising flour, sifted

¼ cup all-purpose flour, sifted

½ cup milk

1 teaspoon ground cinnamon

1 tablespoon superfine sugar, extra

extra butter, melted

preparation: 20 minutes
cooking: 30 minutes
serves: 6–8

1 Preheat the oven to 350°F. Grease a round 8 in cake pan and line the base of the pan with parchment paper.

2 Place the butter and sugar in a bowl and beat with an electric mixer until light and creamy. Add the egg gradually, beating well after each addition.

3 Transfer the mixture to a large bowl. Fold in the sifted flours, alternately with milk. Stir until smooth. Spoon into the prepared pan and smooth the surface. Bake for 30 minutes or until a skewer comes out clean when inserted into the center of the cake. Cool the cake in the pan for 5 minutes before turning out onto a wire rack to cool completely.

4 Combine the cinnamon and extra sugar in a small bowl. Brush the cake with a little melted butter while still warm, then sprinkle with the cinnamon sugar.

nutrition per serve (8)
Protein 3 g; Fat 7.5 g; Carbohydrate 31 g; Dietary Fiber 0.6 g; Cholesterol 44 mg; 203 calories

hint

Cinnamon is the dried bark of the cinnamon tree. Native to Sri Lanka, it is sold ground or in the form of a quill—a stick of cinnamon in the shape of a scroll.

ingredients

2/3 cup butter
1 1/4 cups semi-sweet
    chocolate chips
3/4 cup superfine sugar
3 eggs
1 teaspoon vanilla extract
1 cup all-purpose flour,
    sifted

preparation: 10 minutes +
    cooling
cooking: 40 minutes
makes: 16

1 Preheat the oven to 350°F. Grease the base and sides of an 8 in square cake pan and line the base with parchment paper.

2 Place the butter, chocolate and sugar in a heavy-based saucepan over very low heat. Stir occasionally, until the chocolate has melted and the mixture is smooth. Remove from the heat. Allow to cool.

3 Beat in the eggs and vanilla extract, then fold in the flour. Pour into the prepared pan and bake for 35 minutes, or until firm. Cool in pan before turning out and cutting.

nutrition per brownie
Protein 2.5 g; Fat 12 g; Carbohydrate 25 g; Dietary Fiber 0.5 g; Cholesterol 60 mg; 217 calories

handy tip...

For chocolate fudge walnut brownies, fold 1/2 cup coarsely chopped walnuts into the mixture.
To make rum and raisin brownies, soak 1/2 cup golden raisins in 1/4 cup rum for 10 minutes or until plump. Fold into the mixture.

ingredients

2 cups self-rising flour, sifted
2 tablespoons butter, chopped
1/2 cup milk
milk, extra, for glazing

preparation: 20 minutes
cooking: 12 minutes
makes: 12

1 Preheat the oven to 425°F. Lightly grease a baking sheet.

2 Place the flour and a pinch of salt into a bowl. Add the butter and rub in lightly using your fingertips until fine and crumbly.

3 Make a well in the center of the flour. Combine the milk and 1/3 cup water and add almost all the liquid. Mix with a flat-bladed knife, until the dough comes together in clumps. Use the remaining liquid if necessary.

4 With floured hands, gently gather the dough together, lift out onto a lightly floured surface and pat into a smooth ball. Do not knead the dough or the scones will be tough. Pat the dough out to a 3/4 in thickness. Using a 2 in biscuit cutter, cut into rounds. Gather the dough trimmings together and, without handling too much, cut out more rounds.

5 Place the scones close together on the prepared baking sheet and glaze with the extra milk. Bake for 10–12 minutes, or until golden brown. Serve warm with jam and whipped cream.

nutrition per scone
Protein 2.5 g; Fat 2.5 g; Carbohydrate 15 g; Dietary Fiber 0.5 g; Cholesterol 8 mg; 96 calories

hint

English scones are very similar to baking powder biscuits and are served in much the same way—with jam and whipped cream—as an afternoon treat, rather than at breakfast.

melted caramel choc bar frosting

Chop two 2 oz chocolate-covered caramel nougat bars and place in a saucepan. Add ½ cup whipping cream and stir over low heat until the chocolate melts. Drizzle the mixture over a chocolate cake and allow to cool. Serve with ice cream or cream.

covers 1 round cake

citrus cream cheese frosting

Place 8 oz softened cream cheese, ¼ cup softened butter, 1 teaspoon grated lemon, lime or orange rind and 1 cup sifted confectioners' sugar in a bowl. Beat until thick and smooth. Spread on slices or cakes.

covers 12 muffins

From left to right: Melted caramel choc bar frosting; Citrus cream cheese frosting; Coffee cream frosting; Marshmallow topping; Passion fruit glacé topping; Toffee syrup topping.

coffee cream frosting

Place 1 cup softened unsalted butter, 1 cup sifted confectioners' sugar, 1 tablespoon coffee extract or liqueur and 2 teaspoons milk in a bowl and beat until thick and pale.

covers 1 loaf cake

marshmallow topping

Place ½ cup sifted confectioners' sugar, 2 tablespoons softened butter and 1 tablespoon boiling water in the top of a double boiler and beat until smooth. Add 1 cup chopped marshmallows. Place the insert over simmering water and stir for 3–5 minutes, or until the marshmallows have melted. Allow to cool, then spread over homemade or purchased plain cookies and cupcakes.

covers 20 small oval biscuits

passion fruit glacé topping

Place 1¼ cups sifted confectioners' sugar, and 2 tablespoons fresh passion fruit pulp in the top of a double boiler and place over simmering water. Stir for 5 minutes, or until smooth and glossy. Spread over cookies, bars or plain sponge cales.

covers 24 cup cakes

toffee syrup topping

Place ¾ cup soft brown sugar, 1 cup whipping cream and ¼ cup butter in a saucepan and stir until the sugar dissolves. Bring to a boil, then reduce the heat and simmer for 2 minutes, or until the sauce has slightly thickened. Serve over date loaf or banana cake.

covers 1 small loaf cake

nutrition per muffin
Protein 6 g; Fat 6.5 g; Carbohydrate 40 g; Dietary Fiber 3 g; Cholesterol 45 mg; 235 calories

ingredients

2 cups self-rising flour
1 cup oat bran
3/4 cup superfine sugar
1/4 cup butter, melted
3/4 cup milk
2 eggs, lightly beaten
1 cup mashed, ripe bananas (2 medium bananas)

preparation: 15 minutes
cooking: 15 minutes
makes: 12

1 Preheat the oven to 425°F. Grease a twelve-cup (1/2-cup capacity) muffin pan.

2 Sift the flour into a large bowl, then add the oat bran and sugar. Make a well in the center. Whisk together the butter, milk, eggs and bananas and add to the dry ingredients all at once. Stir with a wooden spoon until just mixed—do not over beat as the batter should remain lumpy.

3 Spoon the mixture into the prepared pans. Bake for 15 minutes, or until puffed and brown. Transfer the muffins to a wire rack to cool.

handy tip...

For muffins with a difference, beat 1/3 cup cream cheese, 2 tablespoons confectioners' sugar and 2 teaspoons lemon juice with an electric mixer until light and creamy. Spread over the muffins and top with dried banana slices.

ingredients

²/₃ cup unsalted butter, softened
2 teaspoons grated orange rind
1 teaspoon grated lemon rind
³/₄ cup superfine sugar
2 eggs, lightly beaten
¹/₃ cup ground almonds
1²/₃ cups self-rising flour, sifted
³/₄ cup plain yogurt

preparation: 10 minutes
cooking: 40 minutes
serves: 8–10

1 Preheat the oven to 350°F. Lightly grease a 9 in ring cake or baba pan with a small amount of butter or oil.

2 Place the butter, orange and lemon rinds and sugar in a bowl and beat with an electric mixer until light and creamy. Add the eggs gradually, beating thoroughly after each addition. Add the ground almonds, flour and yogurt and beat on low speed for 1 minute, or until well combined.

3 Spoon the mixture into the prepared pan. Bake for 40 minutes, or until a skewer comes out clean when inserted into the center of the cake. Turn out onto a wire rack to cool. Serve with cream or an orange glacé frosting, if desired.

nutrition per serve (10)
Protein 5.4 g; Fat 17 g; Carbohydrate 35 g; Dietary Fiber 1.4 g; Cholesterol 77 mg; 314 calories

hint

To make an orange glacé frosting, combine 1 cup sifted confectioners' sugar, 1 teaspoon finely grated lemon rind, 2 teaspoons unsalted butter, and 1–2 tablespoons orange juice in a small heatproof bowl to form a paste. Stand over a saucepan of simmering water and stir until frosting is smooth and glossy.

ingredients

8 oz plain chocolate
    wafers or cookies
1 tablespoon instant
    cocoa mix
1½ cups pecans
¾ cup butter, melted

Caramel topping
½ cup lightly packed soft
    brown sugar
¼ cup butter
13 oz can sweetened
    condensed milk

preparation: 15 minutes +
    chilling
cooking: 35 minutes
makes: 16 pieces

1 Preheat the oven to 350°F. Lightly grease a shallow 11 x 7 in cake pan and line with parchment paper, overhanging two opposite sides.

2 Place the wafers, cocoa mix and a third of the pecans in a food processor and process until finely crushed. Transfer to a bowl and add the melted butter. Mix well, then press into the pan. Press the rest of the pecans gently over the top.

3 To make the caramel topping, place the brown sugar and butter in a saucepan over low heat, until the butter melts and the sugar dissolves. Remove from the heat, stir in the condensed milk, then pour over the cookie base.

4 Bake for 25–30 minutes, or until the caramel is firm and golden— the edges will bubble and darken. Cool, then refrigerate for at least 3 hours.

5 Trim off the crusty edges and cut the layer into squares. If desired, before serving, hold a piece of paper over one half of each piece and sprinkle the other half with confectioners' sugar, then sprinkle the other side with cocoa mix.

nutrition per square
Protein 4 g; Fat 25 g; Carbohydrate 35 g; Dietary Fiber 1 g; Cholesterol 50 mg; 385 calories

handy tip...

Pecans are a smooth-shelled nut containing a ridged kernel, similar in appearance to a walnut. They are native to America, particularly the south central area.
Unshelled nuts can be stored in a cool dry place for up to 6 months—shelled pecans should be stored in an airtight container for up to 3 months.

ingredients

1¼ cups semi-sweet
  chocolate chips
2 cups cornflakes
½ cup golden raisins
½ cup roasted unsalted
  peanuts
½ cup red glacé cherries,
  halved
¼ cup dried currants
1 tablespoon chopped,
  candied citrus peel
⅔ cup sweetened
  condensed milk

preparation: 15 minutes +
  chilling
cooking: 15 minutes
makes: 24 pieces

1 Preheat the oven to 350°F. Line a shallow 11 x 7 in cake pan with foil and lightly grease.

2 Put the chocolate in a heatproof bowl over a small saucepan of simmering water. Stir until melted and smooth. Spread the chocolate evenly into the pan and refrigerate for 15 minutes, or until set.

3 Place the cornflakes, raisins, peanuts, glacé cherries, currants, citrus peel and condensed milk in a bowl. Mix together until all the ingredients are well coated with the condensed milk—try not to crush the cornflakes too much while mixing. Spread the mixture evenly over the chocolate, then bake for 12 minutes, or until the top is light golden.

4 Allow to cool, then refrigerate for 15 minutes to set the chocolate before cutting into squares.

nutrition per square
Protein 2 g; Fat 5 g; Carbohydrate
15 g; Dietary Fiber 0.5 g; Cholesterol
3 mg; 110 calories

hint

This sweet bar is a variation on the traditional Florentine cookies which have plenty of dried fruits, citrus peel and nuts, and are coated with melted chocolate on one side. It can be stored in the fridge for up to two weeks.

ingredients

½ cup butter

½ cup superfine sugar

2 eggs, lightly beaten

1 teaspoon vanilla extract

1½ cups mashed, ripe banana (3 medium bananas)

1 teaspoon baking soda

½ cup milk

2 cups self-rising flour, sifted

preparation: 20 minutes
cooking: 1 hour
serves: 6–8

1 Preheat the oven to 350°F. Lightly grease an 8 in round cake pan with a small amount of butter or oil and line the base with parchment paper.

2 Place the butter and sugar in a bowl and beat with an electric mixer until light and creamy. Add the eggs gradually, beating thoroughly after each addition. Add the vanilla extract and mashed bananas and beat until well combined.

3 Transfer the mixture to a large bowl. Dissolve the baking soda in the milk. Fold in the sifted flour alternately with the milk mixture. Stir until all the ingredients are just combined and the cake mixture is smooth.

4 Spoon into the prepared pan and smooth the surface. Bake for 1 hour, or until a skewer comes out clean when inserted into the center of the cake. Cool the cake in the pan for 10 minutes before turning

onto a wire rack. Delicious on its own or top with butter frosting and toasted flaked coconut.

nutrition per serve (8)
Protein 6 g; Fat 15 g; Carbohydrate 47.5 g; Dietary Fiber 2 g; Cholesterol 87 mg; 345 calories

handy tip...

To make a butter frosting, beat together ½ cup butter, ¾ cup confectioners' sugar and 1 tablespoon lemon juice until smooth and creamy. Spread onto the cooled cake. This is also delicious with the citrus cream cheese frosting on page 282.

ingredients

1 1/4 cups self-rising flour
1/2 cup unsalted butter, chopped
2/3 cup superfine sugar
3 eggs, lightly beaten
1/3 cup buttermilk
2 teaspoons finely grated orange rind

preparation: 15 minutes
cooking: 50 minutes
serves: 6–8

1 Preheat the oven to 350°F. Grease an $8^1/2$ x $4^1/2$ x $2^1/2$ in loaf pan with a small amount of butter or oil. Line the base and sides with parchment paper.

2 Place the flour, butter and sugar in a food processor and, using the pulse button, process the dry ingredients for 20 seconds, or until the mixture is fine and crumbly. Add the combined eggs, buttermilk and orange rind and process for 10 seconds, or until the mixture is smooth.

3 Spoon the mixture into the prepared pan and smooth the surface with the back of a spoon. Bake for 50 minutes, or until a skewer comes out clean when inserted into the center of the cake. Cool the cake in the pan for 5 minutes before turning out onto a wire rack to cool completely.

nutrition per serve (8)
Protein 5 g; Fat 15 g; Carbohydrate 35 g; Dietary Fiber 0.75 g; Cholesterol 108 mg; 289 calories

hint

Yogurt, sour cream or milk can be used instead of buttermilk in this recipe. Decorate with an orange glacé frosting (such as the one suggested in the 'hint' on page 285) and purchased orange sweets, if desired.

ingredients

11 oz package yellow
  cake mix
1/2 cup finely chopped
  fresh pitted dates
1 teaspoon ground mixed
  spice
1 egg, lightly beaten
1/2 cup buttermilk
1/4 cup honey
4 teaspoons unsalted
  butter

preparation: 10 minutes
cooking: 35 minutes
serves: 6–8

1 Preheat the oven to 350°F. Grease an 8 in round cake pan with a small amount of butter or oil. Line the base and sides with parchment paper.

2 Place the cake mix, dates, mixed spice, egg and buttermilk in a bowl and beat with an electric mixer on low speed for 1 minute, or until the ingredients are just combined. Beat on medium speed for 2 minutes, or until the mixture is smooth.

3 Spoon the mixture into the prepared pan. Bake for 35 minutes, or until a skewer comes out clean when inserted into the center of the cake. Cool the cake in the pan for 10 minutes before carefully turning out onto a wire rack.

4 Combine the honey, butter and 1 tablespoon water in a small saucepan. Stir over low heat for 1 minute, or until the butter has just melted. Brush over the warm cake and serve with custard or ice cream, if desired.

nutrition per serve (8)
Protein 5 g; Fat 37 g; Carbohydrate 12 g; Dietary Fiber 2.5 g; Cholesterol 89 mg; 396 calories

handy tip...

Decorate the cake with sifted confectioners' sugar, if desired. This cake is delicious served warm as a dessert.

ingredients

1½ cups whole hazelnuts
¾ cup butter
6 egg whites
1¼ cups all-purpose flour
¼ cup cocoa powder
2 cups confectioners'
    sugar
confectioners' sugar,
    extra, to dust

preparation: 20 minutes
cooking: 40 minutes
makes: 12

1 Preheat the oven to 400°F. Grease twelve ½-cup capacity friandises or muffin cups.

2 Spread the hazelnuts out on a baking sheet and bake for 8–10 minutes, or until fragrant (take care not to burn). Place in a clean dish towel and rub vigorously to loosen the skins. Discard the skins. Cool, then process in a food processor until finely ground.

3 Place the butter in a small saucepan and melt over medium heat, then cook for 3–4 minutes, or until it turns a deep golden color. Allow to cool slightly.

4 Lightly whisk the egg whites in a bowl until foamy but not firm. Sift the flour, cocoa powder and confectioners' sugar into a large bowl and stir in the ground hazelnuts. Make a well in the center and add the egg whites and butter and mix until combined.

5 Spoon the mixture into the friand holes until three-quarters filled. Bake for 20–25 minutes, or until a skewer comes out clean when inserted into the center of each friandise. Cool in the pan for a few minutes, then cool completely on a wire rack. Dust with confectioners' sugar, to serve.

nutrition per friandise
Protein 5.5 g; Fat 25 g; Carbohydrate 30 g; Dietary Fiber 2.5 g; Cholesterol 40 mg; 355 calories

hint

Friandise pans are often oval in shape, however, muffin cups can also be used. Friandises will keep for up to 4 days in an airtight container. Hazelnuts can be substituted with roasted ground almonds or pistachios.

ingredients

4 cups dried mixed fruit
½ cup brandy
1 cup butter
1 cup soft brown sugar
5 eggs
2¾ cups all-purpose flour
1 tablespoon mixed
 spices (cinnamon,
 allspice and nutmeg)
1 teaspoon baking powder

preparation: 15 minutes
cooking: 2 hours 30 minutes
serves: 8–10

1 Preheat the oven to 300°F. Grease an 8 in round cake pan or springform pan and line the base and sides with two layers of parchment paper.

2 Place the mixed fruit in a large bowl, add the brandy and mix together well.

3 Place the butter and sugar in a bowl and beat with an electric mixer until combined. Gradually add the eggs one at a time, beating well after each addition. Sift the flour, mixed spices and baking powder together and fold half of the dry ingredients into the mixture. Stir in the mixed fruit and brandy, then mix in the remaining dry ingredients.

4 Spoon into the prepared pan and smooth the surface. Bake for 2 hours 30 minutes, or until a skewer comes out clean when inserted into the center of the cake. Cover the cake with aluminum foil and allow to cool in the pan.

nutrition per serve (10)
Protein 8.5 g; Fat 3.5 g; Carbohydrate 123 g; Dietary Fiber 5.5 g; Cholesterol 90 mg; 570 calories

handy tip...

Light fruit cake is not as dense as your average Christmas fruit cake, therefore will not last as long. Stored in an airtight container, in the cupboard or refrigerator, it will keep for three weeks.

ingredients

1 large orange
2 eggs, lightly beaten
2 cups shredded carrots
2/3 cup chopped pecans
1/2 teaspoon ground
    cinnamon
1/2 cup oil
2/3 cup superfine sugar
1 1/3 cups self-rising flour

preparation: 15 minutes
cooking: 45 minutes
serves: 6–8

1 Preheat the oven to 350°F. Lightly grease an 8 in square cake pan with a small amount of butter or oil and line the base with parchment paper. Finely grate 2 teaspoons of orange rind and squeeze 1/3 cup of juice.

2 Place the eggs, carrots, orange rind and juice, pecans, cinnamon, oil and sugar in a large bowl and mix together with a wooden spoon.

3 Sift the flour into the bowl and mix together with a wooden spoon for 1 minute, or until the mixture is thick and the ingredients are well combined.

4 Spoon the mixture evenly into the prepared pan and smooth the surface. Bake for 45 minutes, or until a skewer comes out clean when inserted into the center of the cake. Turn out onto a wire rack to cool. Serve the cake warm or cold. Top with a cream cheese frosting *(see hint)* and chopped pecans, if desired.

nutrition per serve (8)
Protein 5 g; Fat 24 g; Carbohydrate 38 g; Dietary Fiber 2.9 g; Cholesterol 45 mg; 383 calories

hint

To make a cream cheese frosting, place 4 oz cream cheese and 3/4 cup sifted confectioners' sugar in a bowl and beat until light and creamy. Add 1–2 tablespoons finely grated lemon or orange rind and beat for another 2 minutes, or until the mixture is smooth and fluffy.
Walnuts can be used instead of pecans, if desired.

recipe developers:

Alison Adams, Laura Ammons, Roslyn Anderson, Anna Beaumont, Wendy Berecry, Janelle Bloom, Anna Paola Boyd, Rosey Brian, Wendy Brodhurst, Janene Brooks, Kerrie Carr, Glynn Christian, Rebecca Clancy, Judy Clarke, Amanda Cooper, Anne Creber, Jane Croswell-Jones, Rosemary De Santis, Alex Diblasi, Michelle Earl, Sheryle Eastwood, Stephanie Elias, Susan Geraghty, Gabrielle Gibson, Jo Glynn, Wendy Goggin, Jenny Grainger, Alex Grant-Mitchell, Lulu Grimes, Margaret Harris, Donna Hay, Eva Katz, Coral Kingston, Kathy Knudsen, Jane Lawson, Michelle Lawton, Michaela Le Compte, Barbara Lowery, Rachel Mackey, Voula Mantzouridis, Tracey Meharg, Rosemary Mellish, Jean Miles, Kerrie Mullins, Denise Munro, Kate Murdoch, Angela Nahas, Liz Nolan, Peter Oszko, Sally Parker, Jackie Passmore, Rosemary Penman, Jennene Plummer, Justine Poole, Tracey Port, Wendy Quisumbing, Zoe Radze, Kerrie Ray, Jo Richardson, Tracy Rutherford, Maria Sampsonis, Chris Sheppard, Deborah Solomon, Stephanie Souvilis, Dimitra Stais, Beverly Sutherland Smith, Alison Turner, Jody Vassallo, Maria Villegas, Lovoni Welch.

home economists:

Frances Abdallaoui, Alison Adams, Laura Ammons, Roslyn Anderson, Anna Beaumont, Anna Paola Boyd, Wendy Brodhurst, Kerrie Carr, Rebecca Clancy, Alex Diblasi, Michelle Earl, Jenny Fanshaw, Leanne Field, Jo Forrest, Maria Gargas, Susan Geraghty, Jo Glynn, Wendy Goggin, Alex Grant-Mitchell, Michelle Lawton, Michaela Le Compte, Melanie McDermott, Rachel Mackey, Voula Mantzouridis, Ben Masters, Tracey Meharg, Beth Mitchell, Kerrie Mullins, Kate Murdoch, Angela Nahas, Bridget O'Connor, Peter Oszko, Justine Poole, Zoe Radze, Kerrie Ray, Jo Richardson, Tracy Rutherford, Maria Sampsonis, Clare Simmonds, Margot Smithyman, Michelle Thrift, Angela Tregonning, Alison Turner, Maria Villegas.

photographers:

Jon Bader, Paul Clarke, Cris Cordeiro, Craig Cranko, Ben Dearnley, Andrew Elton, Joe Filshie, Roberto Jean Francois, Andrew Furlong, Phil Hayley, Chris Jones, Ray Joyce, Tony Lyon, Andre Martin, Luis Martin, Andrew Payne, Peter Scott, Warren Web, Damien Wood.

food stylists:

Wendy Berecry, Anna-Marie Bruechert, Marie-Hélène Clauzon, Amanda Cooper, Rosemary De Santis, Georgina Dolling, Carolyn Fienberg, Kay Francis, Mary Harris, Di Kirby, Vicki Liley, Rosemary Mellish, Lucy Mortensen, Michelle Noerianto, Anna Phillips, Hans Schlupp, Suzie Smith.

food preparation:

Alison Adams, Ann Bollard, Bronwyn Clark, Michelle Earl, Jo Forrest, Wendy Goggin, Cherise Koch, Tatjana Lakajev, Michelle Lawton, Melanie McDermott, Kerrie Mullins, Liz Nolan, Sally Parker, Justine Poole, Tracey Port, Kerrie Ray, Jo Richardson, Tracy Rutherford, Christine Sheppard, Stephanie Souvilis, Dimitra Stais, Alison Turner, Maria Villegas.

The publisher wishes to thank the following for their assistance in the photography for this book:
Country Road
Dulux Paints
Porters Paints
Regeneration Tiles
Studio Ramsay
Wheel & Barrow
Witchery

Published in 2000 by Whitecap Books Ltd,
351 Lynn Avenue, North Vancouver, BC V7J 2C4
Telephone (604) 980 9852   Facsimile (604) 980 8197

Managing Editor: Rachel Carter
Editor: Stephanie Kistner
Designer: Michelle Cutler
Illustrator: Stephen Pollitt
Food Director: Jody Vassallo
Food Editors: Rebecca Clancy, Jane Lawson, Michelle Lawton, Jody Vassallo
Photographer (cover, chapter openers and special features): Joe Filshie
Photographer's Assistant (cover and chapter openers): Paul Tiller
Stylist (cover, chapter openers and special features): Georgina Dolling
Stylist's Assistants: Ben Masters (cover), Kate Murdoch (chapter openers),
Michelle Lawton (special features)
Nutritionist: Thérèse Abbey
Indexer: Russell Brooks
Picture Librarian: Anne Ferrier

CEO & Publisher: Anne Wilson
Associate Publisher: Catie Ziller
General Manager: Mark Smith

ISBN 1-55285-099-4

PRINTED IN SINGAPORE
Printed by Tien Wah Press
First printed 2000. Reprinted 2000.

Distributed in Canada by Whitecap Books (Vancouver) Ltd, 351 Lynn Avenue, North Vancouver, BC V7J 2C4.
Telephone (604) 980 9852   Facsimile (604) 980 8197
or Whitecap (Ontario) Books Ltd, 47 Coldwater Road, North York, ON, M3B 1Y8.
Telephone (416) 444 3442   Facsimile (416) 444 6630.

First published in Australia by Murdoch Books® a division of Murdoch Magazines Pty Ltd,
GPO Box 1203, Sydney NSW 1045, Australia
Customer Service Telephone (612) 4352 7000   Facsimile (612) 4352 7026

IMPORTANT: Those who might be at risk from the effects of salmonella food poisoning
(the elderly, pregnant women, young children and those suffering from immune deficiency diseases)
should consult their GP with any concerns about eating raw eggs.